W9-AWH-162

THE ENCYCLOPEDIA OF
SHARKS

THE ENCYCLOPEDIA OF
SHARKS

STEVE PARKER

FIREFLY BOOKS

Published by Firefly Books Ltd.

Copyright © 2008 Quintet Publishing

All rights reserved. No part of this publication may be
reproduced, stored in a retrieval system, or transmitted
in any form or by any means, electronic, mechanical,
photocopying, recording or otherwise, without the prior
written permission of the Publisher.

Fourth printing, 2014

Publisher Cataloging-in-Publication Data (U.S.)

The encyclopedia of sharks/Steve Parker.
2nd ed.
Original ed. by: Steve and Jane Parker, 2002
[192] p. : col. ill., photos., maps ; cm.
Includes index.
Summary: The life and biology of sharks, including:
anatomy and physiology, reproduction, courtship and
mating, what they eat and how they use their senses to
hunt and survive.
ISBN-13: 978-1-55407-409-9
1. Sharks. I. Title.

597.3 dc22   QL638.9.P375   2008

Library and Archives Canada Cataloguing in Publication

Parker, Steve.
The encyclopedia of sharks / Steve Parker.
2nd ed.
Includes index.
Previous ed. by: Steve and Jane Parker
ISBN 978-1-55407-409-9
1. Sharks. I. Title.
QL638.9.P37 2008
597.3   C2008-900960-6

Published in the United States by
Firefly Books (U.S.) Inc.
P.O. Box 1338, Ellicott Station
Buffalo, New York 14205

Published in Canada by
Firefly Books Ltd.
50 Staples Avenue, Unit 1
Richmond Hill, Ontario L4B 0A7

Printed in China

Conceived, designed, and produced
by Quintet Publishing Limited
6 Blundell Street
London N7 9BH, UK

Project Editor: Ben Hubbard
Designer: Steve West
Illustrator: Julian Baker
Additional Text: David Robson,
    Frances Dipper
Art Editor: Michael Charles
Picture Editor: Victoria Ford
Managing Editor: Donna Gregory
Editorial Assistants: Martha Burley,
    Robert Davies
Publisher: James Tavendale

Cover photography by Corbis

Picture Credits
b = below, c = center, i = inset, r = right, l = left t = top

Alamy: 19b. 98b Ancient Art & Architecture Collection:
R Sheridan/Ancient Art & Architecture Collection Ltd 18b. **Corbis:** Amos Nachoum 4–5 main, Burstein Collection 6–7 main, Gianni
Dagli Orti/Corbis 19c, Chris Rainier 21 main, Bettmann 26br, Tom Brakefield 66 main, Brandon D. Cole 66b, Denis Scott 95 main,
Denis Scott 125B, J. L. Maher/Wildlife Conservation Society 139b, Amos Nachoum 159 main, Jeffrey L.Rotman 160 main, Douglas
P.Wilson 171b, Reuters/Corbis 196 main, Will Burgess/Reuters 197 main, Jeffrey L.Rotman 202main, Jeffrey L.Rotman 213b. **Getty
Images:** Minden Pictures 01rm, Jeff Rotman 2–3 main, Time Life Pictures 26br, Norbert Wu 42 main, Norbert Wu 42b, Brandon
Cole 77b, Minden Pictures 113B, John Warden 138b, Jeff Rotman p139tr, Andrea Pistolesi 139 main, Stephen Frink 149B, Norbert
Wu 157b, Steve Allen 163 main, Nick Caloyianis 175B, Paul Avis 189B, Brandon Cole 190b, Brandon Cole 191 main, David Doubilet
193 main, Brandon Cole 198t, Brandon Cole 198bl, Norbert Wu 199 main, Stephen Frink 200B, Gary John Norman 201 main, Brian
Skerry 210tr, Stephen Frink 214b, Stuart Westmorland 215 main. **Marine Themes:** 8b, 8-9 main, 9b, 10b, 12b, 15 main, 16 main, 17
main, 17b, 20bl, 22b, 23 main, 23b, 24b, 25 main, 25B, 27 main, 28 main, 31 main, 34 main, 34B, 35 main, 35b, 36 main, 36b, 37 main,
37b, 38 main, 39 main, 40 main, 40, 41 main, 41b, 43main, 43BR, 44br, 45 main, 45br, 46 main, 46br, 47 main, 47br, 48 main, 48br, 49
main, 49br, 50 main, 51 main, 51br, 53 main, 53br, 55 main, 55br, 56 main, 57 main, 57b, 58 main, 58br, 59 main, 59br, 60 main, 60br, 61
main, 61br, 62 main, 63 main, 63br, 64 main, 64BR, 65 main, 65br, 66 main, 66br, 67 main, 67br 68 main, 70c, 70bl, 72tr, 74b, 75 main,
75b, 76b, 77 main, 77b, 79 main, 79b, 81 main, 81br, 82r, 83main, 83br, 84b, 85b, 87 main, 87b, 88c, 89tr, 90C, 91 main, 91B, 32171 92,
93 main, 93b, 96-97 main, 98 main, 99 main, 99b, 100t, 101 main, 101br, 103 main, 103b, 104b, 105 main, 106b, 107b, 108b, 109 main,
109b, 110tr, 111 main, 111b, 113 main, 114–115, 116b, 117 main, 117b, 120r, 120b, 120tr 123 main, 123b, 124b, 125 main, 126tr, 127,
129br, 130B, 131 main, 131b, 132B, 133 main, 133B, 134BL, 134R, 135 main, 135b, 136b, 137 main, 137b, 140–141, 142tr, 142BL, 143
main, 143b, 144b, 145 main, 145b, 146B, 146r, 146b, 147 main, 147b, 148b, 149 main, 150b, 151 main, 151b, 153 main, 153b, 154b,
155, 155b, 156b, 157 main, 161 main, 164–165, 166r, 166b, 167 main, 167bl, 168b, 168tr, 169 main, 169b, 170BL, 171 main, 172b, 173b,
175 main, 176b, 176tr, 177 main, 177b, 178b, 178r, 179 main, 179b, 181b, 182b, 183 main, 183b, 184–185, 186b, 187 main, 188b, 189
main, 192b, 195b, 204br, 205 main, 205b, 206br, 207 main, 207br, 208b, 209 main, 209b, 212b, 217br. **Nature Picture Library:** Brandon
Cole 27b, Brandon Cole 30, Jurgen Freund 107 main, Doug Perrine 52 main, Jeff Rotman 52b, Bruce Rasner/Rotman 54 main, Bruce
Rasner/Rotman 54b, Michael Pitts 94b, Mark Carwardine 95b, Jeff Rotman 112, Jeff Rotman 121b, Sinclair Stammers 126B, Brandon
Cole 162t, Doug Perrine 162B, David Shale 163B, Doug Perrine 180, Doug Perrine 181 main, Doc White 187b, Doug Perrine 210B,
Bruce Rasner/Rotman 213 main, Jeff Rotman 215b. **Photolibrary:** 159br. **Science Photo Library:** 158b. **All other images are
the copyright of Quintet Publishing Ltd.** While every effort has been made to credit contributors, Quintet
Publishing would like to apologize should there have been any omissions or errors—and would be pleased
to make the appropriate correction for future editions of the book.

A history of sharks

Sharks have not changed much in the past 350 million years. Their origins stem from as long as 400 million years ago.

John Singleton Copley's *Watson and the Shark* depicts an event in 1749 in Havana, Cuba, when a 14-year-old crew member on a trading ship was attacked by a shark while swimming in the harbor.

What is a shark?

Sharks are fish that have been around for over 400 million years. They came through at least five great mass extinctions, as they competed favorably with bony fish, prehistoric ichthyosaurs, toothed whales and other marine hunters. Today they are among the top predators in the sea.

The variety of sharks

A shark is a sleek, torpedo-shaped hunter with a tall, triangular dorsal fin and powerful scythe-shaped tail. But this is the archetypal shark image. There are many other types too—gigantic filter-feeders resembling whales, sluggish and flabby deep-sea sharks, flattened bottom-dwelling angel sharks, reef sharks with wedge-shaped heads for pushing into cracks and crevices, carpetlike wobbegongs that are camouflaged as coral and seaweed, parasitic cookiecutters with suckerlike mouths and blade teeth, eel-like sharks with frilly gill slits and epaulette sharks that can walk on their fins like salamanders walk on their legs.

Sharks worldwide

A shark is an ocean dweller. But different sharks live in all parts of the seas and oceans, from the bright surface waters to the inky depths and from the tropics to cold polar conditions. There are sharks inhabiting all marine habitats—coral reefs, mangroves, rocky shores, estuaries and the open ocean. The bull shark ventures into tropical freshwater hundreds of miles from the sea, while the Greenland sleeper shark survives even under the Arctic ice.

Humans and sharks

Throughout human history, sharks have been tarred with the same brush and have gained an evil reputation. Much of it was based on myth and folktales, but some was due to the tendency of a few sharks to attack, kill and sometimes devour people.

Luckily for sharks, this negative view is changing. Shark biology and behavior are becoming gradually clearer. These fish have a body language that we are beginning to interpret, as we work toward better understanding why they behave as they do.

Sharks are not all solitary killers looking for the next human victim. Some are social animals abiding by the rules of their own shark society, each individual with its own personal space. If we invade this space, the shark will treat us like any other intruder and attack.

With its flattened body and frilly face, this spotted wobbegong looks nothing like a typical shark. Adapted to life on the seabed, it is found on reefs around southern Australia. Excellent camouflage allows it to lie in wait, ready to ambush passing fish.

The graceful blue shark shows all the features of a typical shark. Its streamlined body and powerful tail enable it to make long journeys across whole oceans in search of food and mates. Because of intense fishing this once abundant shark is now in decline.

New status for sharks

Our developing understanding of sharks is helping to change people's attitude to them. Scientists and photographers now dare work outside their cages, and tourists can attend specially arranged shark banquets. Fear is being replaced with respect. People want to swim with sharks and even stroke or hug them. But we cannot turn sharks into pets. They are wild animals and highly efficient predators. As we understand them more, we realize that many of their attacks against us are due not to their behavior but to our own. We place ourselves in situations where sharks expect to find food, and attacks are often cases of mistaken identity. Sharks do not set out to develop a taste for human blood. They are just living in their own environment, going about their daily lives as top ocean predators.

The first sharks

Fossils show that sharks of various kinds have been around for some 400 million years. Humans can boast less than 2 million years, so we have a long way to go to match the sharks' formidable success.

Early life-forms evolved in the sea, from microscopic single cells into simple, soft-bodied, jellylike animals and floppy plantlike organisms. Around 550 million years ago there was a major development—the appearance of hard materials for animal bodies. Certain creatures evolved a rigid rod of tissue along the inside of the body, like a central supporting column. Bands of muscles on either side of the rod made it bend from one side to the other to create a forward movement. The rod is called a notochord, and the creatures with it were the first chordates.

Design improvements

As evolution continued, the notochord became surrounded by a linked chain of units, the vertebrae (backbones), for extra strength and mobility. Flaplike extensions of the body enlarged to help give better propulsion control. These became the tail and fins. Feathery gills on the sides of the head developed for breathing underwater. The first fish had evolved, although they had no jaws. This was around 450 to 500 million years ago, during the Ordovician period.

Jaws at last

The all-important jaws, with their up-and-down biting action, probably evolved from the rigid arches of tissue that supported the first or front pair of gills. These moved forward, enlarged and became hinged jaws that could grab, snap and slice. The first fish with jaws were Acanthodians, sometimes called "spiny sharks." They were not true sharks (which had not evolved yet), or even the ancestors of true sharks, but they had a sharklike body shape.

Start of an era

Alongside the spiny sharks, other branches of fish evolution were developing. One was the Chondrichthyes—the true sharks and their relatives the skates, rays and chimaeras. They had skeletons of cartilage, not bone. Their skin was covered with tiny toothlike denticles, not bony plates or scales. Their jaws were lined with rows of sharp teeth. From the Carboniferous period these early sharks began to dominate the waters.

Present-day sharks come in a huge variety of sizes and shapes and can be found in many different habitats. This juvenile cloudy cat shark, recently hatched, will grow to around 18 inches (46 cm) long in the warm inshore waters around Japan and China.

The sixgill shark belongs to a small group of primitive sharks, the cow sharks, that have six or seven gill slits instead of the usual five. This group appeared toward the middle of the Jurassic period. Sixgill sharks live in deep water and exceed 16 feet (5 m) in length.

Cladoselache

One of the best-known early sharks is *Cladoselache*, from 350 million years ago. Its remains were beautifully preserved in the black Cleveland shales of Lake Erie and were found in the 1880s by the fossil-hunter Dr. William Kepler. The fine-grained sedimentary rocks contain traces of skeleton, skin and even muscles.

Cladoselache had a slim body about 5 feet (1.5 m) long with two pairs of ventral (underside) fins and two spined dorsal (topside) fins. The rear of the body narrowed and bent upward, with a large caudal or tailfin on the underside. It had large eyes, a short snout and many teeth, indicating an open-ocean predator that hunted by sight.

Shark evolution

We know about the evolutionary history of sharks from fossils. But fossilization is a very rare, chance process and usually happens only to hard parts, like animal shells, bones, teeth or horns. Sharks have no shells or bones—their "skeletons" are slightly softer, less resistant cartilage.

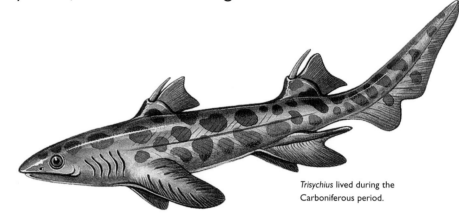

Trisychius lived during the Carboniferous period.

Much of the information available about ancient history and ancestors comes from the harder parts, which are preserved teeth and fin spines. Fossilized sharks' teeth are very common. In life, they were made of enamel and dentine, two of the hardest substances in the animal kingdom. For centuries, people have used them as traditional charms and decorations. Sometimes they were believed to be the teeth of dragons or other monsters. The teeth from different shark species, extinct and living, are fairly distinctive in size, shape and makeup, so they can be used to study evolutionary relationships, both of today and the past.

Fossils of shark skeletons are much rarer. The relatively soft, light, gristly cartilage usually rots after death. The few skeletons that have been preserved, by exceptional circumstances, offer fascinating details about these ancient species. They show that the basic shark shape was established 350 million years ago.

Unusual, usual

One of the strangest of prehistoric sharks was a 3-foot (1 m) long dogfishlike shark with a structure resembling a shaving brush or anvil on its back, where its anterior dorsal fin should be. On the flat upper surface of this structure were tiny hooklike scales. There were also a patch of hooks on the shark's forehead and long streamers trailing from the bases of its pectoral fins.

This creature lived about 350 million years ago and has the name *Stethacanthus*. The function of its strange dorsal appendage has been much debated, with some type of courtship use being an often-quoted theory.

Tristychius was a smallish shark about 2 feet (60 cm) in length, from a similar time period to *Stethacanthus*. Its mouth was rather fishlike, and each of the two dorsal fins had a strong spine at the front. Apart from these features, *Tristychius* was very similar to the modern dogfish. It was probably a cousin of the well-known *Hybodus* shark group, as described on the next page.

This fossilized tooth belonged to the giant *C. Megalodon*, which died out less than two million years ago.

Similar designs

The process of evolution has produced similar solutions to a problem, from different starting points. The prehistoric reptile called the ichthyosaur and today's dolphin (a mammal), tuna (a bony fish) and a typical oceanic shark (a cartilaginous fish) all have the same basic body outline. These animals' similar shapes are not due to close relationships but to similar lifestyles. Nature has streamlined them all to move swiftly and powerfully through the water as fast-swimming, ocean-going hunters. This process is called convergent evolution, and many examples are seen when comparing sharks with other marine creatures.

EVOLUTIONARY TREE OF VERTEBRATES

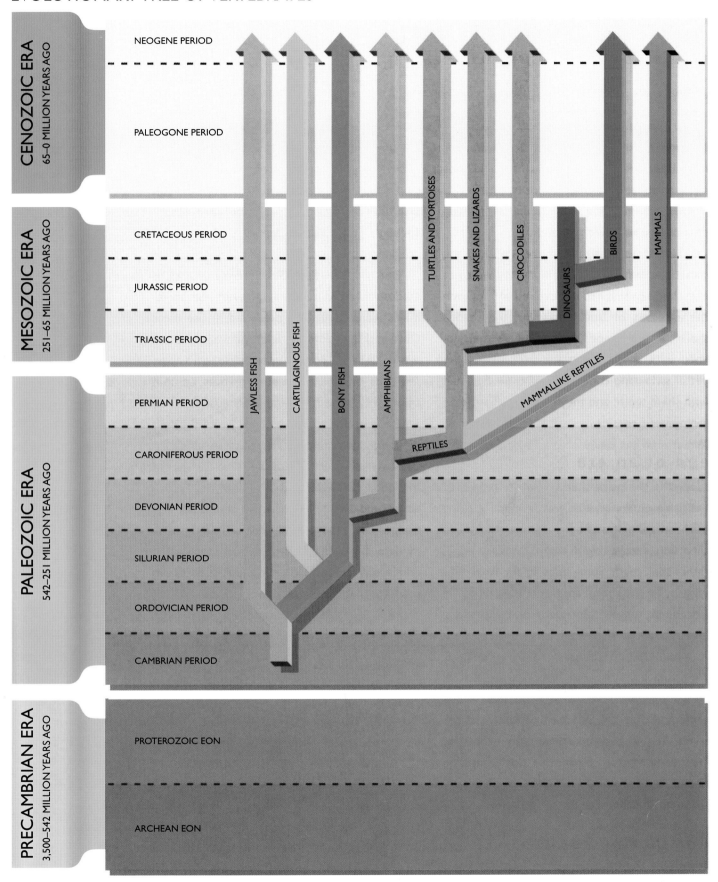

The ancestors of the vertebrates, the Chordates, lived among the invertebrate animals of the Cambrian. Cartilaginous fish evolved from the main vertebrate branch more than 400 million years ago.

The age of sharks

While many of the early sharks were torpedo-shaped and distinctly sharklike, there was a time about 320 million years ago, during the Early Carboniferous (Mississippian) period, when sharks took on all manner of weird shapes. This became known as the "golden age of sharks."

Many fossils of these Carboniferous sharks have been found at Bearsden, a suburb of Glasgow, Scotland, and at Bear Gulch, Montana, United States. An example from the latter site is the unicorn shark, *Falcatus*. It had an L-shaped "horn" extending forward over the top of its head. There is speculation that this had something to do with courtship behavior and may well have been some kind of docking mechanism during mating. Fossils have shown two of these sharks together, one grabbing the "horn" of the other in its mouth.

Long lived

One of the best known, most widespread and longest-persevering of shark genera (groups of species) is *Hybodus*, "humped tooth." Various species came and went over a time span extending from the Middle Permian to the early Late Cretaceous period, about 225 to 90 million years ago. The largest were perhaps 6 feet (2 m) long and had a prominent spine in front of the first dorsal fin. Of special interest are the teeth of *Hybodus*. There are two types: typical sharklike sharp teeth and more flattened, stouter teeth. The former were likely used for grabbing slippery, squirming prey or biting out lumps of flesh, while the latter could have been for crushing and grinding shellfish, as in some bottom-dwelling sharks today.

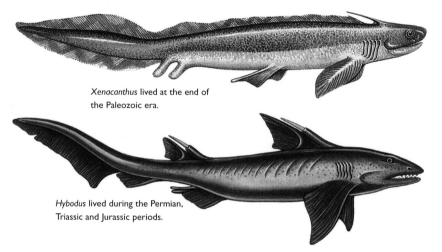

Xenacanthus lived at the end of the Paleozoic era.

Hybodus lived during the Permian, Triassic and Jurassic periods.

Combined evidence from living sharks and fossils shows that some shark types have remained almost unchanged from their prehistoric cousins. One of these so-called "living fossils," the elfin or goblin shark, was first described for science from its fossilized teeth, which are 100 million years old—from the time of the dinosaurs. Then a real, present-day goblin shark was discovered in 1898, near Japan, where it had damaged a submarine telegraph cable. The frilled shark and horned shark are also considered to be very primitive—that is, not simple or backward or stuck in time, but similar to long-disappeared species.

The triangular shape of a fossil *C. Megalodon* tooth is very similar to that of the living great white shark but much larger. A great white's teeth are designed for slicing off chunks of flesh, and *C. Megalodon* also probably hunted large prey like whales.

Megalodon

Perhaps the biggest shark, and fish, that ever lived was *Carcharodon Megalodon*, "big tooth." It is known mainly from huge teeth that resemble those of today's great whites, and similar predatory sharks, but many times larger. *C. Megalodon* fossil teeth have been found around the world and date from more than 15 to less than 2 million years ago. Estimates of this giant's size vary, depending on the growth rate assigned to the teeth and their assumed position in the jaw. Recent reconstructions indicate a body length of 40–60 feet (12–18 m) with a weight of perhaps 50 tons (45 metric tons). This would make *C. Megalodon* bigger than the whale shark and a rival to today's great whales.

Shark relatives

Sharks belong to a large group of fish in which the skeleton is made not of bone but of the slightly lighter, more flexible substance known as cartilage, or "gristle." This fish group is the Chondrichthyes. It also embraces two other subgroups of fish with cartilage "skeletons"—the rays and skates and the ratfish or chimaeras.

Sawfish are unusual rays with a flat, elongated body and an amazing long, sawlike snout. This is used to stun fish and to root out invertebrates from the sandy seabed. (Saw sharks are true sharks with a similar but smaller snout.)

Skates and rays

Also known as batoids, rays and skates are chiefly creatures of the seabed. There are more than 500 species and nearly all are adapted for bottom living. They feed on animals such as flatfish, clams and other shellfish, shrimps and other crustaceans, worms, and carrion. The "wings" on the side of the ray's body are enlarged pectoral fins. As a ray undulates or ripples them, it "flies" through the water. The eyes are on the top of the head, and water is pumped in through the holes, or spiracles, near them, over the gills and out through the gill slits on the underside. Thus a ray can rest on the muddy bottom, breathe easily and keep watch for danger and prey.

Infamous rays include stingrays, with a venomous serrated spine partway along the whiplike tail. The poison is mainly for defense, as the ray lies buried in the sand, waiting for prey. Two stingray species from South American rivers are the only cartilaginous fish completely adapted to freshwater.

The biggest ray is the huge manta, or devilfish, with a "wingspan" of more than 19 feet (5.8 m). It can leap from the water, flopping back with a gigantic splash. Like the biggest sharks, the manta filter feeds on plankton.

Ratfish

There are more than 40 species of ratfish, also known as chimaeras, rabbitfish or ghostsharks. Most dwell in cold, deep seas. A typical ratfish has a disproportionately big head, huge eyes, forward-pointing "beak" formed from large rabbitlike fused front teeth, a poisonous dorsal spine and a long, stringy, ratlike tail. There are only four gill openings, or slits, fewer than a shark. But, as with bony fish, the gills are protected by a platelike gill cover, or operculum.

Ratfish swim awkwardly, by flapping their pectoral fins in the manner of a ray. They spend most of the time resting on the deep seabed, propped up on their fin-tips. Here they feed on bottom-living shellfish, which they crunch up with their strong beak.

The smooth stingray grows to over 13 feet (4 m) long, including its tail with a huge serrated spine. Sharp as a kitchen knife, the spine contains venom that causes excruciating pain. However, stingrays are not aggressive and use their sting only in self-defense.

Electric action

Skates and rays such as the manta (left), like sharks, are sensitive to the electric field produced by active animal muscles. This electrical sense helps them to navigate in dark water and locate prey in sand or mud. Electric rays go a stage further. Blocks of muscles can produce huge bursts of electricity, 300 volts or more. The ray embraces its prey in its wings, shocks it to stunned inaction, then grinds up its body using its flat, slablike teeth.

Shark tales and legends

People have probably been aware of sharks, and the possibility of their attack, since humans began to swim or fish in the sea. Shark teeth and skins have been found at several Neolithic ("new stone age") sites, including Maltese ruins occupied 4,000 years ago.

In ancient times

The first great scientific naturalist, Aristotle (384–322 B.C.E.) of ancient Greece, traveled around the Mediterranean and studied a huge variety of life. He noted differences between fish in general and sharks, including the shark's lack of gill covers, its rough skin instead of true scales and its skeleton of cartilage (gristle) instead of true bone. He mistakenly believed that the "claspers" of a male shark held the female during mating and gave them their confusing name.

The Greek historian Herodotus (485–425 B.C.E.) set the trend for reporting gory shark attacks. He described the scene off Athos, northeast Greece, when many Persian boats sank during a sea battle, and their sailors were eaten by sharks. Vivid accounts of shark attacks have continued since. In the 16th century, the French naturalist Guillaume Rondelet described bodies removed whole from the stomachs of sharks—even a knight in a full suit of armor.

The prospect of being devoured by sharks loomed large in the minds of the old-time mariners—as it still does today. Many old world maps portray fearsome creatures of the deep, including semi-realistic sharks alongside entirely mythical monsters.

Toothy tales

Many tales and stories about the shark originate from the great Pacific Ocean. As ancient peoples "island hopped" in their migrations, cultures developed on each island group, and the much-feared shark featured strongly. New Guinea islanders believed a shark could exert terrible magic and so it must never be caught or harmed in any way. For Solomon Islanders, sharks were incarnations of the spirits of dead ancestors. These spirits needed appeasing, therefore the sharks were fed on meat—from sacrificed human "volunteers."

In Hawaii, the king of the sharks was Kamo Hoa Lii, and his queen was Oahu. People built large stone pens on the seabed where young warriors, armed only with sticks, proved their worth by wrestling Kamo Hoa Lii's all-too-real "subjects." If they failed they were sacrificed to the shark king.

Hawaiian traditions also tell how the mischievous demigod Maui was once insulted by a shark while fishing, so he grabbed the shark and hurled it far into the sky. It can still be seen there, as star patterns within the Milky Way. Another shark managed to escape from Maui's fishing hook and swam away to become the island of Tahiti.

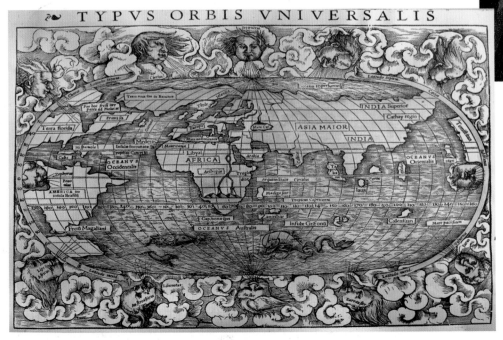

Old maps of the oceans often portray exotic sea creatures with mixed features, some from real animals and others from beasts known only in myth and legend.

Before the days of photography, tales of shark attacks inspired dramatic paintings of "terrors of the deep," menacing sailors and explorers—as in this print, *Killing a Shark*.

Kissing sharks?

Some Pacific islanders believed that kissing a shark rendered it harmless. To this end, kissing ceremonies were performed regularly. The human participants included in this ritual prepared for their ordeal by taking kava, a plant extract with narcotic effects. Often the shark did become harmless—too full of food to threaten anyone else.

Sharks in folklore

Around the world, coastal peoples have taken sharks into their myths, folklores, legends and religions (if not into their hearts!) Those who depended on fishing and sailing were only too aware of the dangers of the deep—especially sharks.

Some responded by worshipping the sharks as gods. Others took a different route, chasing and catching sharks and subjecting them to cruel tortures.

European hatred

Sharks have long been hated by European mariners, not only because they occasionally attacked people, but because they were held responsible for small fish yields. So catching a shark was considered good luck, especially if it was a pregnant female—then there would be fewer sharks in the sea! The unfortunate shark was disemboweled and its tail was cut off, being nailed to the ship's bowsprit as a good-luck trophy. The shark itself, probably still alive, was thrown back into the sea to a chorus of satisfied jeers.

Some sailors believed that sharks could smell a corpse on board, and they would follow the ship relentlessly until the body was committed to the deep—burial at sea. As a consequence, many Europeans refused to eat shark meat, since it could be "recycled" human flesh. Many reports of shark stomach contents encouraged this belief.

The New World

On the other side of the Atlantic, the pirate-ridden Caribbean of the 19th century was home to two legendary man-eating sharks. Port Royal Jack was a large great white who lazily patrolled the harbor entrance at Kingston, Jamaica, waiting for his next meal, probably in a drunken stupor, to fall in. Shanghai Bill

indulged in the same habits off Bridgetown, Barbados. He reputedly died choking on the shaggy coat of a large dog who had gone for a swim.

Around Asia

In ancient Japan there were many gods—including a shark. He was god of storms, and his image symbolized fear. Even today, some Japanese fishermen believe that wearing a long red sash protects against sharks. Along Vietnam's coasts are ancient shrines, apparently dedicated to the mighty whale shark.

Pearl divers descend to amazing depths in the water, holding their breath for two or three minutes and enduring great pressures. They were exposed to another danger as they were struggling back into their boats—the menace of sharks. In Ceylon (now Sri Lanka), the divers employed snake-charmers to adapt their technique and to subdue the marauding fish.

In a shark-aware region, any pointed prominence lends itself to decoration, such as these rocks bordering a coastal highway in California.

Decorative sharks

Through the ages many coastal peoples have used sharks' teeth for ceremonial necklaces, bracelets and ear decorations and also to tip their daggers, spears and other weapons. The traditions continue today, and souvenir stores in tropical holiday resorts bristle with sharks' teeth jewelry, whole jaws as trophies and even walking sticks made from the dried, gristle-like backbones. Sadly, much of this trade contributes to the hunting or persecution of rare sharks, as described at length in chapter nine.

Sharks still feature prominently in tribal customs and traditions to this today. This shaman from Kontu in Papua New Guinea is calling sharks to his canoe by blowing on a conch. When the shark approaches he will slip a ring collar over its head to capture it.

Catching sharks

There are 60 to 70 reported shark attacks each year, of which perhaps 20 result in human fatalities. That's about one ton of people. Meanwhile, humans catch and kill more than half a million tons of sharks, and their close relatives the skates and rays, yearly. This includes commercial fishing by large boats for profit, local and traditional fishing for mainly domestic needs and angling as a sport.

Shark fisheries

Commercial fishing for sharks has some, but limited, success. Sharks breed relatively slowly, so local stocks are soon wiped out by modern, efficient boats. The smaller-scale, opportunistic pursuit of individually valuable fish is usually more productive.

However, some sharks support a regular trade. The dogfish, also known as the rough hound or lesser spotted dogfish, is common in European waters, from the Shetland Islands south to the Mediterranean. Popular for fish dishes, several thousand tons are caught by trawlers every year. It is sold under various names, such as rock salmon, rock eel, flake and huss.

Another North Atlantic commercial target is the spiny dogfish, or spurdog. Over 50,000 tons (45,360 metric tons) were once taken from around the coast of Britain alone every year. But this species does not breed until at least five years of age, so the replacement rate is low.

Since the early 1980s, catches have declined, but other species are still caught commercially around the world. Blue sharks supply the Japanese soup market, and threshers are caught for food and oil production.

A sporting chance?

Sports angling is big business and is affecting the populations of some sharks, particularly the great white. Even if the sharks themselves are not hooked, commercial fishing boats are catching many other kinds of fish for human consumption, thus depriving the sharks of food. Some people like to demonstrate their dominance over the supposed "terror of the deep" with ever more sophisticated methods of catching and killing their trophies.

Not surprisingly, very large specimens of sharks have become hard to find. The mako is a favorite sports fish because it puts up a long, spirited and spectacular fight, leaping repeatedly from the water. The great white is less exciting since it dives to deeper water when hooked and uses sheer strength to try to escape. In British waters, the blue shark is popular with sea anglers—but it's less so with trawler crews, who say that these sharks attack their catches and cause damage to the nets.

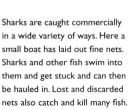

Sharks are caught commercially in a wide variety of ways. Here a small boat has laid out fine nets. Sharks and other fish swim into them and get stuck and can then be hauled in. Lost and discarded nets also catch and kill many fish.

Line fishing for sharks is a popular sport. In the past, angling competitions needlessly killed many thousands of sharks. Nowadays, the sharks are often released after capture and may also be tagged, providing useful information to shark biologists.

Record-breakers

The largest fish ever caught on rod and line was a great white shark, 16.8 feet (5.1 m) long and weighing 2,664 pounds (1.2 metric tons), in Australia in 1959. (A large human averages 176 pounds/80 kg.) Other record-breaking shark catches include:

- A porbeagle of 507 pounds/230 kg (in 1993)
- A bigeye thresher of 802 pounds/364 kg (1981)
- A hammerhead of 991 pounds/450kg (1982)
- A shortfin mako of 1,221 pounds/554 kg (2001)
- A Greenland shark of 1,709 pounds/775 kg (1987)

Traditional shark uses

Many types of shark flesh are edible; indeed, some are very tasty and popular. Shark steaks have long been a daily staple food in some regions and have featured increasingly on restaurant menus as an exotic and expensive treat. However, there are growing concerns about pollutants such as heavy metals being concentrated in shark flesh.

Shark flesh is eaten in various forms—fresh or dried or even raw. There are shark fillets, steaks, fishcakes, sharkburgers, fishpastes and, of course, shark's fin soup. The fins of several species can be used, but the most famous is the tope, the soupfin shark. Traditionally the fins are cut off, dusted with salt or lime, sun-dried and processed into dried fibrous disks. These dissolve when boiled to produce a fish-flavored gelatinous soup.

If a shark's flesh is not considered good enough for the meat market, it can be rendered down, together with leftover entrails and other parts, to produce fish oil and meal for animal feed or fertilizer.

Shark-liver oil

For its body size, a shark has an enormous liver. A big basking shark could produce more than 400 gallons (1,514 L) of liver oil, which is rich in minerals and vitamins, especially vitamin E. The oil has also been used in cosmetics, paints, lubricants, candles, lighting fuel and leather tanning.

The shark liver industry was once substantial. During the early 20th century, Scandinavians caught 30,000 or more Greenland sharks yearly. Cheaper synthetic alternatives mean that this trade has largely disappeared in many areas. But some people still seek the benefits of shark liver oil. One of its ingredients, squalene, is purified and sold in capsules as a cure-all health tonic.

Shark skin

Shark skin was once a sought-after product—stronger than cowhide, flexible and often attractively marked. Removed from the carcass, trimmed, soaked in brine for several weeks and treated, it becomes shagreen. This still bears the tiny pointed, toothlike "scales," dermal denticles, and was used as a sandpaperlike abrasive for smoothing and polishing. It also served as a grip for swords and daggers—nonslip even when blood soaked—and as a novelty covering for books, cigarette lighters and trinkets. Tope, carpet sharks, zebra sharks and kitefin sharks have made good-quality shagreen.

Tanning shark skin removes the denticles to produce a soft leather for shoes, purses, briefcases and books. Nurse, tiger, silky, carpet and lemon sharks all have beautiful markings that made them targets for the shark-leather trade. Like many aspects of shark use, this is now controlled by conservation laws, including the CITES agreement, as described on page 210.

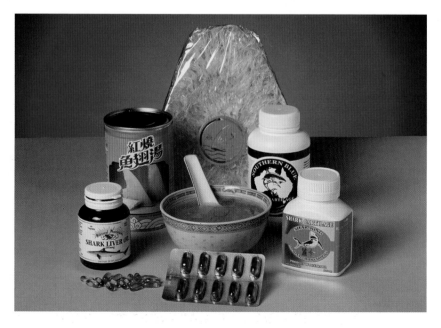

Shark products are sold fresh, dried and processed, with the largest markets being China and Southeast Asia. Dried shark's fin for homemade soup, tinned shark's fin soup, and shark liver oil (squalene) capsules are some of the most popular products.

Dried shark fins can be seen for sale in many Asian markets along with dried sea cucumbers and other marine creatures. Shark fins are very valuable, but their trade is leading to over exploitation of many shark species. The shark body is often discarded.

Shark-based medicines

Traditional treatments for human ailments using parts of sharks have been many and varied around the world:

- Shark's bile or gallbladder extract for eye cataracts;
- Baked shark ashes for teething pains and ringworm;
- Dried shark brain to prevent dental decay and ease labor pains;
- Powdered sharks' teeth for gallstones and excessive bleeding.

However, scientific evidence that these remedies work is lacking or controversial.

Sharks in war

Enemy action isn't the only threat the military has to worry about in times of conflict—shark attacks have been responsible for serious loss of life in wartime, too.

Air-sea catastrophes involving military personnel are often compounded by shark attack, most famously in the Pacific during the Second World War, but also throughout history. In the 5th century B.C.E. Herodotus described a shark attacking a sailor shipwrecked during a battle between the Greeks and the Persians—and the problem has only worsened with intense activity and serious shipwreck incidents during modern warfare.

Attacks in the Mediterranean

Shark attacks in the Mediterranean are rare, despite the huge numbers of tourists swimming in the waters. During wartime, however, the problem worsens. It is likely that many shark attack incidents remained unreported because of the sheer scale of casualties during the World Wars of the twentieth century; but incidents like that in August 1943, when U.S. pilot Lieutenant R. Kurtz crashed into the sea south of Naples and was seriously injured by shark bites to his hands and arms, are unlikely to have been isolated.

Stealth sharks

U.S. military engineers have long harbored hopes of manipulating sharks' natural abilities, making them a tool of warfare rather than a hazard of combat. In 2006, military engineers in Virginia came a step closer to creating cyborg sharks when they built a neural implant designed to allow remote control of a shark's brain signals. The Pentagon is developing it so that the shark's movement can be directed remotely, transforming the fish into an intelligence agent. The shark, gliding quietly through the water, could trail a ship or submarine without being detected—and would not be identified as a threat by the crew of the vessel it was following. Remote-controlled sharks will also allow us to monitor more closely the natural behavior of sharks, and the device could also help researchers trying to restore movement to paralyzed humans.

Tiger sharks (right) are a potentially dangerous species, but they live relatively close to shore rather than in the open ocean. So they would only be a threat to shipwreck survivors in inshore tropical areas. Offshore, the main threat is from oceanic whitetip sharks.

USS Indianapolis disaster

The most notorious wartime incident was the sinking of the *USS Indianapolis*, a U.S. cruiser, by a Japanese submarine in 1945. The ship, returning to the United States from an airbase in the Pacific, was struck by a torpedo and sank. The ship went down with 300 men; the remaining 900 crewmembers were left floating in the ocean, clinging to wreckage. This is how they stayed, with no one discovering or reporting the loss of the vessel until four days later. When rescuers arrived, they found just 300 men still alive—the remainder having been killed, in front of their shipmates, by attacking sharks. The sharks, mainly blue sharks and oceanic whitetips, began to circle two days after the *Indianapolis* went down, soon massing in their hundreds and picking the men off gradually. Testimony given by the survivors suggests that they were at their most active in the late afternoon, when the screams of the men they attacked filled the air. The ship's captain, Charles Butler McVay III (pictured), survived the attack

and became the only captain of a U.S. vessel to be court-martialed during World War II. He was found responsible for the deaths of his crew, though was later exonerated by President Clinton.

Given the stimulus of blood in the water, almost any large shark may become excited enough to attack. Blue sharks have attacked shipwreck survivors, divers and even small boats. Here whitetip reef sharks hunt at night.

Types of shark

Although sharks all have the same basic body plan, they vary widely in the details of their design.

The strangely shaped head of a hammerhead shark makes it instantly recognizable. Its large, wide-set eyes give it excellent vision.

How sharks are classified

The true sharks are a relatively well-studied animal group. But their classification is tricky. Even the number of individual kinds or species varies, from less than 350 to more than 400, averaging around 370–380 in many schemes.

Sharks are of course in the kingdom Animalia, along with well over two million other scientifically described species (possibly over 10 million), from gnats to ourselves. Within the kingdom, sharks belong to the phylum (major animal group) Chordata—the chordates, animals that possess a notochord or a backbone derived from it. This phylum is then split into subphyla. The sharks' subphylum is Vertebrata, the vertebrates, taking in animals with a vertebral column, or backbone. This includes all fish, amphibians, reptiles, birds and mammals.

Fishy groupings

Among the fish, sharks are in the class Chondrichthyes, cartilaginous fish. Other fish, with skeletons made of bone, are known as Osteichthyes. With nearly 30,000 known species, these bony fish far outnumber sharks and their cartilaginous cousins.

The Chondrichthyes class is usually split into two subclasses. These are Elasmobranchii, including sharks, skates and rays, and Holocephali, the ratfish or chimaeras.

Elasmobranchii were once grouped into two main super-orders: Batoidea, skates and rays, and Selachimorpha (Selachii), true sharks. The living sharks are divided into several orders, varying from about six to more than 10, depending on the scheme being followed.

Changing ideas

The science of taxonomy—classifying and grouping living things—has changed considerably in recent years. Using the modern method of cladistics, living things are grouped according to their evolutionary origins and relationships. The basic group is the clade, which includes an original common ancestor, all of its descendants and no others. This system shows that some sharks are more closely related to skates and rays than to other sharks. So the sharks, skates, and rays in the Elasmobranchii are split into two main clades (see next page for details):

• Galea, which includes bullhead sharks, carpet sharks, mackerel sharks and ground sharks.

• Squalea, encompassing frilled sharks, cow sharks, bramble sharks, dogfish sharks, angel sharks, saw sharks, and skates and rays.

Species

Every type of living thing described by scientists is given an internationally accepted two-part name, known as its binomial nomenclature. The first part is the genus (group of closely related species), and the second is the individual species. The tongue-twisting words are often derived from Latin or Ancient Greek and describe some aspect of the organism. A few examples: are

• The great white is *Carcharodon carcharias*, "sharp/jagged tooth."

• The megamouth shark is *Megachasma pelagios*, "a shark of open ocean with a huge mouth."

• The Galapagos shark is *Carcharhinus galapagensis*, "sharp nose of the Galapagos."

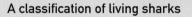

A classification of living sharks

Phylum	Chordata (possessing a notochord)
Subphylum	Vertebrata (possessing a backbone)
Superclass	Gnathostomata (jawed vertebrates)
Class	Chondrichthyes (cartilaginous skeletons)
Subclass	Elasmobranchii (ribbonlike gills)
Super-order	Euselachii* (shark-shaped)

* See the main text for how ideas have moved away from putting all sharks into one group with skates and rays in another.

The sixgill shark, *Hexanchus griseus*, belongs to a small group (order) of sharks that includes the frilled sharks and the cow sharks, called Hexanchiformes. All these sharks have either six or seven pairs of gill slits in front of the pectoral fins and live in deep water.

The silky shark belongs to the largest and most varied order, the ground sharks or Carcharhiniformes. Within this group are many subgroups, with the silky shark belonging to the requiem sharks found mainly in the tropics.

Shark relatives

Skate

Manta ray

Blue shark

Although skates and rays are easily confused with some types of sharks, the biggest difference lies in the way they swim: sharks usually propel themselves with their caudal fin, whereas rays and skates swim using their elongated pectoral fins, which look like wings. The key difference between skates and rays is the way they reproduce: skates lay eggs, whereas rays give birth to live young.

Main shark groups

Sharks are divided into between six and 10 groups, called orders. Each order is then subdivided into families. Families are further subdivided into genera and species. Some of the orders include dozens of species, while others include just one.

Saw sharks

The order Pristiophoriformes contains nine species of saw shark which have an elongated, flat snout edged with sharp teeth, similar to the "saw" of a sawfish. Saw sharks are flattened for bottom-dwelling like their close cousins the skates and rays.

Angel sharks

The Squatiniformes takes in 15 species of angel shark, which are sometimes called sand devils or monkfish. They are flat and lie waiting on the bottom for prey.

Dogfish

In the order Squaliformes are 97 species in seven families. Examples are the Squalidae, including the spiny dogfish (also known as spurdog) and roughskin dogfish; sleeper sharks (Somniosidae); lantern sharks (Etmopteridae); and rough sharks (Oxynotidae).

Bramble sharks

The Echinorhinus are the two genera of bramble sharks, named for their knobbly skin. In North America this group is generally included in the dogfish shark order (see above), as the family Echinorhinidae.

Cow sharks

The Hexanchiformes are the frilled sharks and cow sharks, or sixgill and sevengill sharks. They are among the most ancient types of living sharks. The five species dwell in deep water, have only one dorsal fin and possess comblike teeth on the lower jaw.

Frilled sharks

Though generally considered a family of the Hexanchiformes order, the frilled sharks, or Chlamydoselachidae, are treated by some as a separate order. The group includes just one living family, Chlamydoselachidae, with a sole species, the frilled shark, *Chlamydoselachus anguineus*. It is named for the covers to its four or five pairs of gill slits. It closely resembles its prehistoric relatives from over 350 million years ago.

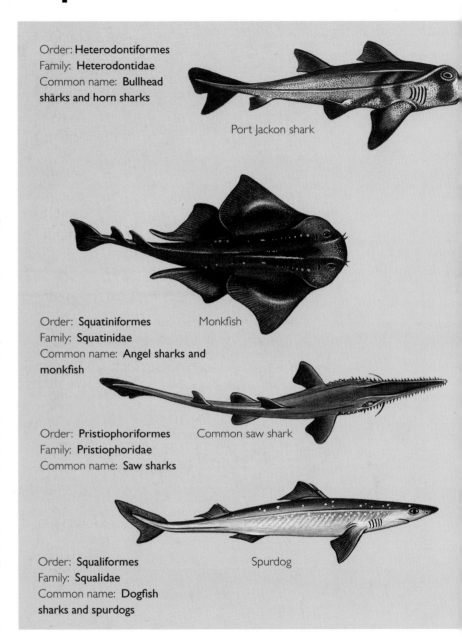

Order: **Heterodontiformes**
Family: **Heterodontidae**
Common name: **Bullhead sharks and horn sharks**

Port Jackon shark

Order: **Squatiniformes** Monkfish
Family: **Squatinidae**
Common name: **Angel sharks and monkfish**

Order: **Pristiophoriformes** Common saw shark
Family: **Pristiophoridae**
Common name: **Saw sharks**

Order: **Squaliformes** Spurdog
Family: **Squalidae**
Common name: **Dogfish sharks and spurdogs**

Bullhead sharks

The Heterodontiformes—"different teeth"—are known as bullhead sharks. Similar species lived in the seas 220 million years ago, when the first dinosaurs appeared on land. Today there are about nine species, including the horn and Port Jackson sharks.

Carpet sharks

The order Orectolobiformes has 31 species in seven families. Among them are carpet sharks, wobbegongs, epaulette sharks, nurse sharks, blind and zebra sharks. They tend to lie or swim slowly on the seabed. One family within this order, Rhincodontidae,

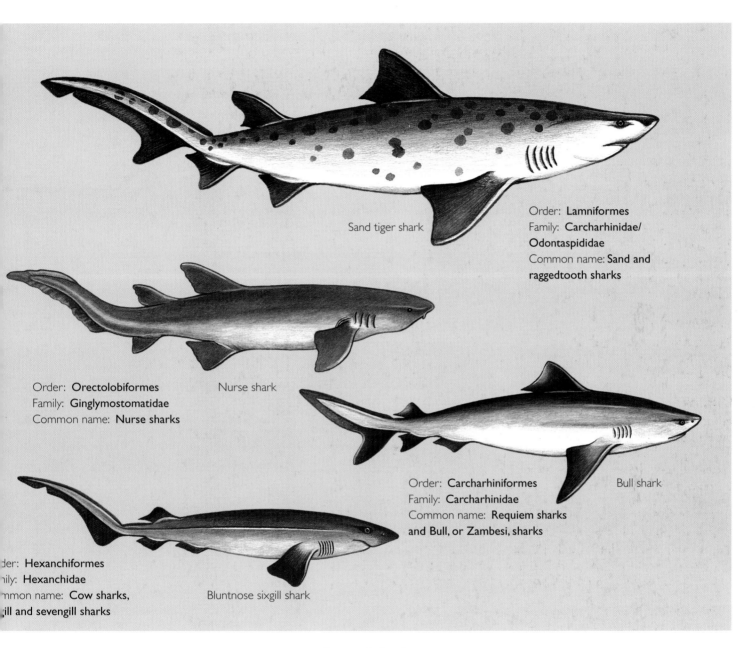

Sand tiger shark

Order: **Lamniformes**
Family: **Carcharhinidae/ Odontaspididae**
Common name: **Sand and raggedtooth sharks**

Order: **Orectolobiformes**
Family: **Ginglymostomatidae**
Common name: **Nurse sharks**

Nurse shark

Order: **Carcharhiniformes**
Family: **Carcharhinidae**
Common name: **Requiem sharks and Bull, or Zambesi, sharks**

Bull shark

der: **Hexanchiformes**
ily: **Hexanchidae**
mmon name: **Cow sharks,**
ill and sevengill sharks

Bluntnose sixgill shark

contains only one species, the whale shark.

Mackerel sharks

The Lamniformes are 15 species in seven families. Known generally as mackerel sharks, they vary from the basking shark (Cetorhinidae) to the white, mako and other "typical" mackerel sharks (Lamnidae). Other groups are threshers (Alopiidae), crocodile sharks (Pseudocarchariidae), goblin sharks (Mitsukurinidae), and sand tigers, or gray nurse. The megamouth has its own family, Megachasmidae.

Ground sharks

The 200 species of Carcharhiniformes are the most "sharklike" of sharks, as streamlined hunters of open water. The main family, Carcharhinidae, is also known as requiem sharks and includes tigers, whitetips, black-tips and blues. Other families are the hammerheads and bonnethead sharks (Sphyrnidae); hound sharks, topes, and smooth dogfish such as the soupfin and leopard shark (Triakidae); barbeled hound sharks (Leptochariidae); weasel sharks (Hemigaleidae); cat sharks such as the nursehound and swell shark (Scyliorhinidae); finback cat sharks (Proscylliidae); and false cat sharks (Pseudotriakidae).

Representatives of several shark families are shown here, displaying variety in shape and form. The relationships between them are determined by features unique to those groups.

Worldwide distribution

Classification

Phylum: Chordata
Class: Chondrichthyes
Subclass: Elasmobranchii
Order: Hexanchiformes
Family: Chlamydoselachidae
Genus and species: *Chlamydoselachus anguineus*

Shark stats

Length: Up to 6 feet (1.8 m)
Weight: Not recorded
Habitat: Deep water, outer continental shelves and slopes
Depth: 330 to more than 4,000 feet (100–1,219 m)
Colors and markings: Generally brown or gray, few distinguishing markings
Sexual maturity: Male 3½ feet (1 m), female 4½ feet (1.4 m)
Mating season: Unknown
Reproduction: Ovoviviparous
Gestation: Possibly more than 3 years
Litter: 6–10 young averaging 22 inches (56 cm) long
Life span: Unclear, possibly 50-plus years

Range

Known from widely separated sites in all oceans, from cool to tropical waters

In captivity

Unknown in captivity

Frilled shark

The frilled shark is very like some of the early prehistoric sharks such as *Cladoselache*; it is rarely caught in deep-sea trawls and even more rarely sighted at the surface. Its many unusual features include a long, sinuous, eel-like body, a single dorsal fin sited far back, near the tail, and an anal fin. Its snout is blunt and its mouth terminal, that is, at the front of its head, with nostrils on top. (Modern sharks have their mouths and nostrils on the head's underside.) Its teeth are also primitive in shape, trident-like—each with three long prongs—and arranged in 20–25 sets with five teeth in each. The six pairs of gills are another unusual feature, rather than five as found in most other sharks. The gills are frilly looking due to protruding tissues, and the slits are elongated, with the first pair joining at the base, across the throat.

This shark can protrude and gape its jaws widely, to engulf its deep-water prey of octopus, squid and bony fish. From the shape of the tail and position of the dorsal, pelvic and anal fins, it may be a stealth predator that accelerates to strike suddenly. The frilled shark also still has a rod of cartilage, the notochord, running along the center of its body from skull to tail. Its lateral-line system for sensing vibrations and movements in the water is an open groove, rather than being in a part-buried tube in the skin, as with other sharks.

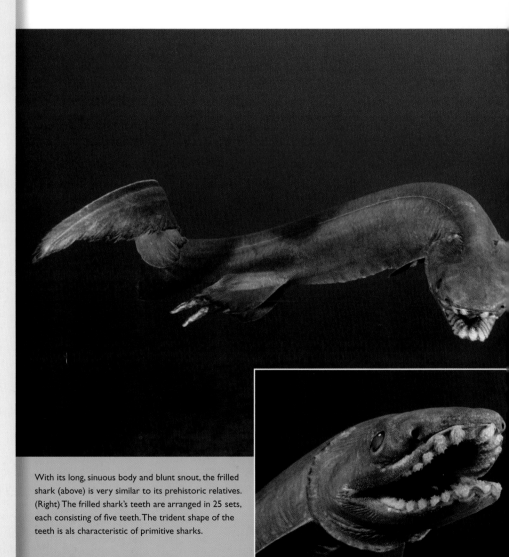

With its long, sinuous body and blunt snout, the frilled shark (above) is very similar to its prehistoric relatives. (Right) The frilled shark's teeth are arranged in 25 sets, each consisting of five teeth. The trident shape of the teeth is als characteristic of primitive sharks.

Worldwide distribution

Classification

Phylum: Chordata
Class: Chondrichthyes
Subclass: Elasmobranchii
Order: Hexanchiformes
Family: Hexanchidae
Genus and species: *Hexanchus griseus*

Shark stats

Length: 16½ feet (5 m), occasionally 18 feet (5.5 m)
Weight: Large specimens in excess of 1,100 lb (499 kg)
Habitat: Deep water by day in most marine habitats, ascending at night
Depth: Down to 6,000 feet (1,829 m) by day, as shallow at 100 feet (31 m) at night
Colors and markings: Light brown to gray, dark sliver or black, paler underside, paler lateral line, spotty or patchy flanks, blue-green eyes
Sexual maturity: 14–14½ feet (4.3–4.4 m)
Mating season: Probably May–September
Reproduction: Ovoviviparous
Gestation: Unclear, possibly more than 2 years
Litter: 20–100 young averaging 2¼ feet long
Life span: Unclear, possibly 80-plus years

Range

Worldwide, one of the widest distributions of any shark

In captivity

Has not survived in captivity for any length of time

Sixgill shark

The sixgill shark, or bluntnose sixgill, is characterized by its possession of six gill slits, rather than the usual five. This is a primitive trait, as in the frilled shark, opposite. The sixgill is a very large shark, the biggest member of its family, with a heavy, powerful body, a single dorsal fin set toward the rear and a rear-sited anal fin. This design is usually associated with sudden bursts of speed in an otherwise slow, sluggish lifestyle. There are five to seven rows of sharp teeth, and the diet is thought to consist of other fish, including smaller sharks and rays, also squid, crabs and similar shellfish and, in some reports, marine mammals such as seals. Fish prey found in the stomach contents from sixgill sharks caught in different locations include deep-sea lampreys and hagfish, hake in the North Atlantic, Pacific salmon and Cape anchovies.

Drably colored apart from intense greeny-blue eyes with black pupils, a light lateral line and fin margins, and perhaps vague spots along the sides, the sixgill shark is a little-known species. The pups are paler than the adults, which may be for camouflage in shallower waters. The adults frequent deep water by day, perhaps coming up to depths of 100 feet (31 m) or less at night, when they may be encountered by divers. During the middle six months of the year these sharks tend to frequent shallow water more often, perhaps as part of their breeding cycle.

The sixgill shark lives in the deep sea for most of the year, but they are known to frequent shallower waters during the mating season.

Most modern sharks feature five gill slits, but this shark's six gills betray its primitive ancestry. Its bulky body is capable of producing sudden bursts of speed to catch prey.

Worldwide distribution

Classification

Phylum: Chordata
Class: Chondrichthyes
Subclass: Elasmobranchii
Order: Heterodontiformes
Family: Heterodontidae
Genus and species: *Heterodontus portusjacksoni*

Shark stats

Length: Up to 5½ feet (1.7 m), usually 3 feet (0.9 m)
Weight: 15–33 pounds (6.8–15kg)
Habitat: Coastal waters, rocky seabed, occasionally mud, sand or sea grass, estuaries
Depth: Down to 650 feet (198 m), usually 300 feet (92 m) or less
Colors and markings: Light gray-brown body with black bar across head and cheeks, dark stripes along the sides and back forming a characteristic harness-type pattern, black tail stripe
Sexual maturity: Male 1½–2½ feet (45–76 cm), females 2¼–2½ feet (70–76 cm)
Mating season: Winter and early spring
Reproduction: Oviparous
Time to hatching: 9–12 months
Litter: 10–15 eggs laid, newly hatched young averaging 10 inches (25 cm) long
Life span: Unknown, possibly 30 years

Range

Off the coasts of Australia (apart from the far north) and nearby islands, rarely New Zealand; migratory in most parts of the range

In captivity

A common aquarium inhabitant which usually thrives on varied foods and makes a decorative and interesting resident

Port Jackson shark

A member of the bullhead family, the Port Jackson shark has a blunt, piglike snout, a large, cone-shaped bulky head, scroll-like nostrils, a prominent ridge across the forehead and above each eye and a body that tapers steadily from head to tail. Each of the two similar-sized dorsal fins has a stout spine at the front, and there are very large pectoral fins with the pelvics placed just behind. The gill system is unusual in that the first of the five gills has a single row of filaments while the others have two, also there is an accessory opening, the spiracle, behind each eye, as seen in many rays. In addition, this shark can lie motionless and breathe by muscular pumping action, taking water in through the first gill slit and forcing it out through the other four, leaving the mouth free. Thus the Port Jackson shark can eat and respire at the same time, an unusual ability within its group.

Port Jackson sharks migrate north in summer to warm inshore waters to breed in traditional areas of gullies and caves, which are used year after year. The sharks travel back south for winter, and for some the return journey totals more than 900 miles (1,448 km).

This shark feeds mainly at night. Its mouth is on the underside, and the powerful jaws bear small, pointed teeth at the front and large, flattened crushing teeth at the back. These grind up mainly bottom-dwelling prey, especially sea urchins and starfish but also shellfish, crabs, lobsters, octopus and seabed fish.

The Port Jackson shark scours the seafloor for sea urchins, starfish and shellfish. The large nostrils of the Port Jackson shark (right) have a rolled or scroll-like shape.

Worldwide distribution

Classification

Phylum: Chordata
Class: Chondrichthyes
Subclass: Elasmobranchii
Order: Squaliformes
Family: Squalidae
Genus and species: *Squalus acanthias*

Shark stats

Length: 3 feet (0.9 m), occasionally 5 feet (1.5 m)
Weight: 11–22 pounds (5–10 kg)
Habitat: Coastal and inshore waters, temperatures below 60°F (16°C)
Depth: Usually 100–300 feet (30.5–92 m), occasionally down to 3,000 feet (915 m)
Colors and markings: Gray, silver, brown or a combination of these hues, occasionally almost black, paler underside, often pale or white spots along the back
Sexual maturity: Male 2 feet (60 cm), female 2½ feet (76 cm)
Mating season: Winter
Reproduction: Ovoviviparous
Gestation: Up to 2 years
Litter: 6–7 young averaging 9–12 inches (23–30 cm) long
Life span: At least 40 years

Range

Cool to temperate coastal waters (45–60°F/7–15°C) of the Pacific and west Atlantic, including Europe, southern Africa, Australia, Japan, western North and South America; absent in warmer waters

In captivity

Commonly kept in sea-life centers and aquaria in temperate regions, and a regular subject in education as a live biological specimen or for anatomical dissections

Spiny dogfish

Also known as the spurdog, grayfish and piked dogfish, the spiny dogfish is one of about 15 species in the genus *Squalus*. It is a chiefly coastal fish frequenting mid water and the sea bed, and lacks an anal fin. Slow moving, when troubled it arches its back and thrashes, at which time the spine at the front of each dorsal fin can inflict painful wounds with a mild venom produced by a gland at the base of the spine—as testified by generations of commercial fishing workers and anglers. In the early 20th century it was a pest for fishing fleets, but after intense exploitation as a target species, from the 1960s its numbers have fallen drastically.

The spiny dogfish's diet is crabs and other crustaceans, molluskan shellfish, sea anemones, squid and especially fish such as herring, sprat, pilchards, flatfish, cod, garfish and sand eels. It forms large single-sex schools, which has long made it a commercial catch for fishing fleets. Its flesh is sold mainly in Europe under many names such as "rock salmon" or "sea eel," and its body parts are processed into oils, pet foods, fertilizers, low-cost versions of shark's fin soup and many other products. Because of overfishing, its very slow growth rate, long reproductive cycle and small litters, the species is now in great trouble and a target for conservation. Its stock levels are critical in the northeast Atlantic, around European coasts, where it has been the most heavily fished. Tagging studies have shown individuals travel widely from warmer to cooler waters.

The spiny dogfish's two spines, one in front of each dorsal fin, and its lack of an anal fin, are typical characteristics of the dogfish family of sharks. Like all spiny dogfish, which may vary in color from gray to chocolate brown, this shark is countershaded, with a lighter belly and darker gray back.

Worldwide distribution

Classification

Phylum: Chordata
Class: Chondrichthyes
Subclass: Elasmobranchii
Order: Squaliformes
Family: Squalidae
Genus and species: *Cirrhigaleus barbifer*

Shark stats

Length: 4 feet (1.2 m)
Weight: 20 pounds (9 kg)
Habitat: Outer continental shelves and slopes, mainly deeper waters
Depth: Rarely less than 300 feet (92 m), usually 500–1,500 (152–457 m) feet, may descend below 2,000 feet (610 m)
Colors and markings: Gray, brown or some combination of these on the upper parts; paler underside; fins have pale to white edges
Sexual maturity: Male 2½ feet (76 cm), female 3½ feet (1 m)
Mating season: Unknown
Reproduction: Ovoviviparous
Gestation: Unknown
Litter: Unclear, possibly 10 young
Life span: Unknown, possibly 20-plus years

Range

West Pacific from Japan to New Zealand

In captivity

Almost unknown in captivity

Mandarin dogfish

Also called the mandarin shark, this species is characterized by its very enlarged barbels (feeler tendrils) developed from the anterior nasal flaps. These are elongated, fleshy and very sensitive, especially to touch, water currents and chemical substances. The shark probably trails these over the seabed to locate prey. The resemblance of the barbels to the long moustache formerly worn by Chinese men of rank led to the common name.

The mandarin dogfish has a short rounded snout, a smallish head and a spiracle behind each eye. The body is stout and wide. Each dorsal fin has a long, stout spine at the front. In the first dorsal fin the spine approaches the height of the fin itself, while in the second the spine may be as tall as the fin. The first dorsal is set just behind and above the pectoral fins, likewise the second dorsal is just behind and above the pelvics. The pectorals are large with rounded tips. The tail is very long and has a tall, upright upper lobe and a much smaller lower lobe. There is no anal fin, but there are lateral keels, or side ridges, on the caudal peduncle, where the body narrows to the base of the tail.

The blade-shaped teeth, 26 or 27 in the upper jaw and 22 to 26 in the lower jaw, interlock closely when the jaws close behind the pectoral fins below. Details of the mandarin shark's diet are scarce; it probably eats bottom-dwelling fish and various invertebrates, such as crabs.

They may look like a dog's whiskers, but the mandarin shark's barbels are precise sensors, capable of feeling its environment and detecting water currents and chemical changes. Mandarin sharks live on continental shelves and insular shelves at depths of more than 300 feet (92 m).

Worldwide distribution

Classification

Phylum: Chordata
Class: Chondrichthyes
Subclass: Elasmobranchii
Order: Squaliformes
Family: Somniosidae (Dalatiidae)
Genus and species: *Somniosus microcephalus*

Shark stats

Length: 18-plus feet (5.5+ m)
Weight: Occasionally more than 2,200 pounds
(907 kg)
Habitat: Cold deep water, usually
35–45°F (2–7°C), occasionally comes into
shallower bays and estuaries
Depth: Usually deep water at about 1,000 to
2,000 feet (305–610 m), down to 6,500 feet
(1,981 m)
Colors and markings: Generally dark gray to
brown, occasionally purplish, violet or black,
possibly dark or pale patches on the flanks,
few definite distinguishing marks
Sexual maturity: Unclear, probably at least
9 feet (2.7 m) for females
Mating season: Unknown
Reproduction: Ovoviviparous
Gestation: Unknown
Litter: Unclear, possibly up to 10 averaging
13–16 inches (33–41 cm) long
Life span: Unclear, possibly more than
100 years

Range

Cold waters of the North Atlantic, especially
the northwest—occurs father north than
almost any other shark species and as far
south as the Gulf of Saint Lawrence

In captivity

Has not survived for any appreciable time
in captivity

Greenland shark

One of the biggest of all sharks, the Greenland shark rivals the great white in size and appetite. Its many names include sleeper shark, gurry shark, ground shark, eqalussaq (an Inuit name) and håkjerring (in Norwegian). Its size, power and opportunistic scavenging habits—especially as a nuisance to local people and commercial fleets catching fish and whales—mean that this species features in many local tales and legends of Northern cultures.

Usually sluggish, this shark seems to be capable of bursts of speed, as indicated by the broad tail and the finding that it consumes fast-swimming fish, such as salmon, as well as squid, narwal, beluga (white whale) and right whales. It seizes prey with its 100 or so relatively small teeth, which are narrow, smooth-edged and sharp on the upper jaw, and wider and larger with pointed tips on the lower jaw. Its two dorsal and pectoral fins are relatively small, and there is no anal fin.

The Greenland shark has a varied diet, both pursuing live prey, such as fish, squid and seals, and scavenging. Its stomach contents include caribou, whales, such as the narwhal, beluga, white whale, right whale and bowhead, and it is known to be cannibalistic.

Many individuals are partly or completely blind due to the parasitic copepod *Ommatokoita* (a type of crustacean), which attaches to the outer part of the front of the eye, the cornea. However, the shark can use its other senses, especially smell, since it hunts in deep, dark waters. Its flesh is poisonous when fresh, causing problems similar to alcohol intoxication, but the poison can be negated by repeated boiling in water.

Because of their large size, Greenland sharks are common characters in Inuit legends. Although they are not known to be dangerous to humans, some legends tell of the shark attacking kayaks.

Worldwide distribution

Classification

Phylum: Chordata
Class: Chondrichthyes
Subclass: Elasmobranchii
Order: Squaliformes
Family: Centrophoridae
Genus and species: *Deania calcea*

Shark stats

Length: Up to 4 feet (1.2 m)
Weight: Up to 15 pounds (6.8 kg)
Habitat: Deepwater insular slopes, usually near the seafloor
Depth: 200–5,000 feet (61–1,524 m)
Colors and markings: Gray-brown all over
Sexual maturity: Males and females 2½ feet (76 cm)
Mating season: Unknown
Reproduction: Ovoviviparous
Litter: Up to 12 pups, usually 7 (range 1–17) averaging 12 inches (30 cm) in length
Life span: Probably more than 30 years

Range

The eastern Atlantic Ocean as far south as southern Africa, southern Australia, southern Indian Ocean, and eastern and western Pacific Ocean

In captivity

Rarely kept in captivity

Brier shark

The brier shark's long, flattened nose has given rise to a number of alternative nicknames, including the birdbeak dogfish and the shovel-nosed shark. It is gray-brown in color, and it features a spine in front of each dorsal fin.

Apart from its unusual dorsal fins, the brier shark lacks an anal fin. Its diet includes various kinds of bony fish, especially those found in the 1,500–3,000 feet (457–914 m) range such as myctophids—better known as lanternfish—as well as squid, octopus and other cephalopod mollusks, and crustaceans such as shrimps and crabs.

The brier shark's flesh is edible but not especially prized. The species has been caught chiefly for its liver, which contains high levels of the substance squalene, used in various processes and preparations in the pharmaceutical and cosmetic industries.

Squalene is less dense than water, and scientists believe that the high levels of this oil stored in the shark's liver help to keep its body buoyant in the sea. Shark-liver oil is not the only source of squalene, which is also found in amaranth seeds, wheat germ and olives, and many environmentalists argue that it would be better to extract the chemical from these vegetable sources instead of from sharks.

The brier shark can be identified by its front dorsal fin, which has a long base and lies close to the shark's body. For its weight, the brier shark's body is long and streamlined with a powerful tail. It feeds on fish and crustaceans.

Worldwide distribution

Classification

Phylum: Chordata
Class: Chondrichthyes
Subclass: Elasmobranchii
Order: Squaliformes
Family: Dalatiidae
Genus and species: *Euprotomicrus bispinatus*

Shark stats

Length: 9–11 inches (23–28 cm)
Weight: 1/3 ounce (9–28 g)
Habitat: Deep, temperate waters with little sunlight
Depth: Down to 6,500 feet (1,981 m) during the day, swims upward at night to feed on prey at roughly 650 feet (198 m)
Colors and markings: Black body with a lighter gray underside and a luminescent belly
Sexual maturity: Male 6 inches (15 cm), female 7 inches (18 cm)
Mating season: Unknown
Reproduction: Ovoviviparous
Eggs: 8 eggs—8 young of 6–10 cm
Life span: Unknown

Range

Tropical and subtropical seas worldwide

In captivity

Hardly ever kept captive, rarely survives being caught

Pygmy shark

At just 9–11 inches (23–28 cm) in length, the pygmy shark is one the smallest species of shark, matched only by its close relative the dwarf lantern shark. Its back is covered in dark gray markings, and it has a paler underside and white tips to its fins. The pygmy shark's most notable characteristic is its startling glow-in-the-dark belly, full of photo-luminescent chemicals. Scientists believe this confuses predators prowling in deeper waters, which are looking for a dark silhouette against the light background of the ocean's surface.

This pygmy shark can also be recognized by its proportionally large bulbous snout, big eyes, fleshy lips and very small dorsal fins, the first of which is extremely short and set well to the rear along the body. Its tail is paddle-like. Its small size means that the pygmy shark is relatively harmless to humans, although it does have large, knifelike lower teeth that it uses to shred squid, shrimps and other mid-water fish.

For most of the day this shark lives in deep water at about 6,500 feet (1,981 m) below the surface, but each night the shark rises to depths of just 650 feet (198 m) to hunt for its prey. In addition to hiding it from predators, the pygmy shark's bright underside may help it catch fish looking for the bright light of the surface water.

This photo shows the pygmy shark's characteristic white-tipped fins, bulbous snout and sleek, streamlined shape. It is very rare and barely ever seen by divers.

Worldwide distribution

Classification

Phylum: Chordata
Class: Chondrichthyes
Subclass: Elasmobranchii
Order: Pristiophoriformes
Family: Pristiophoridae
Genus and species: *Pristiophorus cirratus*

Shark stats

Length: 3 feet (0.9 m), occasionally
4½ feet (1.4 m)
Weight: Up to 22 pounds (10 kg)
Habitat: Mainly continental shelf
Depth: 130–980 feet (39–299 m) over varied
seabed, especially sand and mud
Colors and markings: Mix of yellows, grays
and browns, generally a pale background with
variable dark patches, blotches and bands in
the neck and gill region between the pectoral
fins and on the back in the region of the
dorsal fin
Sexual maturity: Unclear, male and female
probably 20–30 inches (51–76 cm)
Mating season: Summer
Reproduction: Ovoviviparous
Gestation: About 1 year
Litter: 10 (range of 3–22) young averaging
12–14 inches (30–36 cm) long
Life span: At least 15 years

Range

Southern coasts of Australia and nearby
islands in the south-east Indian Ocean and
south-west Pacific

In captivity

Occasionally kept in captivity, but tends not
to thrive in the typical densely populated
public aquaria

Longnose saw shark

There are about eight species of saw sharks in the genus *Pristiophorus*, which are broadly similar in anatomy and habits. The body is flattened from top to bottom, or dorsoventrally, and there is a very distinctive long, sawlike snout, or rostrum. In the longnose saw shark this forms more than one quarter of the total body length, with about 20 teeth along each side, which are dark edged and white underneath and usually alternate in size, slightly smaller and larger. A pair of long, fleshy sensory barbels, or tendrils, are situated about halfway along the saw. A spiracle is present near the eye, and the gill slits are on the sides of the head. There are two dorsal fins, the rear ones being slightly smaller, and 40–50 rostral teeth which are extremely sharp. The pups' very sharp teeth are folded back, presumably to avoid injuring the mother during birth; the teeth then straighten to allow feeding. Older individuals have toothlike denticles on the pectoral and pelvic fins.

The longnose saw shark eats small fish such as cornets, also shrimps, prawns and squid. It uses its pair of barbels for touch, and its electrosense and smell to find prey. The saw can be swiped sideways at victims or used to grub in the mud and dislodge animals. This species is commercially fished for the very flavorsome, high-quality flesh, which has severely depleted some longnose saw shark populations.

Other saw shark species include the Japanese saw shark, *Pristiophorus japonicus,* the Bahamas saw shark, *Pristiophorus schroederi*, and the shortnose saw shark, *Pristiophorus nudipinnis*. The sixgill saw shark is in a different genus, *Pliotrema warreni.*

The longnose saw shark is so called with good reason—the snout occupies between a quarter and a third of the total length of its body.

In addition to being a vicious weapon, the rostrum is a sensitive organ capable of detecting vibrations and bioelectricity. The whiskers, or barbels, are sensitive to pressure and chemical concentrations.

Worldwide distribution

Classification

Phylum: Chordata
Class: Chondrichthyes
Subclass: Elasmobranchii
Order: Squatiniformes
Family: Squatinidae
Genus and species: *Squatina sp. A*

Shark stats

Length: 4½ feet (1.4 m) rarely 5 feet (1.5 m)
Weight: Up to 45 pounds (20 kg)
Habitat: Seabed from the mid to outer continental shelf on mud and sand, also pebbles and rocks
Depth: 300–1,000 feet (92–305 m)
Colors and markings: Brown, varying from yellow-brown to rich chocolate brown, with darker, small white-centered spots and also large brown areas, paler on the underside
Sexual maturity: Unclear, probably 39–43 inches (99–109 cm)
Mating season: Late winter to late summer
Reproduction: Ovoviviparous
Gestation: 8–12 months
Litter: 10–15 (up to 20) young averaging 6–8 inches (15–20 cm)
Life span: Unknown, probably more than 20 years

Range

Eastern Australia from Victoria north round to Cairns, Queensland

In Captivity

Rarely kept in captivity

Eastern angel shark

Like the other angel sharks in the genus *Squatina*, this species resembles a ray or skate, rather than a shark. The body is flattened from top to bottom, and the pectoral and pelvic fins are held out to the side and are large and winglike (hence the name angel shark). The blunt, broad snout bears nasal barbels or tendrils with fringed edges and tips. The eyes are smaller than the spiracles, the head is slightly dished, or concave, between the eyes and there are orbital thorns, or enlarged dermal denticles, in the eyebrow region. The rear of the body and tail are more typically sharklike—the two small dorsal fins, the front one slightly larger, are set far back, between the pelvic fins and tail.

Angel sharks are principally bottom-dwellers and ambush predators. They lie part buried in sand, mud, fine pebbles or seaweeds, with just the eyes and top of the head showing, then lurch upward with a fast lunge to grab passing victims. There are small, sharp teeth in the upper and lower jaw, and the jaws protrude as the mouth opens and snap shut like a trap. The diet is bottom-dwelling or mid-water fish, including smaller sharks, skates and rays, flatfish, cuttlefish, octopus, crabs, prawns and other crustaceans. Among the 15 similar species in the widespread genus *Squatina* are the African angel shark, *Squatina africanas,* Atlantic angel shark or sand devil, *Squatina dumeril,* Japanese angel shark, *Squatina japonica* (the largest of the group at up to 6 feet (2 m), Pacific angel shark, *Squatina californica*, and angel shark, angelfish, or monkfish, *Squatina squatina*.

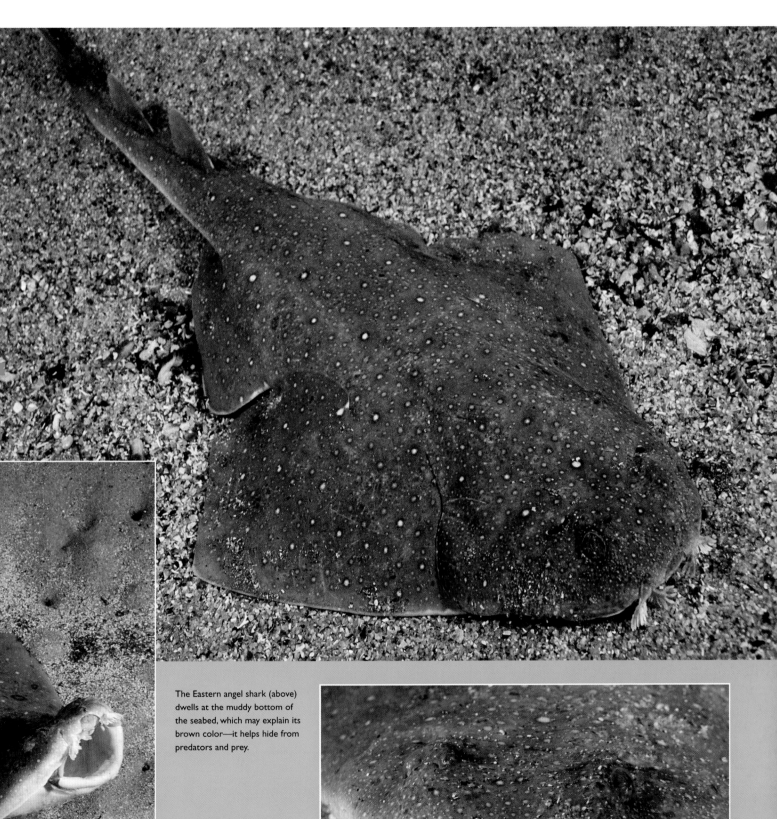

The Eastern angel shark (above) dwells at the muddy bottom of the seabed, which may explain its brown color—it helps hide from predators and prey.

The angel shark (left) buries itself until its unsuspecting prey, which can include small sharks, fish and prawns, passes by. Then it lunges up and grabs its victim with its small, sharp teeth.

Worldwide distribution

Classification

Phylum: Chordata
Class: Chondrichthyes
Subclass: Elasmobranchii
Order: Lamniformes
Family: Cetorhinidae
Genus and species: *Cetorhinus maximus*

Shark stats

Length: 26–33 feet (7.9–10 m), rarely exceeds 40 feet (12 m)
Weight: 2,200 pounds (998 kg) occasionally more than 11,000 pounds (4,990 kg) of which one quarter may be the liver
Habitat: A pelagic species found in all waters, from near coasts to the open ocean, rarely on or near the seabed
Depth: Generally less than 300 feet (92 m), moves to deeper water down to 3,300 feet (1,006 m) in winter
Colors and markings: Very variable, dark blue or gray or brown above, fading to pale or white on the belly, with individual patterns of indistinct patches and streaks mainly on the fins and flanks
Sexual maturity: Unclear, probably male 16 feet (4.9 m), female 23 feet (7 m)
Mating season: Unknown
Reproduction: Ovoviviparous
Gestation: Unclear, probably 12 to 16 months
Litter: 6 young (very few cases recorded) averaging 5–10 feet (1.5–3 m) long
Life span: Unknown, probably more than 50 years

Range

Worldwide in temperate seas and oceans with waters between about 45°F and 60°F (7–15°C), including bays and inshore and open ocean

In captivity

Smaller specimens have not survived for any appreciable time

Basking shark

Famed as the second-largest fish in the world, after the whale shark, this plankton-feeding species may be seen in large schools in the summer in many oceans, following the drifting planktonic food. It is wide bodied and stout with a tall, triangular dorsal fin about halfway along the body, midway between the pectoral and pelvic fins, a much smaller dorsal fin near the tail, the anal fin below that fin and ridges, or sideways-projecting keels, at the caudal peduncle where the body tapers toward the tail. The tail is lunate, with the lower lobe almost as large as the upper.

The basking shark has a conical snout projecting above a huge mouth up to 3 feet (0.9 m) in width, which it gapes open while feeding. The shark swims forward slowly so that a ram-jet action pushes water into the mouth, over the gill rakers and out through the gill slits, which almost join at the top and bottom to encircle the head. It was believed that in winter, when the food supply is scarce, basking sharks shed their gill rakers and rested on the seabed. It is now known they are active all year, and they dive to feed on deeper plankton in winter, and the rakers are shed and regrow at regular intervals. These sharks, also known as elephant sharks or bone sharks, often swim lazily at the surface even when not feeding, on their side or their back, and may roll over. Despite their bulk and slow habits, they can leap or breach almost clear of the water.

The basking shark is sometimes mistaken for the great white shark. However, its large, cavernous jaw and long gill slits are two distinctive characteristics.

The basking shark is most often seen in this way, swimming through the water with its mouth open as it filters the water for plankton, fish and invertebrates.

Worldwide distribution

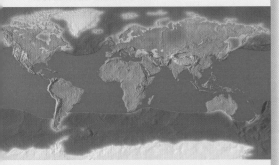

Classification

Phylum: Chordata
Class: Chondrichthyes
Subclass: Elasmobranchii
Order: Lamniformes
Family: Lamnidae
Genus and species: *Isurus oxyrinchus*

Shark stats

Length: 8–10 feet (2.4–3 m), occasionally over 11 feet (3.4 m)
Weight: 330 pounds (150 kg) rarely more than 1,100 pounds (499 kg)
Habitat: Most marine habitats, including inshore, offshore and open ocean, preferring water at 60–70°F (16–21°C), shows migratory patterns
Depth: From the surface down to 2,500 feet (762 m), depending on water temperature and prey availability
Colors and markings: Often called "metallic" blue on the back and upper sides, sharply demarcated from the pale to white lower sides and belly; mouth area is white (in the longfin mako it is blue); color tends to darken with age
Sexual maturity: Male 6½ feet (2 m), female 8–10 feet (2.4–3 m)
Mating season: Variable
Reproduction: Ovoviviparous
Gestation: 15–18 months
Litter: After intrauterine cannibalism, 8–10 young (range 4–20) averaging 28 inches 71 cm) long
Life span: Unclear, probably 20 years or more

Range

Worldwide in all tropical and temperate waters, as far north as the UK, Japan and the north Pacific and as far south as the tips of South America, Africa and New Zealand

In captivity

Not suited to life in captivity

Shortfin mako

Sleek and streamlined, the spindle-shaped shortfin mako holds the record as the fastest shark and one of the quickest of all fish. It can cruise at great speed, covering more than 1,200 miles (1,931 km) in less than 40 days. It is renowned for its fighting power when hooked and can leap more than 20 feet (6 m) above the surface.

This mako (the name is taken from a New Zealand Maori word for "shark") has a fairly pointed snout, large black eyes, gill slits just in front of the pectoral fins, a smallish dorsal fin set between the pectorals and pelvics, relatively small pectoral fins, which are nevertheless larger than the pelvics, and small second dorsal and anal fin, sited well back, near the tail. The tail is crescentic, or lunate, with the lower lobe almost as large as the upper, and there is a longitudinal ridge, or lateral caudal keel, projecting on each side from the rear body and tail (caudal peduncle).

The teeth are long, hooklike and pointed, with very sharp but smooth (non-serrated) edges and triangular bases. They number about 30 in each row of each jaw and are visible when the mouth is closed, especially in the lower jaw. The diet is mainly other fish, including sharks, tuna, bonitos, bluefish and swordfish, as well as squid and, less commonly, marine mammals, such as sea otters, porpoises and small seals, and marine turtles.

The closest relative of the shortfin mako is the longfin mako, *Isurus paucus*, which has bigger eyes and pectoral fins.

The shortfin mako's teeth are long and smooth. They protrude so much that they are visible even when the shark's mouth is closed.

The mako's powerful body allows it to swim very quickly. Angry makos have even been known to jump on board a ship if they are caught by a fishing hook.

Worldwide distribution

Classification

Phylum: Chordata
Class: Chondrichthyes
Subclass: Elasmobranchii
Order: Lamniformes
Family: Lamnidae
Genus and species: *Carcharodon carcharias*

Shark stats

Length: Much exaggerated, 16–20 feet (1.8–6 m), rarely 21 feet (6.4 m)
Weight: Usually up to 2,200 pounds (998 kg), rarely more than 4,400 pounds (1,996 kg)
Habitat: All waters, from coastal shallows and bays to the open ocean, more generally recorded inshore, even into the surf
Depth: Usually from the surface down to 800 feet (244 m) but has been tracked to 4,000 feet (1,219 m); usually cruises near the surface or seabed
Colors and markings: Gray, gray-brown, bronze or bluish above with vague light and dark areas, pale to white underside, relatively distinct but irregular demarcation between the two running through the snout/eye areas and along the lower flanks
Sexual maturity: Male 11–13 feet (3.4–4 m), female 15 feet (4.6 m)
Mating season: Variable, usually summer
Reproduction: Ovoviviparous
Gestation: 10–12 months
Litter: After intrauterine cannibalism from up to 40 embryos, 2–10 young, average length 3–4½ feet (0.9–1.4 m)
Life span: Unknown, possibly more than 40 years

Range

Worldwide in subtropical to cool seas and oceans, generally with the water temperature range 53–75°F (12–24°C); shows marked migratory behavior

In captivity

None have survived for any appreciable time

Great white shark

Also known as the white pointer, blue pointer, white shark, white death and man-eater, this is one of the most famous animals on the planet. Yet, despite its reputation, relatively little is actually known about its life cycle. The great white has a heavy, muscular body; pointed snout; black eyes; a tall, triangular slightly backswept dorsal fin; very small second dorsal fin set well back, just above the equally small anal fin; large sickle-shaped pectoral fins; a large central girth when well fed; caudal keels near the tail; and a crescentic tail with the lower lobe almost as large as the upper.

The upper jaw houses 25–30 large, triangular, serrated-edged teeth, which saw off lumps of the prey with a side-to-side head motion, while the lower teeth are similar in number, narrower, more pointed and serrated. Great whites consume a wide array of generally large prey items, including large fish, such as tuna, rays and smaller sharks, marine mammals, including seals, sealions, dolphins, porpoises and small whales, seabirds and sea turtles. Juveniles take smaller fish and squid. They may also scavenge on large whale carcasses.

The great white shows the behavior known as "spy-hopping," when it holds its body vertically and exposes its head, presumably to look around—unusual among sharks but common in many kinds of whales and dolphins. Migration can be marked—one tagged individual was tracked from southern Africa to Australia and back, a distance of more than 11,000 miles (17,703 km), which it covered in less than nine months.

(Above) The great white shark's countershading—with a dark back and white underbelly—confuses prey by breaking up the shark's outline when viewed head on. A terrifying sight (right) for nearby swimmers and divers, this is a great white shark "spy-hopping," lifting its head out of the water to view its surroundings.

Worldwide distribution

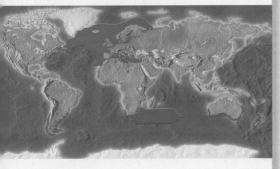

Classification

Phylum: Chordata
Class: Chondrichthyes
Subclass: Elasmobranchii
Order: Lamniformes
Family: Lamnidae
Genus and species: *Lamna nasus*

Shark stats

Length: Up to 12 feet (3.7 m)
Weight: up to 550 pounds (249 kg)
Habitat: Cool waters (below 60°F/16°C) on continental shelves or inshore
Depth: Down to 1,200 feet (366 m)
Colors and markings: Dark gray, blue or intermediate on back, fading to pale underneath, characteristic white area on rear edge of the dorsal fin
Sexual maturity: Male 5½ feet (1.7 m) female 7 feet (2.1 m)
Mating season: late summer/early fall
Reproduction: Ovoviviparous
Gestation: 8–9 months
Litter: Usually about 4 pups (range 2–6) averaging 2–3 feet (61–91 cm) at birth
Life span: Estimated at more than 40 years

Range

Across the North Atlantic, as far north as Iceland and northern Norway, and cooler waters around most of the Southern Hemisphere

In captivity

Not generally well suited to life in captivity

Porbeagle

You wouldn't think so to look at it, but the stout and heavy porbeagle shark is actually one of the fastest swimmers in the sea. It is also one of the few sharks capable of jumping fully out of the water. Like the salmon shark, one of its close relatives, it has two keels on the caudal fin, which help to propel it to great speeds when swimming.

Measuring up to 12 feet (3.7 m) in length and with a dark gray back and white underbelly, the porbeagle is often mistaken for its relative—the great white shark. Its key distinguishing feature is a white smudge on the back-edge of the dorsal fin.

Unlike most sharks, which are cold blooded, the porbeagle is capable of raising its body temperature 14°F (8°C) above the temperature of the water. This is in part due to the design of its blood vessels, which ensure that blood traveling from the cold extremities of the animal flows near to the hotter blood that has just left its warm muscles. Heat passes between the ingoing and outgoing blood to ensure that it stays at a warmer temperature in certain vital body parts.

Although the porbeagle has been known to attack humans, its usual diet is small bony fish like mackerels and herrings. It has long, sharp teeth, which it uses to spear its prey and stop it from escaping. These teeth are not capable of shredding the meat, so the prey is generally swallowed whole.

While its manic eyes and sharp teeth suggest a vicious and dangerous predator, the porbeagle's diet is usually bony fish, such as mackerel and herring, which it usually swallows whole.

Worldwide distribution

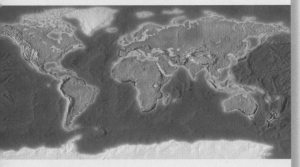

Classification

Phylum: Chordata
Class: Chondrichthyes
Subclass: Elasmobranchii
Order: Lamniformes
Family: Mitsukurinidae
Genus and species: *Mitsukurina owstoni*

Shark stats

Length: Up to 12 feet (3.7 m)
Weight: Rarely exceeds 450 pounds (209 kg)
Habitat: Deeper warm to temperate waters,
usually on or near the seabed but also at
middle levels
Depth: 650–4,300 feet (198–1,311 m)
Colors and markings: Often the body is
pink, but sometimes gray, blue and white
underneath, and sometimes redish brown
Sexual maturity: Thought to be 7½ feet
(2.3 m) for both males and females
Mating season: Uncertain
Reproduction: Thought to be ovoviviparous
Gestation: Uncertain; no pregnant goblin shark
has ever been found
Litter: Uncertain
Life span: Currently not known

Range

Specimens are rare and isolated but are
known from areas around Japan, the west and
east Atlantic, off western Europe, west and
southern Africa, and in the east Pacific off the
shores of California

In captivity

A goblin shark caught in Tokyo Bay in 2007
was taken to the Tokyo Sea Life Park for
display and study but died 2 days later;
no other specimen has ever been taken
into captivity

Goblin shark

The goblin shark, or *tenguzame* as it is known in Japan, is named after the goblinlike creature *tengu* from Japanese folklore, which it closely resembles due to its very long, pointed snout. It is a very strange-looking fish, with large jaws that protrude prominently from its face during feeding but otherwise lie inside its head. Scientists believe the goblin shark's long snout may contain extra electrical sensors that help the shark to find its way around the deep ocean, where there is little light.

The goblin shark is also unusual because of its blushing pink color, which is due to a semitransparent skin covering many small blood vessels. For this reason, the goblin shark bruises very easily. Its fins are small and rounded.

The goblin shark is rarely seen, and reports suggest only 45 specimens have ever been scientifically studied. Unsurprisingly, not much is known about them. One of the biggest mysteries surrounding the goblin shark is the reason for its large liver, which accounts for up to 25 percent of its body weight. Possibly because of their strange appearance and their rarity, the remains of the goblin shark are very valuable when caught: collectors will pay up to U.S. $4,000 for the skeleton of their jaws. Despite its rarity, the goblin shark is found across the world, and its numbers are not thought to be in significant decline, since humans rarely manage to catch or kill this elusive shark.

A case for some serious orthodontic treatment? The goblin shark is surely one of the most distinctive creatures in the sea, with its prominent, moveable jaws that protrude from its face during hunting.

Worldwide distribution

Classification

Phylum: Chordata
Class: Chondrichthyes
Subclass: Elasmobranchii
Order: Lamniformes
Family: Alopiidae
Genus and species: *Alopias vulpinus*

Shark stats

Length: Up to 18 feet (5.5 m)
Weight: 900 pounds (408 kg), rarely more
Habitat: Preferably open ocean but also
inshore when pursuing prey
Depth: Surface to 1,300-plus feet (396+ m)
Colors and markings: Shiny brown to blue
or gray on the upper side, pale to white
underside, variable mottling mainly along the
flanks, especially near and behind the pectorals,
and perhaps extending to the underside
Sexual maturity: Male 9 feet (2.7 m),
female 10 feet (3 m)
Mating season: Summer
Reproduction: Ovoviviparous
Gestation: 8–10 months
Litter: After intrauterine cannibalism, 4–6
young averaging 4–5 feet long (1.2–1.5 m)
Life span: Unclear, probably more than
25 years, possibly 50 years

Range

Worldwide in cool to warm waters, less
common in the warmest regions, migrate to
higher latitudes for summer breeding

In captivity

Small threshers have survived reasonably well
in captivity

Thresher shark

Also called the thin-tailed or long-tailed thresher, foxshark, spindletail, swiveltail, common and Atlantic thresher, this species is immediately distinguished by its extremely long upper tail lobe, which expands at the tip and has a slight notch and triangular, downward-pointing lower lobe at its base. The tail may be half the length of the body and is thick skinned and leathery. The snout is short and abrupt, the head small, the body stout, the pectoral fins long, sickle shaped and pointed, and the pelvic fins have concave trailing edges. The pectorals and pelvics may have darker patches and blotches. The second dorsal and anal fins are tiny, with the former set just in front of the latter.

The thresher's teeth are small, curved, smooth-edged and extremely sharp and of much the same shape in both jaws. Its prey is mainly schooling fish, such as lancets, bluefish, menhaden, mackerel and herring, as well as squid, octopus and crustaceans. Various reports describe the shark thrashing its tail to herd the fish together and to wound or stun them. Observers have also noted that two threshers or even more may work together to gather a fish school. Seabirds are also taken, again reportedly slapped with the tail.

Threshers are migratory, swimming away from the tropics to cooler waters in spring for summer breeding and returning in autumn. The bigeye thresher, *Alopias superciliosus*, is similar to the common thresher and named for its large, dark eyes; it is thought to be a deep-water inhabitant. The smallest of the three species in the genus is the pelagic thresher, *Alopias pelagicus*.

The large eyes of this thresher (above) help it to see in the darkest depths of the ocean. This thresher shark (right) has beautiful, shimmering purple-gray skin, but they can range from gray-brown to blue. All threshers have a paler underside.

Worldwide distribution

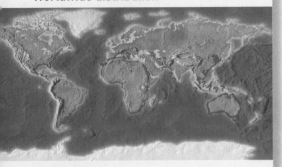

Classification

Phylum: Chordata
Class: Chondrichthyes
Subclass: Elasmobranchii
Order: Lamniformes
Family: Odontaspididae
Genus and species: *Carcharias taurus*

Shark stats

Length: 6½–10 feet (2–3 m), occasionally 10½ feet (3.2 m)
Weight: Up to 350 pounds (159 kg)
Habitat: Coastal waters and shallows, especially over sandy seabeds, even into the surf zone; also rocky or gravelly areas and reefs, moving to deeper water in winter
Depth: Usually less than 500 feet (152 m), occasionally down below 650 feet (198 m)
Colors and markings: Gray, brownish, greenish or bronze above, fading gradually to paler below, with red or brown spots along the flanks to the tail that diminish with age
Sexual maturity: Male 6–7 feet (1.8–2.1 m) female 7–7½ feet (2.1–2.3 m)
Mating season: Winter and spring
Reproduction: Ovoviviparous
Gestation: Unclear, reports vary from 6 to 12 months
Litter: After intrauterine cannibalism, usually 2 young averaging 3 feet (0.9 m) long
Life span: 16 years in captivity

Range

Warmer and tropical seas worldwide, migrating to higher latitudes in spring and back toward the equator in autumn

In captivity

Due to its sharp teeth, its tendency to swim with its mouth open, which presents a fearsome appearance, and its shallow-water habitat, this is perhaps the most popular aquarium species of sizeable shark

Sand tiger

Not to be confused with the tiger shark (see page 56), or variously but vaguely named sand sharks, the sand tiger nevertheless has many alternative names, such as gray nurse, spotted ragtooth, ground shark and slender-toothed shark. The mouth is elongated, extending behind the eye when seen from the side. The first dorsal fin is medium sized and set nearer the pelvics than the pectorals, and the second dorsal is only slightly smaller. There are large triangular pectoral fins, and the tail is very asymmetrical, with an enlarged upper lobe and a smaller triangular lobe pointing down and "mirroring" the anal fin just in front of it.

The sand tiger's teeth are long but slim, like spikes and there are usually three rows of 40–50 in each jaw. The cusps are smooth edged rather than serrated, and each one has two very small side points, or cusps. The narrow teeth give a gap-toothed or "snaggle-like" appearance. They are suited to relatively small prey which they hunt at night, especially a varied array of bony fish—flatfish, herrings, snappers, hake, bass, remoras, sea robins and many others—and also smaller sharks and rays, squid and crustaceans such as crabs and shrimps.

These sharks have been observed feeding cooperatively, surrounding prey to concentrate them and make feeding dashes into the school more successful. The sand tiger also has an unusual ability to alter its buoyancy by swallowing in or belching (ejecting) air at the surface, thereby enabling it to stay at a certain depth with little energy expenditure.

The sand tiger has an elongated jaw that extends beyond the level of its eyes when viewed from the side.

The sand tiger's gappy teeth have lead to many unflattering alternative names, such as the ragged-toothed shark, the spotted ragtooth and the slender-toothed shark.

Worldwide distribution

Classification

Phylum: Chordata
Class: Chondrichthyes
Subclass: Elasmobranchii
Order: Lamniformes
Family: Megachasmidae
Genus and species: *Megachasma pelagios*

Shark stats

Length: Up to 18 feet (5.5 m), possibly more
Weight: Up to 2,650 pounds (1,202 kg)
Habitat: Open water in warmer tropical oceans, rarely inshore
Depth: Probably 650 feet (198 m) or more by day, coming nearer to the surface during nightly vertical migrations
Colors and markings: Brown or gray-blue to black above, fading to pale on the underside with paler fin-tips, a white band on the upper front of the snout in the "upper lip" area and few other distinguishing marks
Sexual maturity: Unclear, possibly male 13 feet (4 m), female 16 feet (4.9 m)
Mating season: Unknown
Reproduction: Unknown
Gestation: Unknown
Litter: Unknown
Life span: Unknown

Range

The rarity of this shark makes judgments difficult, with most sightings and catches in the northwest Pacific, but, as data build, it is thought to occupy tropical and warmer waters worldwide

In captivity

No chance!

Megamouth shark

Discovered only in 1976 and averaging not much more than one new sighting each year, the large, flabby, sluggish megamouth has nevertheless achieved charismatic status to become one of the most fascinating of shark species. Its stout body has soft, loose skin and flesh. The blunt, wide, long head bears the mouth at the front tip (rather than underslung as in typical sharks), a bulging forehead, deep-set eyes above the mouth line and a small spiracle just behind each eye. The large pectoral fins resemble whale flippers and contrast with the reduced pelvic fins. The smallish, low front dorsal fin is set behind the pectorals, with a much smaller second dorsal fin back toward the tail and an even smaller anal fin almost at the lower base of the tail. There is a very long upper lobe to the tail, reminiscent of, but not as extreme as, that of the thresher shark.

The megamouth's hundreds of small hooked teeth are in up to 50 rows in the upper jaw and 75 in the lower, lining the jaw edges. The mouth's interior might be silvery or reflective; whether or not the lips and mouth are bioluminescent is much debated.

One of only three species of filter-feeding sharks, the others being the whale and basking sharks, the megamouth opens its huge, rubbery-lipped mouth and protrudes its jaws to sieve plankton, especially the euphasiid shrimps called krill and soft-bodied creatures, such as jellyfish. From depths of perhaps hundreds of feet by day, the megamouth comes toward the surface after dark, rising to 65 feet (20 m) or less.

The megamouth's large, rounded mouth and broad snout sometimes lead it to be mistaken for a young orca. Its bioluminescent lips may attract plankton, which it feeds on.

Worldwide distribution

Classification

Phylum: Chordata
Class: Chondrichthyes
Subclass: Elasmobranchii
Order: Carcharhiniformes
Family: Carcharhinidae
Genus and species: *Triaenodon obesus*

Shark stats

Length: 4½–5 feet (1.4–1.5m), rarely 6 ½–plus feet (2+ m)
Weight: 44 pounds (20 kg) rarely more than 55 pounds (25 kg)
Habitat: Chiefly on and around coral reefs
Depth: Usually 32–131 feet (9.8–40 m), though rarely down to 1,000 feet (305 m)
Colors and markings: Gray, brown or gray-brown above, paler below and darker dorsal, anal and caudal (tail) fins with distinctive white tips to first dorsal and upper caudal fins
Sexual maturity: 5 years
Mating season: Autumn–winter
Reproduction: Viviparous
Gestation: 5-plus months
Litter: 1–5 averaging 20–23 inches (51–58 cm) long
Life span: 20-plus years

Range

Tropical and subtropical seas of the Pacific and Indian oceans, especially around coral reefs

In captivity

Due to their docile nature, whitetip reef sharks are relatively common aquarium and sea-life center species, and they are also maintained in marine research laboratory tanks for scientific study. Examples include the specimens kept at Waikiki Aquarium, Honolulu, and the Steinhart Aquarium, San Francisco

Whitetip reef shark

The whitetip reef shark is medium sized and generally gray or gray-brown with a pale, even white underside. The characteristic white tips on the first dorsal and upper caudal fins may also be present on the pelvic fins. The second dorsal fin is relatively large and helps to distinguish this reef shark from the silvertip and oceanic whitetip sharks. The wide, short snout and underslung nostrils are also distinctive, and the teeth are smooth edged rather than serrated. The tough skin and comparatively flexible fins allow the whitetip to maneuver among cramped, sharp-edged coral.

Whitetip reef sharks rarely stray from the central regions of their reef, leaving the reef edges and plunging shelves to other reef shark species. By day they rest in caves or cracks, sometimes in groups, being able to pump water across their gills while stationary. Often a shark returns to its favorite secluded day site for months on end. At night the shark becomes active and hunts a variety of prey, such as eels, parrotfish, damselfish, triggerfish, goatfish, squirrelfish and other fish, as well as shellfish such as crabs, lobsters, prawns and shrimps, and octopus. It is surprisingly agile and energetic among the coral cracks and crevices and sometimes hunts in groups with its own kind or with other reef sharks.

This shark is generally not aggressive and coexists with others of its kind with few disputes over territory or food. If approached by humans it tends to swim away but may attempt to bite if cornered or repeatedly harassed.

The distinctive white tips are most noticeable on dark gray individuals (above), but they can also be seen on yellow-skinned whitetip reef sharks.

Worldwide distribution

Classification

Phylum: Chordata
Class: Chondrichthyes
Subclass: Elasmobranchii
Order: Carcharhiniformes
Family: Carcharhinidae
Genus and species: *Galeocerdo cuvier*

Shark stats

Length: 10–12 feet (3–3.7 m) occasionally 16-plus feet (4.9+ m)
Weight: Up to 1,300 pounds (590 kg)
Habitat: Most habitats—from coasts, including harbors, bays, estuaries and inlets, to offshore reefs and open ocean
Depth: Down to 1,000 feet (305 m) by day, moves inshore to shallower water at night
Colors and markings: Gray-green or gray-blue shading to black above, pale underside may be cream, light gray or muddy yellow
Sexual maturity: Male 8 feet (2.4 m), female 10 feet (3 m)
Mating season: Spring
Reproduction: Ovoviviparous
Gestation: 12 months
Litter: 20–50 young averaging 20–30 inches (51–76 cm) long
Life span: 25-plus years

Range

Tropical and subtropical seas worldwide, ventures into warm temperate regions in summer or with warm ocean currents

In captivity

Many aquaria and sea-life centers have kept tiger sharks, occasionally for three or four years, including in recent times at Maui Ocean Center in Hawaii, Veracruz Aquarium in Mexico, Beijing Aquarium in China and Shark Bay Gold Coast by Sea World in Australia

Tiger shark

The young tiger shark, up to about 6 feet (1.8 m) long, has a mottled or striped appearance, with dark blotches on a light background, especially on the dorsal fin. These may merge into vertical stripes, hence the name "tiger" and the alternative names of leopard and spotted shark, but the markings tend to fade with age. The tiger shark has a large head, a short, bluntly rounded snout and its exceptionally sharp "rooster comb" teeth are very serrated with deep notches. The first dorsal fin is larger than the second.

This shark is mainly a solitary wanderer. Although appearing sluggish, it can burst into action and attain a speed of more than 20 miles per hour (32 km/h) within a couple of seconds but cannot maintain this for long. Most of its time is spent slowly cruising, covering distances of 45 miles (72 km) or more every 24 hours in search of food and feeding mainly at night.

The tiger shark is famed for its scavenging habits and consumption of inedible items. It will take almost any nearly dead or dead meat, including fish, shellfish, squid, octopus, reptiles such as turtles and sea snakes, all kinds of seabirds and mammals including seals, dolphins and whales. It may also actively hunt prey such as eels and smaller sharks (including its own kind). Tales abound of tiger sharks caught and cut open to reveal all kinds of strange objects in their guts, from bottles and lumps of wood to bags of coal and potatoes, clothing, car tires and even a tom-tom drum. The tiger shark has a notorious reputation and is perhaps second only to the great white in numbers of recorded attacks on humans.

Tiger sharks generally hunt by themselves. They are known to drift sluggishly through the sea until they see something of interest, when they can produce rapid bursts of speed for short periods.

Although the tiger shark's markings are more evident in the young and tend to fade with age, they can be seen clearly on the side of this adult shark.

Worldwide distribution

Classification

Phylum: Chordata
Class: Chondrichthyes
Subclass: Elasmobranchii
Order: Carcharhiniformes
Family: Carcharhinidae
Genus and species: *Carcharhinus leucas*

Shark stats

Length: Males up to 7 feet (2.1 m),
females up to 11½ feet (3.5 m)
Weight: Males up to 200 pounds (91 kg)
females up to 700 pounds (318 kg)
Habitat: Coastal waters of warm oceans and
both salt- and freshwater rivers and lakes
Depth: Usually no deeper than 100 feet
(31 m), but up to 500 feet (152 m)
Sexual maturity: Male 5¼ feet (1.6 m),
females 6½ feet (2 m)
Mating season: Summer
Reproduction: Viviparous
Gestation: 1 year
Litter: Up to 13 young, each about 2 feet
(60 cm) long
Life span: Up to 32 years

Range

Just off the Pacific and Atlantic coasts of North
and South America; around much of the coast
of sub-Saharan Africa; far along the Amazon
and Mississippi river systems; along the shores
of India, Southeast Asia and Australia

In captivity

The bull shark is thought to be hardy and
well suited to a long life (up to 25 years) in
captivity; examples include uShaka Marine
World in South Africa and Sea World Florida
in the U.S.

Bull shark

With its plain gray markings and broad, flat snout, the bull shark is not known for its
beauty. It is significantly wider than other sharks of a comparable length (a relatively
large 11½ feet/3.5 m), giving it a beefy frame, and it is also known for its aggressive
and unpredictable behavior—all features that contribute to its "bullish" reputation.
Its long and tapered back fin is also instantly recognizable.

The bull shark is one of the few sharks capable of living in freshwater rivers and
lakes as well as saltwater in the sea—it has even been known to survive 2,500 miles
(4,023 km) up the Amazon River system. Most sharks' blood contains minerals
at the same concentration as saltwater, and swimming in freshwater, which is less
concentrated, can disrupt this balance, leading to illness and death. Bull sharks
living in freshwater have adapted by drinking lots of water, which has the effect of
reducing the concentration of their blood to match the water outside. But this has
an unpleasant side effect—bull sharks living in freshwater produce 20 times more
urine than those living in saltwater.

Bull sharks are solitary hunters that cruise through shallow waters. Once prey has
been spotted, they are capable of great bursts of speed. They have been known
to attack humans in the Ganges River in India and along the Natal coast of South
Africa. Given their size and ferocity, few animals scare them, although they have been
known to be the victim of attacks by alligators and larger sharks.

The bull shark's long, tapered back fin, seen very
clearly here, is one of the its most recognizable
characteristics. The bull shark's beefy frame
and broad snout, and its unpredictable bullish
temperament, all gave rise to its name.

Worldwide distribution

Classification

Phylum: Chordata
Class: Chondrichthyes
Subclass: Elasmobranchii
Order: Carcharhiniformes
Family: Carcharhinidae
Genus and species: *Carcharhinus longimanus*

Shark stats

Length: Around 10 feet (3 m), up to 14 feet (4.3 m) on occasion
Weight: Up to 375 pounds (170 kg)
Habitat: Deep open water at temperatures between 68–82°F (20–28°C)
Depth: Down to 500 feet (152 m)
Colors and markings: Gray, brown or gray-brown above, paler below, darker dorsal, anal and caudal (tail) fins with distinctive white tips to first dorsal and upper caudal fin
Sexual maturity: Male 6 feet (1.8 m), female 7 feet (2.1 m)
Mating season: Early summer in the northwest Atlantic and southwest Indian Ocean; apparently year-round in the Pacific
Reproduction: Viviparous
Gestation: 1 year
Litter: 1–15 young, each 2 feet (60 cm) long
Life span: Males 12 years, females 16 years

Range

Deep open waters between 68°F and 82°F (20–28°C), in a wide band extending around the world's ocean from the U.S. and Portugal in the north to Chile, South Africa and Australia in the south

In captivity

Due to their aggressive nature they need either a private environment or specially chosen tank mates. Examples include the Monterey Bay Aquarium in the U.S.

Oceanic whitetip

The oceanic whitetip shark can be recognized by the distinctive white rings at the tips of almost every fin on its body. Its predominant color is between bronze, brown and bluish gray, depending on where it was born, and it is also known for its large, winglike pectoral and dorsal fins.

Some experts believe that the old-fashioned term for sharks as "sea dogs" stemmed from the oceanic whitetip's habit of following ships—often in packs—in a doglike manner. Its movement resembles a playful and bashful puppy, cautiously approaching the boat but backing away to a safe distance at the least sign of danger. This behavior probably arises from their instinct to follow schools of tuna and squid—two of their favorite foods.

It may sound cute, but frequently this taste for following boats can take on a more menacing nature. In 1945, the *USS Indianapolis* was torpedoed by an enemy submarine, and experts believe that many of the sailors on board were eaten by a pack of oceanic whitetip sharks. Similar attacks on other shipwrecks and fallen planes were reported throughout the 20th century, and although not all these deaths have been officially attributed to the oceanic whitetip, the numbers may amount to thousands—makings its death count even greater than the great white shark.

However, the tide may now be turning on the oceanic whitetip shark, and its numbers are dwindling rapidly. Its large fins are considered a delicacy, and they are used as the chief ingredient in shark fin soup, a popular Cantonese dish; it is also facing stiff competition from fisheries for its diet of bony fish. Considered one of the most abundant large creatures in the sea in the late 1960s, studies have revealed that its numbers dropped by as much as 70 percent in the western areas of the Atlantic Ocean between 1992 and 2000; it is now considered "vulnerable" on the IUCN Red List of threatened species (see page 212).

The oceanic whitetip's coloring can vary from brown to blue-gray. However, all have the distinctive white smudges at the tips of their fins.

Worldwide distribution

Classification

Phylum: Chordata
Class: Chondrichthyes
Subclass: Elasmobranchii
Order: Carcharhiniformes
Family: Carcharhinidae
Genus and species: *Negaprion brevirostris*

Shark stats

Length: Normally 8–10 feet (2.4–3 m), although a 12-foot (3.6 m) shark was once recorded
Weight: Up to 400 pounds (181 kg)
Habitat: Shallow tropical waters, including reefs, bays and mangrove swamps
Depth: Shallow waters, to 300 feet (92 m)
Colors and markings: Darker back in shades of yellow, brown, olive, gray or some combination of these grading to paler yellow or creamy underside, no obvious markings
Sexual maturity: Male 7 feet (2.1 m), female 8 feet (2.4 m)
Mating season: During the spring months
Reproduction: Viviparous
Gestation: 10–12 months
Litter: 4–17 young averaging 23–26 inches (58–66 cm) in length
Life span: Unknown

Range

Tropical coasts of the Americas, including Pacific, Caribbean and Atlantic, and West Africa

In captivity

Lemon sharks are widely kept as they survive better than many other species. They are therefore one of the best known sharks in terms of behavior and ecology. Famously, Dr. Samuel Gruber at the University of Miami has studied captive lemon sharks since the late 1960s

Lemon shark

The lemon shark is known for its golden-brown color and pale, off-white underbelly. It can also be recognized by its big dorsal fins, both of equal size, and its wide, flat head. This shark suffers from very poor eyesight, but it makes up for this with extraordinarily sensitive magnetic sensors in its nose, which it uses to locate food, predators and sexual partners.

Unlike many sharks, the lemon shark can survive in shallow water with very low oxygen content, allowing it to live in the mangroves, reefs and river mouths of Latin America and the Caribbean. These sharks rarely venture into the deep sea during their day-to-day life, but recent genetics work has shown they are willing to travel over hundreds of miles to find a mate, with Florida seeming to be a preferred breeding ground.

Despite its large size (it can grow up to 12 feet/3.6 m in length), the lemon shark is of little danger to humans or other mammals, preferring instead to feed on shellfish, bony fish and other sharks. There have been just 22 reported attacks on humans since 1580, with none of them fatal.

In fact, these sharks are of great use to scientists because they live quite happily in captivity; other species, such as the great white shark, refuse to eat when held captive. This has led to them being the most well-understood shark in terms of both their behavior and ecology.

The lemon shark has adapted to life in shallow water with very low oxygen content, meaning it can survive in reefs, bays and mangrove swamps.

The lemon shark's distinctive golden-brown coloring and its wide, flat head help to differentiate it from other sharks. It suffers from poor eyesight but makes up for this with magnetic sensors.

Worldwide distribution

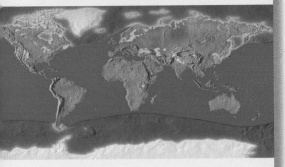

Classification

Phylum: Chordata
Class: Chondrichthyes
Subclass: Elasmobranchii
Order: Carcharhiniformes
Family: Carcharhinidae
Genus and species: *Prionace glauca*

Shark stats

Length: Up to 13 feet (4 m)
Weight: Usually 300–400 pounds
(136–181 kg)
Habitat: Deep temperate and tropical waters
Depth: Sometimes swims at the surface, but
ranges as deep as 1,100 feet (335 m)
Colors and markings: Deep indigo blue from
above and a vibrant blue on its sides, changing
to white underneath
Sexual maturity: Male 6 feet (1.8 m),
female 7 feet (2.1 m)
Mating season: Summer
Reproduction: Viviparous
Gestation: 9–12 months
Litter: 25–50 (range 4–135) young averaging
15–17 inches (38–43 cm) long
Life span: 20-plus years

Range

Found off the coasts of every continent
except Antarctica, from the northern tip of
Norway to the southern point of Chile

In captivity

Generally not well suited to life in captivity for
more than a few months

Blue shark

With its distinctive blue coloring that varies from deep indigo on its back to a vibrant
sea blue on its sides and its large, circular eyes, the blue shark is instantly recognizable.
This shark is very long and slender, reaching lengths of around 12–13 feet (3.7–4 m).
Its streamlined shape and long pectoral fins allow the blue shark to move very quickly
when hunting prey.

The blue shark enjoys a varied diet, including squid, cuttlefish, octopuses, shrimps,
crabs and fish such as cod, haddock and mackerel. Its feeding is not restricted to small
fish, however, and it is quite capable of attacking larger animals if the opportunity
arises—studies have found seal and whale meat in blue shark intestines. While their
large size means that no other predators (except humans) pose a serious threat, they
do suffer from several parasites, including tapeworms.

The blue shark's mating ritual is vigorous: the male blue shark often violently bites
the female's back and fins. As a result, the female has evolved a skin that is at least
twice as thick as the male's to help protect her from serious damage. Despite this,
she still suffers from heavy scarring—a feature that is often used to determine the
sex of a specimen. Following mating, the female blue shark is capable of holding
and nourishing the male's sperm for months or even years as she awaits ovulation.
However, the trials of the conception may be worth it, as blue sharks are well known
for very large litters, which can vary from 4 to 135 pups.

The blue shark's long
pectoral fins (seen above
and left) help to steer the
shark in the right direction.

Worldwide distribution

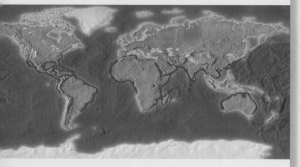

Classification

Phylum: Chordata
Class: Chondrichthyes
Subclass: Elasmobranchii
Order: Carcharhiniformes
Family: Sphyrnidae
Genus and species: *Sphyrna mokarran*

Shark stats

Length: 16 feet (4.9 m) occasionally
20 feet (6 m)
Weight: 550 pounds (249 kg), rarely over 800
pounds (363 kg)
Habitat: Mainly offshore, but also coastal areas,
reefs and occasionally estuaries; may come
inshore when pursuing food
Depth: Surface down to about 300 feet
(92 m), sometimes 1,000 feet (305 m)
Colors and markings: Gray, brown or olive-
green on the back, grading to pale or white on
the underside, few distinguishing marks
Sexual maturity: Male 7–8 feet (2.1–2.4m),
female 8–9 feet (2.4–2.7 m)
Mating season: Spring–summer
Reproduction: Viviparous
Gestation: 11 months
Litter: 20–40 (range 6–55) young averaging
24–28 inches (61–71 cm) long
Life span: Unclear, possibly 30 years

Range

Tropical to warm-temperate waters
worldwide, including the southern
Mediterranean; migrate to higher latitudes in
summer, returning toward the topics
for winter

In captivity

Has survived well on occasion in captivity,
but the hammerheads are more usually
represented by other species, such as the
scalloped hammerhead

Great hammerhead

Hammerheads are identified at once by their distinctively hammerlike heads with enlarged, angular lateral lobes. However, distinguishing the nine species is more awkward. Seen from above, the front edge of the snout of the adult great hammerhead (the largest species, also called the squat-headed hammerhead) is relatively straight with a shallow central indent or notch in the middle. This edge is more curved and scalloped in the scalloped hammerhead, *Sphyrna lewini*, and more curved but smoother in the smooth hammerhead, *Sphyrna zygaena*.

Most species of hammerheads have a slightly humped back, a very tall swept-back dorsal fin and a second dorsal fin that is about half the height but similar in shape to the first and notched in its trailing edge, like the anal fin below. The upper tail lobe is much larger than the lower. The pectoral fins resemble the dorsal fin in their swept-back, or the falcate profile, and the pelvics have concave trailing edges.

The teeth are triangular with marked serrations along the edge, wider in the upper jaw than the lower and numbering about 25 in each jaw. An active predator, the great hammerhead takes a wide range of fish, including catfish, jacks, groupers, grunts and flatfish, as well as squid, octopus and crustaceans such as lobster. A regular prey item is the stingray—even the venomous tail sting is consumed—and other sharks are also hunted. The great hammerhead is known to be cannibalistic. It is also one of the few shark species that attacks humans, but more rarely than is popularly perceived, since it is rarely aggressive.

Hammerhead sharks are known for their swept-back dorsal and pectoral fins and their large upper tail lobe.

The different hammerhead sharks can be differentiated by the shapes of their heads. The great hammerhead (left) has a relatively straight snout, whereas the snout of the scalloped hammerhead (above) has a more pronounced curve.

Classification

Phylum: Chordata
Class: Chondrichthyes
Subclass: Elasmobranchii
Order: Carcharhiniformes
Family: Scyliorhinidae
Genus and species: *Cephaloscyllium ventriosum*

Shark stats

Length: 3 feet (0.9 m), occasionally 3 ½ feet (1 m)
Weight: 10–20 pounds (4.5–9 kg), rarely 25-plus pounds (11 kg)
Habitat: Inshore, continental shelf and upper slope, especially on weed-covered kelp or other algal beds, less often over rocks, sand and mud
Depth: Extreme shallows down to 1,600 feet (488 m), usually less than 160 feet (49 m)
Colors and markings: Generally yellow-brown but variable, ranging from pale to dark with darker patches, spots and central saddle areas, and lighter spots, the marks extending onto the fins, while the underside is paler but still with spots and markings
Sexual maturity: 27–30 inches (69–76 cm)
Mating season: Unknown
Reproduction: Oviparous
Time to hatching: 7–11 months, temperature dependent
Eggs: 2 eggs laid, newly hatched young averaging 5–6 inches (13–15 cm) long
Life span: Unknown, probably more than 8 years

Range

Eastern Pacific Ocean, mainly subtropical waters from central California south to Mexico and off Chile and possibly Peru

In captivity

An occasional species in aquaria and sea-life centers, where individuals may lie piled on top of each other when resting

Longnose swell shark

The swell shark is so named because it expands its body by gulping in water (or air at the surface) to make itself larger. The shark arches its body, bites and holds its tail fin and gulps water or air into the cardiac (forward) portion of its stomach. The girth around the middle of its body can double, deterring many predators. In a rocky crevice, swelling makes removal of the shark impossible. It is also called the puffer shark or balloon shark.

The swell shark has a large head, a short, rounded snout and a long, wide, underslung mouth extending behind the large, catlike oval eyes. In fact, relative to body size, the swell shark's mouth is larger than the great white's. The first dorsal fin is set well back, just behind the pelvic fins below, and has a rounded upper tip. The second dorsal fin is about half the size of the first, similar to the anal fin directly below it. The pectorals are broad with straight, rear-facing trailing edges. The upper lobe of the tail is low with a basal notch, and the lower lobe is broadbased and triangular.

There are up to 60 small teeth in each jaw. The teeth are extremely sharp with a long, daggerlike central cusp and two smaller cusplets. Generally a slow-swimming bottom-dweller, the swell shark hides in weeds, caves and crevices by day, then emerges to hunts bony fish, crabs, shrimps, prawns and other crustaceans and carrion. This shark has been seen charging through a school of small fish to grab and swallow them with a forceful, suction-powered gulp.

The swell shark hides in weeds and crevices on the ocean floor. The swell shark's yellow-brown color with darker spots is a very effective camouflage, helping it to hide from both predators and prey.

Worldwide distribution

Classification

Phylum: Chordata
Class: Chondrichthyes
Subclass: Elasmobranchii
Order: Orectolobiformes
Family: Orectolobidae
Genus and species: *Orectolobus maculatus*

Shark stats

Length: 5–6½ feet (1.5–1.7 m), occasionally exceeds10 feet (3 m)
Weight: Up to 175 pounds (79 kg)
Habitat: Shallow water, rocky and coral reefs, sandy areas and seagrass pastures into lagoons and rockpools
Depth: Less than 3 feet (0.9 m) down to about 300 feet (92 m)
Colors and markings: Extensively marked in shades of yellow, green, brown and perhaps gray, with pale spots forming clusters and O-rings around darker patches and saddlelike areas on the back
Sexual maturity: Unclear, male and female probably 2¼–3 feet (70–90 cm)
Mating season: Unclear, possibly winter
Reproduction: Ovoviviparous
Gestation: Unclear, likely 1–2 years
Litter: 20 (up to 37) young averaging 28 inches (71 cm) long
Life span: Unknown, probably exceeds 30 years

Range

Eastern Indian Ocean and around Australian coasts, from western Australia south and east to southern Queensland

In captivity

Various types of wobbegongs, especially the tasselled and ornate wobbegongs, are kept in captivity, both by commercial aquaria and sea-life centers, and by capable fish hobbyists

Spotted wobbegong

One of about 5 species in the genus *Orectolobus*, the spotted wobbegong, or "wobby," is the largest of that group, which are all members of the carpet shark family. It has a wide, flattened body, a large spiracle near each eye and the mouth is in front of the eyes. Long barbels, or tendrils, next to the nostrils and up to 10 dermal lobes below the eyes form projections shaped like seaweed fronds. These wave in the current and are part of the wobbegong's complex camouflage.

The two small dorsal fins are set well back on the body, and the pectoral and pelvic fins are broad and low set. The small, short tail has a very reduced lower lobe. The wobbegong rests on the bottom in water as shallow as 3 feet (0.9 m); it may even drag itself between pools with its upper parts exposed. It typically hunts at night, lurching up or sideways to grab animals that pass unsuspectingly, since the shark has an amazing camouflage of complex markings, like a heavily patterned rug or carpet, and seaweedlike tassels and fringes around the mouth. Its food includes lobsters, crabs, crayfish, octopuses and bottom-dwelling fish such as flatfish, scorpionfish, sea basses and luderick. There are many slim, sharp, fanglike teeth in its protruding jaws, which can reach forward to grab as the mouth and throat exert a powerful suction to engulf the prey in a traplike mechanism.

Other species include the tasselled wobbegong, *Orectolobus dasypogon*, the Japanese wobbegong, *Orectolobus japonicus*, the ornate wobbegong, *Orectolobus ornatus*, and the northern wobbegong, *Orectolobus wardi*.

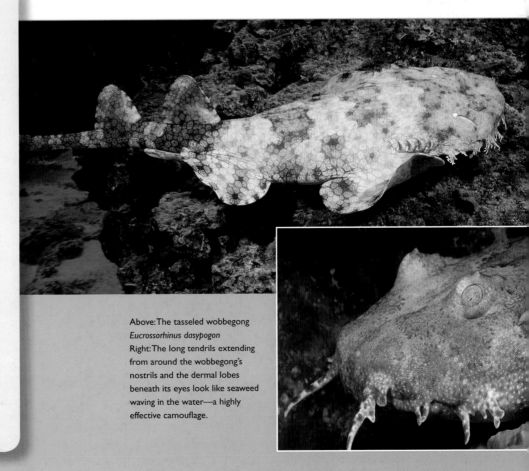

Above: The tasseled wobbegong *Eucrossorhinus dasypogon*
Right: The long tendrils extending from around the wobbegong's nostrils and the dermal lobes beneath its eyes look like seaweed waving in the water—a highly effective camouflage.

Worldwide distribution

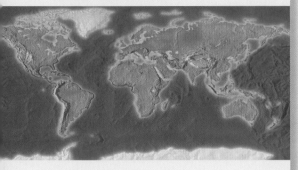

Classification

Phylum: Chordata
Class: Chondrichthyes
Subclass: Elasmobranchii
Order: Orectolobiformes
Family: Ginglymostomatidae
Genus and species: *Ginglymostoma cirratum*

Shark stats

Length: Up to 10 feet (4.3 m)
Weight: Up to 240 pounds (109 kg)
Habitat: Tropical and subtropical waters close to the shoreline, typically around reefs, sand flats and mangrove swamps
Depth: Between 3 and 40 feet (0.9–12 m)
Colors and markings: Generally gray to dark brown, dirty white underneath
Sexual maturity: Male 7 feet (2.1 m) female 7½ feet (2.3 m)
Mating season: June/July
Reproduction: Ovoviviparous
Gestation: 6 months
Litter: 20–30 pups averaging 10–12 inches (25–30 cm)
Life span: Up to 25 years

Range

The eastern Pacific around California and around the coast of South America from Mexico to Peru, the western Atlantic from Rhode Island in the U.S. to southern Brazil; also the west coast of Africa and possibly Europe

In captivity

A generally docile and reliable member of aquaria and sealife centers and also kept by proficient amateur aquarists, but it soon grows too big for most of their tanks

Nurse shark

The nurse shark is a large, sluggish species found at the bottom of the ocean. Its skin is dark gray-brown, and it is generally smoother to touch than most shark skin. Younger nurse sharks are marked with lighter brown spots on their body, but these normally fade with age. Like the catfish, the nurse shark seems to have whiskers on its upper jaw. These thin, fleshy organs, called barbels, are actually sensors that help the nurse shark to taste and feel its way around the seabed.

Nurse sharks are most active during the night, when they hunt alone for a diet of lobsters, shrimp and squid. When hunting, the nurse shark expands its large throat cavity to suck in water and prey with it. They are also known to graze on algae and coral. Some experts have suggested that this sucking sounds like a baby feeding from its mother's breast, giving rise to the nurse shark's name. Others have argued that the name comes from the Old English word for seafloor shark: *hurse*.

During the day, nurse sharks can be found lolling around the ocean floor in large, inactive groups of up to 40 individuals. Their common habitats include reefs and sand flats, and each shark often picks a favourite ledge or crevice that it will return to night after night.

The nurse shark is not known to be aggressive unless provoked, but its placid reputation means it is sometimes the victim of harassment from foolhardy divers and swimmers, who try to ride or walk on top of the shark. The shark may take revenge with a violent bite that can cause some damage; in spite of their small teeth, it is very difficult to free oneself from their strong jaws.

The nurse shark often cruises just above the sea bed then swoops down to mouth in the sand or mud for prey, from stingrays to sea squirts.

The two slim barbels or tendrils are next to the nostrils and sense touch, water currents and pressure and various chemical substances including the blood and body fluids of other animals.

Worldwide distribution

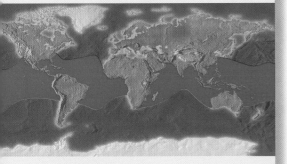

Classification

Phylum: Chordata
Class: Chondrichthyes
Subclass: Elasmobranchii
Order: Orectolobiformes
Family: Rhincodontidae
Genus and species: *Rhincodon typus*

Shark stats

Length: Subject to debate, 33–36 feet (10–11 m), rarely more than 40 feet (12 m)
Weight: 10-plus tons (9-plus tonnes), rarely over 22 tons (20 tonnes)
Habitat: Mainly open ocean; congregates to feed near coasts and around reefs; may enter lagoons and estuaries
Depth: Surface down to 2,300 feet (701 m)
Colors and markings: Gray, greenish, or bluish on the back and sides, paling to white on the lower flanks and underside, with a complex pattern of pale cream, yellow, or gray spots and stripes in the checkerboard fashion on the back and sides and spots on the head
Sexual maturity: Unknown, possibly 30 years or 26–30 feet (7.9–9.1 m)
Mating season: Unknown
Reproduction: Ovoviviparous
Gestation: Unknown
Litter: Number unclear; one harpooned female bore 300 developing pups; newborn young average 20–26 inches (51–66 cm) in length
Life span: Not known, probably more than 60 years, some estimates exceed 100 years

Range

Worldwide in tropical to warm oceans ranging from 68–86°F (20–30°C)

In captivity

More than 10 whale sharks have been or are being held in captivity, mainly in Japan (Osaka, Okinawa) and the U.S. (Atlanta, Georgia)

Whale shark

The world's biggest shark is also the world's biggest fish, but despite its enormous size and power, the whale shark, or chagrin, is a slow, peaceful filter-feeder that takes little notice of divers or boats unless molested.

The whale shark has a wide, flat head, and the mouth is terminal, that is, at the front tip of the snout, and up to 5 feet (1.5 m) wide. There are hundreds of tiny teeth that are not involved in feeding, small eyes with a spiracle (respiratory opening) just behind each and a humped back. The first dorsal fin forms a tall equal-sided triangle and is set just behind the midway point of the body; the second dorsal fin is about half the height of the first and directly above the even smaller anal fin. The rearmost one or two of the five large gill slits are positioned over the front of the wide-based, slightly swept-back pectoral fins. Three usually well-defined ridges run lengthways along the upper sides, and the tail is very tall and scythe shaped with an upper lobe almost twice the height of the lower lobe.

Whale sharks may congregate in areas rich in food but are otherwise solitary. They filter feed by actively sucking in water and sieving it through their gill rakers. The shark does not have to swim forward to feed—it can do so while stationary and even when upright. Its main food items are small planktonic animals, such as shrimplike euphausiids or krill, and small fish, squid and jellyfish.

A gentle giant, the whale shark is the largest fish in the sea, but it normally takes little notice of divers or boats unless it is harassed. This whale shark (right) is filter-feeding by taking in large volumes of water through its huge mouth, which it sieves for plankton through its gill rakers.

The biology of sharks

The shark is far from a primitive killing machine—it is a complex organism that is very well adapted to the difficulties of living in a harsh marine environment.

Sharks have a heart and a liver, guts, muscles, kidneys, blood, brain and nerves. They also have a skeleton, yet they have no bones.

Shark skin and scales

To the shark, skin is much more than just an ornamental cover—it functions for protection, camouflage, sensation and movement.

Like the skin of all vertebrates, including ourselves, the shark's skin is made of two layers, the outer epidermis and the inner dermis. The dermis is composed of connective tissue, muscle fibers, sensory nerve cells and blood capillaries. The epidermis above it consists of dead cells that are produced constantly by the dermis, which continuously wear away on the outside. It has been discovered that in many species of large shark, the skin is thicker than a human finger, with the whale shark's skin some 6 inches (15 cm) thick.

Skin scales—dermal denticles

Dermal denticles are tiny, toothlike scales that cover a shark's skin and are unique to the group. Also called placoid scales, these denticles are different from the scales of bony fish and very similar in structure to the shark's actual teeth—to the teeth of all vertebrates.

A dermal denticle arises in the dermis, anchored by a basal plate. Its point pushes up through the epidermis. A nerve and blood vessel grow through the plate into the soft tissue within the denticle, called the pulp cavity. Around this is a layer of one of nature's hardest substances, dentine. And this is covered by an even harder material, enamel. Once a denticle reaches its full size it stops growing, eventually falls out and is replaced by another, just like the shark's teeth.

Dermal denticles vary widely in shape and size between shark species. The bramble or briar shark *Echinorhinus* has knobbly denticles the size of shirt buttons, each with a tuft of sharp, curved thorns in the

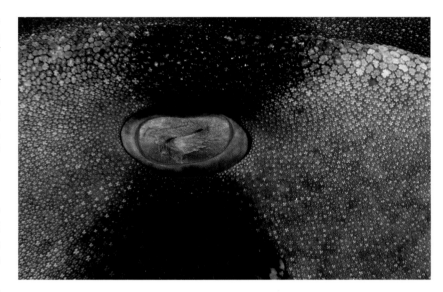

center. On other sharks the denticles are tiny fractions of an inch long.

On an individual shark the denticles may vary over the body. On an individual shark the denticles may vary over the body. For example, on the belly, the denticles are flatter and shield shaped, forming a chainmail suit of armour to protect the skin while the shark is resting on the bottom or feeding.

The bramble shark's denticles are very large—the size of shirt buttons—with a tuft of sharp, curved spikes toward the center. However, the size and shape may vary across the shark's body.

Go faster

Under the microscope, the scales along a typical shark's flanks look like tiny keeled hydrofoils or spoilers, as used on fast boats and cars. As an object moves through a fluid it creates eddies, whirls, vortices and general turbulence. This slows the object and wastes energy. The shark's denticle design minimizes this problem by directing the water's flow and allowing it to slip by more smoothly. In recent years several sports and diving companies have experimented with swimsuits bearing tiny drag-reducing projections, modeled on shark scales, that allow swimmers to go faster.

Shark skin

Shark skin scales, or denticles, have the same composition as teeth. The scales serve different functions in various species. Those of the bramble shark are knobbly and prickly and may be for protection and defense. The overlapping keeled scales of the whale shark and the ridged scales of gray sharks reduce water resistance.

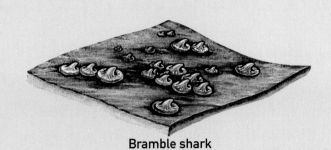

Bramble shark

Bramble shark

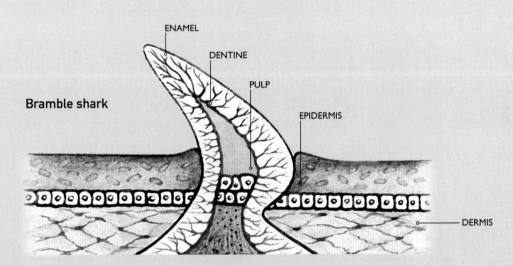

ENAMEL

DENTINE

PULP

EPIDERMIS

DERMIS

Denticles

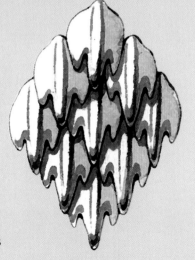

Gray shark skin scales (from above)

Gray shark skin scales (from rear)

Whale shark skin scales (from above)

Whale shark skin scales (from rear)

Shark skeletons and muscles

The shark skeleton provides a flexible framework for muscles to pull and move. It is made of cartilage, a lightweight, gristly, pearly-translucent, slightly elastic and pliable substance.

Cartilage is not unique to sharks—skates, rays and ratfish have skeletons made of it, while most other vertebrates have some cartilage parts to their skeletons. It is composed of fibers of proteins such as collagen and elastin embedded in a matrix of various salts and minerals.

Bone is cartilage that has been hardened by a process called mineral calcification, during which calcium crystals give extra stiffness and hardness. Ossification occurs in a shark's vertebrae (in the spinal column) and in parts of the jaws, teeth, fin rods and dermal denticles or skin scales.

Joints

In the shark skeleton, where one component butts up against another, the contact surfaces are made from extra-smooth cartilage. This reduces wear and tear. There is a shock-absorbing bag of fluid, the synovial capsule, between them, for cushioning and to minimize friction. Strong, elastic, straplike ligaments hold the joint stable, allowing a degree of movement but not too much. This whole joint structure is very similar to that found in other vertebrates.

In the spinal column each vertebra articulates slightly with the vertebrae in front and behind it. The joints for

the jaws and the branchial arches that support the gills are more flexible, so the shark can open its mouth or its gills wide when necessary. Many small joints between the fin's basal rods of cartilage and the internal girdles of the skeleton allow a complex range of movements.

Muscles

In the basics of their muscular system, sharks are much like other vertebrate animals. They have three main types of muscle tissue:
• Cardiac muscle in the heart that is specialized to work continually and tirelessly.
• Layered visceral muscle that is found in internal parts such as the guts, excretory and reproductive organs, and blood vessels. It pushes contents through these cavities and tubes.
• Skeletal muscles that move the skeleton. The main pairs of muscles along a shark's body are on either side of the spinal column. When they shorten on one side the muscles on the opposite side relax, and the spinal column flexes. Alternate flexing produces the shark's swimming motion (see page 100).

The shark's spine is made from hard, ossified cartilage as opposed to the softer cartilage of the rest of its skeleton. This vertebra, from the shortnose spurdog, has been dyed to show how the vertebrae grow in concentric rings.

Two types of muscle

Sharks have two types of skeletal muscle:
• About one-tenth is red muscle in narrow strips along the body's sides, just beneath the skin. Its generous blood supply means it can work for long periods without tiring. It is used mainly for the small, smooth movements of cruising.

• The rest is white muscle. It has a poorer blood supply and is used for short bursts such as when chasing prey. A shark on the attack may suddenly turn and cruise away because its white muscle is "tired."

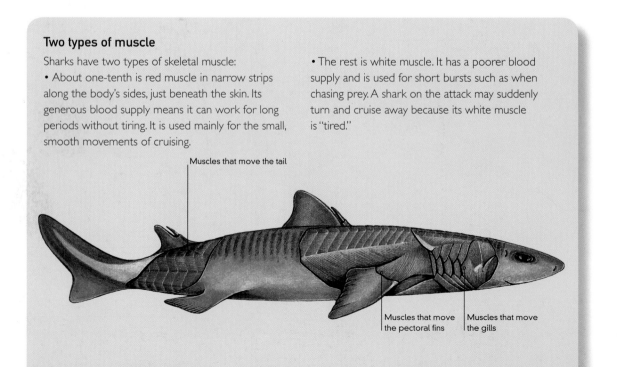

Muscles that move the tail

Muscles that move the pectoral fins

Muscles that move the gills

The cartilaginous skeleton of a shark

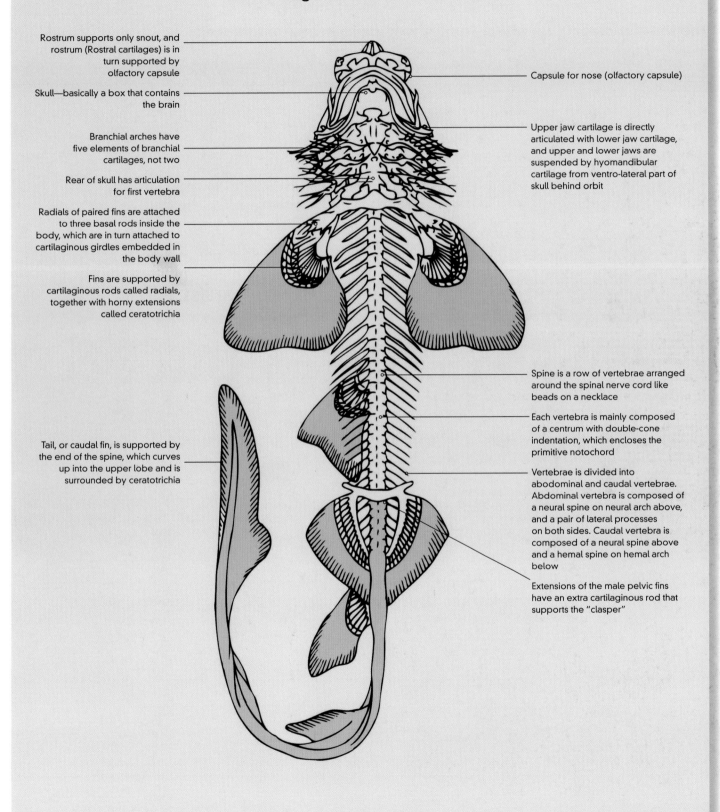

Rostrum supports only snout, and rostrum (Rostral cartilages) is in turn supported by olfactory capsule

Skull—basically a box that contains the brain

Branchial arches have five elements of branchial cartilages, not two

Rear of skull has articulation for first vertebra

Radials of paired fins are attached to three basal rods inside the body, which are in turn attached to cartilaginous girdles embedded in the body wall

Fins are supported by cartilaginous rods called radials, together with horny extensions called ceratotrichia

Tail, or caudal fin, is supported by the end of the spine, which curves up into the upper lobe and is surrounded by ceratotrichia

Capsule for nose (olfactory capsule)

Upper jaw cartilage is directly articulated with lower jaw cartilage, and upper and lower jaws are suspended by hyomandibular cartilage from ventro-lateral part of skull behind orbit

Spine is a row of vertebrae arranged around the spinal nerve cord like beads on a necklace

Each vertebra is mainly composed of a centrum with double-cone indentation, which encloses the primitive notochord

Vertebrae is divided into abodominal and caudal vertebrae. Abdominal vertebra is composed of a neural spine on neural arch above, and a pair of lateral processes on both sides. Caudal vertebra is composed of a neural spine above and a hemal spine on hemal arch below

Extensions of the male pelvic fins have an extra cartilaginous rod that supports the "clasper"

Breathing underwater

Sharks—and all other animals—depend on oxygen for the release of energy from food.

Sharks, like other aquatic creatures, depend on oxygen dissolved in water. They extract it with their gills. Water comes in through the shark's mouth, flows over the gills and exits through the gill slits.

Structure of gills

Most fish, including the majority of sharks, have five pairs of gill openings on the sides of the head. In a shark, each arch-shaped gill is supported by a cartilage branchial bar that curves around the side of the throat cavity. This arch carries a double fringe of hundreds of feathery-looking gill filaments. In turn, each filament is made of tiny, leaflike branches called lamellae. This design creates a very large surface area for absorbing as much oxygen as possible.

How gills work

The delicate, thin-walled lamellae contain microscopic blood vessels called capillaries. As blood flows through these, it is very close to the water outside. Oxygen seeps, or diffuses, from its relatively high concentration in the water to the lower concentration in the blood. The body's waste product, carbon dioxide, passes in the opposite direction, from the blood out into the water. The efficiency of the system is improved by the countercurrent principle. Water flows over the gills from front to back. Blood flows within the gills from back to front. This raises the contrast between the concentrations of oxygen in water, where it is higher, and blood, where it is lower, to encourage its transfer.

Constant flow

Gills need a constant supply of new water. In some sharks, muscular action draws water into the mouth, shuts the mouth and squeezes the water over the gills and out through the gill slits, as more water is sucked into the mouth. To aid this pumped flow most sharks swim forward. The open-ocean hunting sharks depend almost entirely on their forward motion to provide a "ram jet" water flow over the gills.

Bottom-living sharks like the wobbegong do not keep swimming, and they also risk blocking their gills with debris stirred up from the seabed. So they have a modified system, breathing in through an extra hole just behind each eye, the spiracle, and out through gill slits, like skates and rays. The Port Jackson shark, another bottom-dweller, pumps water in through its first pair of gill slits and out over the other four.

Stirred debris from the seafloor could block the gills of bottom-dwelling sharks, such as these Port Jackson sharks, potentially starving them of oxygen.

Most modern sharks have just five gills on each side of the head, but some more primitive species, such as this broadnose sevengill shark, have more gill slits, as their prehistoric cousins.

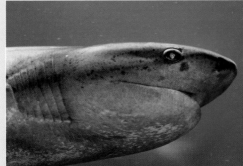

More from less
- Fresh air contains about 21 percent gaseous oxygen.
- Our lungs can extract about one-quarter of this oxygen.
- Cold surface seawater contains up to four percent dissolved oxygen, and this proportion reduces to less than 0.025 percent in warm or deep water.
- Fish gills can extract some four-fifths of this dissolved oxygen.

Sharks' lifeblood

Blood is an amazing fluid. It distributes vital substances such as oxygen, nutrients from digested food, hormones for coordinating inner processes, disease-fighting antibodies and much more throughout the body. It also collects bodily wastes and by-products for removal.

Shark blood is fairly typical of a vertebrate. It consists of a straw-colored liquid, plasma, in which microscopic cells float. Plasma is a watery solution of hundreds of body chemicals, salts, nutrients, hormones and waste. There are two main kinds of blood cells, or corpuscles. Red blood cells contain a red-colored substance, hemoglobin, which bonds strongly to oxygen. There are millions of red cells in just one drop of blood. They absorb oxygen in the shark's gills and give it up to the tissues around the body. White blood cells help to protect the body against diseases and infections as part of the immune system.

Hormones and lymph

The shark's hormone, or endocrine, system consists of many glands throughout the body. They include the pituitary near the brain, the thymus, thyroid and parathyroid glands in the "neck" region, the adrenals near the kidneys and the sex glands—ovaries in the female, testes in the male. These glands make chemical messengers called hormones, which circulate in the blood and control many of the shark's body processes, such as using energy, removing waste, growth and sexual maturation.

A second transport fluid is lymph. This consists of general body fluids in the tissues, blood that "leaks" out of its vessels and liquids that ooze out of microscopic cells. Lymph flows slowly through a fine network of open channels and tubes, propelled mainly by the squeezing motions of body muscles as the shark moves. It collects in bigger tubes and eventually empties back into the veins of the main blood system. Lymph assists blood by delivering nutrients, collecting waste and fighting infections.

Hot stuff

Most fish are cold-blooded. More accurately, they are poikilothermic or ectothermic. Their body temperature is almost the same as that of the surrounding water. But several species in the mackerel shark group, including the great white, shortfin mako, porbeagle, salmon shark and thresher, are warm-blooded, or homeothermic. Parts of their body can be more than 20°F (11°C) above ambient water temperature. The heat is produced by muscle activity and biochemical reactions in the tissues. It is conserved by networks of tiny blood vessels called rete mirable, and this warmer blood flows mainly to the swimming muscles, parts of the gut and the brain. A rise in temperature of 50°F (10°C) in the swimming muscles allows them to work three times harder and faster. So the shark is more active and speedier than the colder creatures around it—but it also uses up more energy, which must be taken in as extra food.

The cold-blooded blue shark (left) feeds on a ball of krill to give it the energy it needs to survive.

The shortfin mako shark (above) and the great white shark (left) are both warm-blooded, which means that they can raise their body temperature above the temperature of the seawater. However, this comes at a cost—the sharks need more food to maintain their warmth.

Heart and other organs

The shark's heart is the pump for its circulatory system. Being a very ancient group, sharks have a slightly different heart design compared with other vertebrates. Blood goes from the heart to the gills to gather oxygen, then onward around the body to deliver the oxygen before returning to the heart.

From the heart

The shark's heart is just behind its lower jaw. It is effectively a thickened part of the main blood vessel, the aorta, folded back on itself and divided into four chambers. The walls are composed of strong muscle that contracts rhythmically, pushing blood through. Valves make the blood flow one way only, on a steady and never-ending circuit.

Vessels that carry blood away from the shark's heart are arteries. They have thick, muscular walls that bulge or pulse with the pressurized surge of each heartbeat. The main artery, the ventral aorta, carries low-oxygen blood from the heart directly to the gills. Here it divides into branched pairs, one for each gill arch. Each branch divides into microscopic, thin-walled blood vessels, called capillaries, within the gill filaments. Oxygen passes from the water into these.

Around the body

Coming away from the gills, the capillaries join and become wider, finally forming the dorsal aorta. This branches into smaller arteries that convey blood to all of the body. The arteries divide repeatedly to form capillaries, whose walls are so thin that oxygen, nutrients and other substances can pass out into the tissues. Wastes and by-products pass the other way, from the tissues into the blood.

Capillaries join together into larger tubes, veins and even larger sinuses or spaces. Since blood by then has passed through two or even three capillary systems, it has lost its high pressure and pulse. So vein walls, unlike artery walls, are thin and floppy.

The veins and sinuses empty into the first chamber of the heart, the sinus venosus. From here the blood passes into the second chamber, the auricle or atrium, and is then sucked into the third chamber, the thick-walled ventricle. This provides the main power to force the blood into the fourth chamber, a valved bulb called the conus arteriosus, at the base of the main artery. From here it passes out into the ventral aorta.

Pump and suck

The heart of a shark, or other elasmobranch, is both a pressure pump and suction pump. When the heart relaxes between beats it also sucks blood in from the veins. This happens because the heart is encased in a fairly rigid, boxlike chamber, the pericardium.

As the heart itself contracts and becomes smaller, it causes the pericardium to collapse inward, like sucking in your cheeks. This produces a low pressure inside the pericardial chamber, allowing blood flow in from the veins to refill the heart.

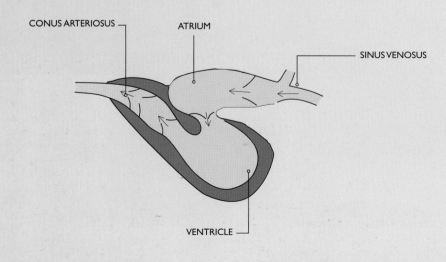

CONUS ARTERIOSUS — ATRIUM   SINUS VENOSUS

VENTRICLE

The shark's heart is essentially a thickened blood vessel folded back on itself and divided into four separate chambers. Each chamber, particularly the third one, helps to make the flow of blood throughout the body uniform and steady.

All sharks, including this leopard shark (above) and the prickly dogfish shark (left), rely on a very similar mechanism to take up oxygen from their gills and pump it around their body in their blood.

Kidneys and waste

In sharks, as in other vertebrates, most of the by-products and waste collected from the tissues by blood are filtered by the main organs of excretion, the kidneys. Along with excess water, and various unwanted minerals and salts, they make the liquid waste called urine.

A shark's two long, narrow kidneys lie on either side of the vertebral column, approximately under the dorsal fin. Like our own kidneys, they consist of many microscopic tubes (renal tubules) closely intertwined with tiny blood vessels (capillaries). The very thin walls of both tubules and capillaries are specially adapted to regulate the passage of salts and water. The renal tubules of sharks are among the largest of any vertebrate—bigger than those in our own kidneys.

Wanted and unwanted

In the renal tubules, water and dissolved substances from the blood are processed so that desirable substances stay within the body. Unwanted waste such as urea and excess water—urine—stay in the tubules, which join together into urinary ducts. These carry the urine into a urinary sinus, which is the shark's bladder. The sinus from each kidney joins to the dual-purpose excretion-reproduction opening, the cloaca. From here the urine is voided into the sea.

The problem of saltwater

Seawater has a relatively high concentration of salts. Similarly, the body fluids inside a shark also contain dissolved salts. These two sets of salts being unbalanced could cause problems due to osmosis—the natural tendency for concentrations to even out—during which water or salts pass from one solution to the other. This process is called osmoregulation.

Most seawater fish have fluids and tissues that have lower salt concentrations than the salty water around them. So water tends to leave their bodies, meaning they must drink large amounts of seawater. Sharks have another answer. They keep the salts in their body fluids and tissues at the same concentration as the surrounding seawater, or even slightly higher, by maintaining unusually high concentrations of waste products, especially urea, in the blood. They also have another substance, TMAO (trimethylamine oxide), which counteracts the damaging effects of too much urea. As a result, sharks produce very little urine for their size. Comparing a human and a human-sized shark, the former would make perhaps 10 times more urine than the latter.

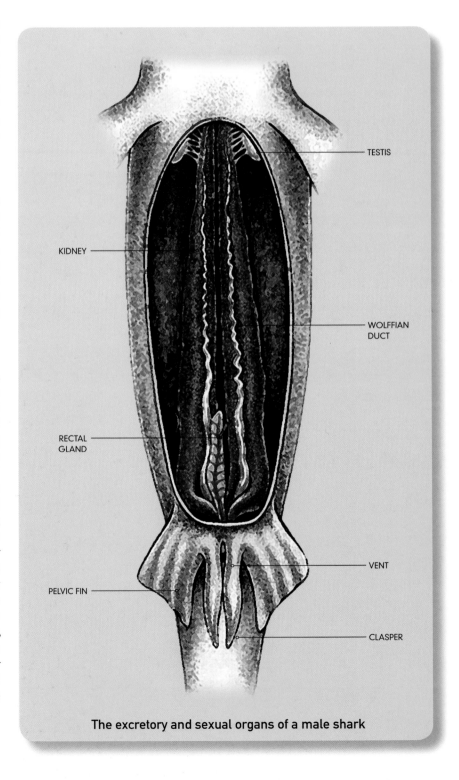

The excretory and sexual organs of a male shark

TESTIS

KIDNEY

WOLFFIAN DUCT

RECTAL GLAND

VENT

PELVIC FIN

CLASPER

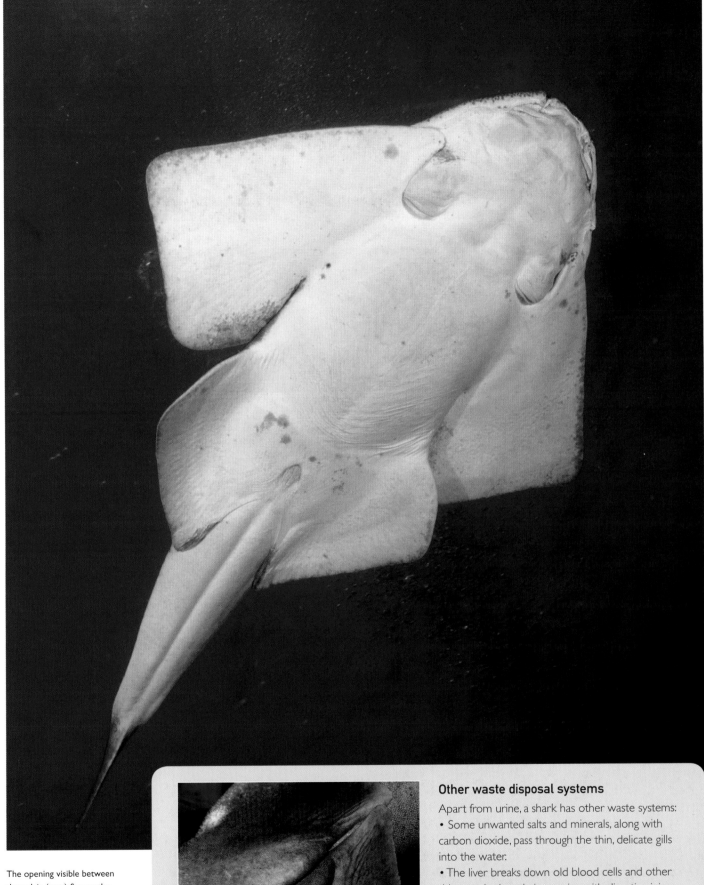

The opening visible between the pelvic (rear) fins on the underside of this Japanese angel shark is called the cloaca. The gut, the kidneys, and oviducts both open into this shared duct, and feces, urine, and babies are expelled from it.

Other waste disposal systems

Apart from urine, a shark has other waste systems:
• Some unwanted salts and minerals, along with carbon dioxide, pass through the thin, delicate gills into the water.
• The liver breaks down old blood cells and other things and mixes their remains with digestive juices to form a yellow fluid called bile. This is stored in the gall bladder, squeezed into the gut to help with digestion and eventually voided with the feces.
• Undigested waste from the gut form the feces.
• The rectal gland concentrates and secretes excess salts.

The shark's brain

The shark's brain is the control and coordination center for its whole body. With the spinal cord, which is the main nerve projecting from the brain along the vertebral column, it makes up the central nervous system.

The networks of stringlike nerves that carry information between the central nervous system and the muscles and organs all over the body make up the peripheral nervous system. Information is sent around in the form of coded patterns of tiny electrical pulses, called nerve signals.

Each nerve is made of hundreds or thousands of long but microscopically thin "wires," called nerve fibers or axons. These are parts of nerve cells or neurons. Those that carry nerve signals from the sense organs around the shark's body to its spinal cord and brain are called sensory neurons. Their information is processed in the brain. In response, signals are sent out to the various muscles and organs by motor neurons, to make the shark move and react.

Parts of the brain

The typical shark brain is partly hollow, containing fluid-filled chambers, known as ventricles, and has three main regions.

• The forebrain consists partly of large bulges called olfactory lobes. These deal with information coming in from the smell and scent detectors. The forebrain part called the cerebrum is involved mainly in processing this olfactory information and in other aspects of perception and "thought"—especially in birds and mammals, the cerebrum is the site of intelligence and learning. In ourselves it makes up nine-tenths of the brain volume.

• The midbrain contains the optic lobes, which receive

signals sent in from the eyes, concerning vision. It is also the region where most of the sensory information is coordinated and from where instructions are sent out along motor nerves to the muscles to control the shark's movements.

• The hindbrain is comparatively large in all fish, including sharks. The wrinkled part on top, known as the cerebellum, coordinates muscle movements. Involved in rapid, instinctive reactions is the amygdaloid center. The brainstem, in the manner of an airplane's autopilot, controls basic life functions such as heartbeat, blood pressure, digestion and excretion and merges into the spinal cord.

As it lies resting on the seabed, this tawny nurse shark's brain is probably rather inactive, with just the brainstem keeping all its basic functions going. When using its sense of smell to find buried clams, the olfactory lobes in the forebrain will be very active.

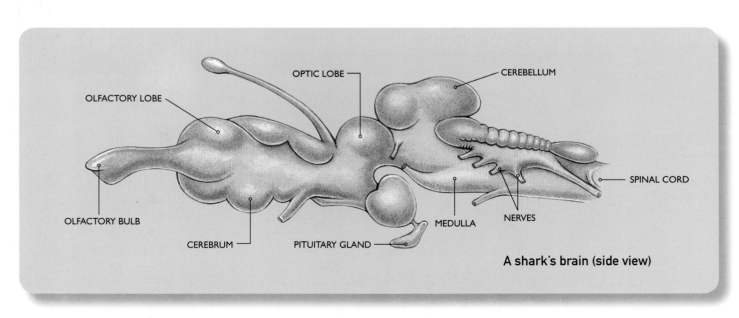

OPTIC LOBE — CEREBELLUM

OLFACTORY LOBE

OLFACTORY BULB

CEREBRUM — PITUITARY GLAND — MEDULLA NERVES

SPINAL CORD

A shark's brain (side view)

This tawny nurse shark has seen two approaching snorkelers and is swimming away from them. The visual signals sent to its brain from its eyes will be processed in the optic lobes in the mid-brain area. These sharks have small eyes and their vision is probably rather poor.

Brain to body size ratio

The comparison of a creature's body size with its brain size, in terms of weight, is often said to reflect what we term "intelligence."

- A 15-foot (4.6 m) long great white has a brain almost 2 feet (60 cm) long. It's brain:body ratio is around 1:10,000.
- This ratio for certain other sharks, and especially rays, is much higher at 1:1,000 to 1:500, similar to some birds and mammals.
- In general, sharks have bigger brains for body size than other fish.
- In ourselves, the brain:body ratio is about 1:50.

However, much of the typical shark's brain is involved in analyzing the mass of information from its "supersenses." The olfactory, optic and other lobes are relatively large. The parts involved in learning and adaptation, such as the cerebrum, are relatively small.

Super scents

The ocean is full of scents carried by dissolved substances. The importance of smell in a typical shark's life is shown by its brain. The olfactory lobes, which analyze smell information, can make up to one-fifth of the brain's total weight.

Site of smell

The olfactory organs that detect scents and smells are a pair of nasal sacs near the front of the shark's snout. Their openings are the shark's "nostrils," or nares. In most sharks the nares are closed sacs used only for smell and not for breathing.

Each nasal sac is shaped so that water flows in, passes over the wrinkled inner surface and flows out again as the shark swims. The wrinkled lining within the sac is covered with microscopic olfactory cells that detect smell-carrying substances in the water. The cells send nerve signals along the olfactory bulb that surrounds the nasal sac. The signals are filtered and part-sorted in the olfactory bulb and also in the olfactory tract, the large bundle of nerves that conveys them to the olfactory lobe of the brain.

What can sharks smell?

Most sharks can smell only a limited range of substances, especially those produced by predators, prey (blood or body fluids) or mates (communication chemicals called pheromones). But for these selected substances the shark is supersensitive. Experiments show that sharks respond strongly to the body fluids and secretions of injured or distressed animals. If the same animals are healthy and uninjured the shark reacts less strongly.

Blood is high on the list, causing responses at concentrations of less than one part per million— about one teaspoonful in an average swimming pool. However, tales of sharks swimming unerringly toward prey from 10 miles (16 km) or more are probably exaggerated.

A shark may home in by following the increasing strength of the scent trail in the water. As it zigzags across the odor trail and swings its head from side to side, the brain compares the strength of the smell in each nare, and the shark turns toward the stronger side. Another possibility is that the shark detects an odor and then turns its body to swim into the current bringing the odor, using its lateral-line system.

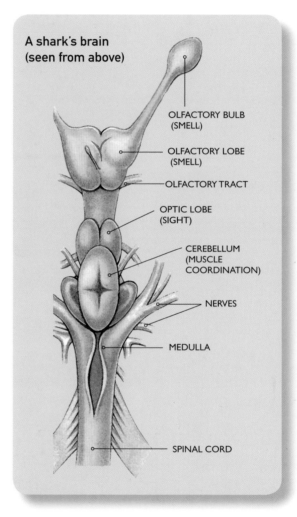

A shark's brain (seen from above)

- OLFACTORY BULB (SMELL)
- OLFACTORY LOBE (SMELL)
- OLFACTORY TRACT
- OPTIC LOBE (SIGHT)
- CEREBELLUM (MUSCLE COORDINATION)
- NERVES
- MEDULLA
- SPINAL CORD

Now safe on the beach, this California sea lion has been bitten on the head and body by sharks. In the water, the blood and body fluids from its wounds would quickly attract other sharks as well as help its initial attacker to find it again.

A tuna caught on a hook and line will soon attract sharks, which home in on the vibrations it creates in the water as it struggles, as well as the smell of any blood in the water. Sometimes anglers find only half a fish left on their line, the rest having been bitten off by a shark.

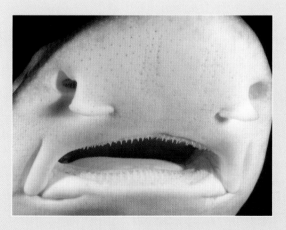

Taste

Sharks have microscopic taste buds scattered around the lining of the mouth and throat. Each taste bud is like a minute rounded cave with a narrow opening onto the surface. Inside are spindle-shaped gustatory cells that respond to certain chemicals dissolved in the water. These cells send nerve signals to the brain. Most sharks can discern only a few basic flavors, such as bitter, sweet and salty. Some bottom-living sharks have whiskerlike barbels that bear taste buds to "taste" the seabed.

Shark vision

The shark's eye is typical of most vertebrates, including humans. The jelly-filled eyeball is protected in a socket, or orbit, in the skull.

At the front of the eyeball is a transparent "window"—the cornea. Light passes through this, through a hole called the pupil in a ring of muscle known as the iris, through a hard, ball-shaped lens, through the clear jelly within the eyeball and shines onto the light-sensitive layer on the rear eyeball lining—the retina.

Muscles that support the lens can move it forward or backward to focus on distant or nearby objects. The iris muscles contract automatically, the brighter the light, to make the pupil smaller and protect the sensitive retina from overexposure. In some shark species this makes the pupil into a slit shape; in others it becomes a series of tiny holes.

Rods and cones

In most sharks, the retina contains millions of microscopic rod cells. These are sensitive to light levels and send patterns of nerve signals along the optic nerve to the optic lobe of the brain. But rod cells cannot distinguish colors. Recent research shows that many sharks, especially those frequenting clear waters, also have light-sensitive retinal cells called cones, which pick out colors. Whether the shark perceives them in the way we do is not known.

Behind the retina is the tapetum, a layer of cells containing a silvery pigment. It works like a mirror to reflect any light that passes through the retina back into it for greater sensitivity. It also means the shark's eye appears to shine in the dark—like a cat's. Sharks have another device, too, unique among vertebrates. In very bright light the tapetum can be covered with darkly pigmented cells, which works like sunglasses to cut down reflections and protect the sensitive retina.

Eyes on the sides

Most sharks have eyes on the sides of the head, facing outward rather than to the front. They can see all around, but with no area of overlap in the views from the two eyes, they cannot judge distances well by binocular or stereoscopic vision, as we do with our forward-facing eyes.

Sharks that live in gloomy mid-water have bigger eyes to catch more light. The bigeye thresher's eyes are the size of human fists. The dark shy shark, or shy-eye shark, is so named because it curls its tail over its eyes when caught.

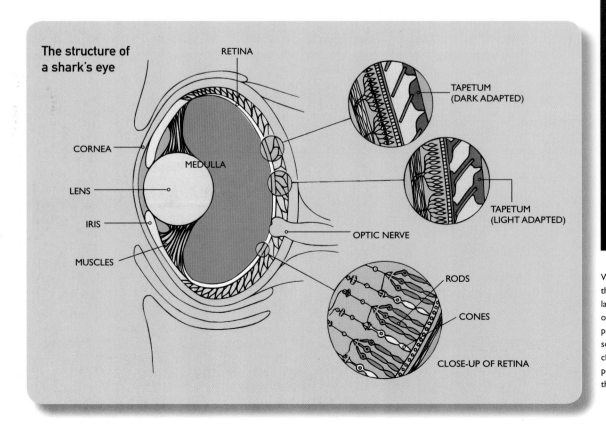

The structure of a shark's eye

RETINA

TAPETUM (DARK ADAPTED)

TAPETUM (LIGHT ADAPTED)

CORNEA

MEDULLA

LENS

IRIS

OPTIC NERVE

MUSCLES

RODS

CONES

CLOSE-UP OF RETINA

With relatively large eyes, the shortfin mako hunts largely by sight. Out in clear oceanic waters it can spot prey fish and squid from some distance and then close in rapidly—this shark is possibly the fastest shark in the ocean.

Three eyelids?

A typical shark has upper and lower eyelids to protect the eyeball. But the two eyelids do not always meet. Some species, such as the requiem group (Carcharhinidae), have a third eyelid—the nictitating membrane—to draw across the eye for protection. This may close at the moment of biting. Other sharks lack the nictitating membrane. When they bite they roll their eyeballs up under their true upper eyelids, exposing the fibrous underside of the eyeball to give a white-eyed appearance.

Sounds of the sea

The seas are full of sound—swishing water currents, passing creatures such as fish and squid, waves splashing at the surface and shore, singing whales, grunting seals and, increasingly, ship engines and churning propellers.

Sharks detect sounds with two sets of sensory organs: the ears and the lateral-line system (see page 90).

In the sea, sounds and vibrations travel as ripples of water pressure. Both the shark's ears and lateral-line detect these using sets of microscopic sensors called hair cells. The cell's microhairs are swayed by pressures and movements in the outside water. As they bend, they stimulate the hair cells and send signals to the brain.

Shark ears

Sharks' ears are two tiny holes on the sides of the head, behind the eyes. Each leads along a narrow tube to the inner ear, which is a fluid-filled cavity on the outside of the back of the skull. The inner ear consists of a series of connected tubes, called a labyrinth, which are themselves filled with fluid. The labyrinth's lining contains clusters of hair cells. The cell's microhairs are stimulated by movements of the nearby otoliths, which are tiny, stony lumps suspended in the fluid around them.

A shark's flesh has a similar density to that of seawater. As such, the pressure waves and vibrations of sounds pass not only along the fine tubes to the inner ears but straight through the shark's head, which is, in effect, acoustically transparent. The waves strike the much denser, stony otoliths in the inner ear and cause them to move, thereby stimulating the hair cells

to produce nerve signals.

It is doubtful whether sharks respond to a wide range of sounds, both in volume (loud or soft) and pitch or frequency (high or low), as we hear in air. Bull sharks react to sounds with a frequency of 20 to 1,000 hertz (cycles per second), which for us would range from deep booms like thunder to the higher notes of the human voice. Lower frequencies have more effect, especially when they are irregular—as generated by an injured, thrashing animal. These pressure waves can be detected more than 650 feet (198 m) away.

Some of the loudest sounds in the ocean are made by humpback whales (right main). The whales communicate with each other over long distances using a series of complex "songs." These huge animals have little to fear from most sharks, but sharks might be attracted by the calls of a distressed calf.

Research submersibles such as the Johnson Sea Link (top right) create sound and vibrations easily detected by sharks. This may make it difficult for the scientists to study deep-sea sharks such as cow sharks, which may be frightened by unusual noises.

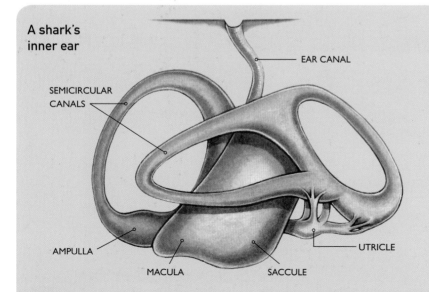

A shark's inner ear

- EAR CANAL
- SEMICIRCULAR CANALS
- AMPULLA
- MACULA
- SACCULE
- UTRICLE

The balanced approach

The upper part of the shark's inner ear labyrinth is for balance. It consists of a chamber, the utricle, and three C-shaped semicircular canals, each arranged at right angles to the other two. The linings of these chambers bear hair cells. As the shark moves, the tiny, stonelike otoliths lag behind for a fraction of a second. Their swaying moves the nearby microhairs of the sensory hair cells, which send signals to the brain. This information is combined with the inner sense of proprioception, described on page 91.

Touch at a distance

We have no directly equivalent sense to the lateral-line system of a fish. As its name implies, it is a line-shaped sensory organ that runs along each side of the shark's body, with three or more branches around the head. Each lateral-line system consists of a tiny, tunnellike canal just under the skin and connected to the outside by numerous tiny tubes that open at holes in the shark's skin.

The canal is lined with hundreds of neuromasts, which are bunches of sensory hair cells as described on page 88. The microhair tips of each bunch are embedded in a jelly lump, the cupola, or simply project into the water in the canal. As the shark swims the outside water swishes past its skin and sets up currents in the water within the lateral-line canal. These currents push and sway the cupolas and hairs, which stimulate their hair cells to send signals to the brain.

Touchy subject

Our skin can feel light touch, heavier pressure, small variations in heat and cold and surfaces that are rough or smooth, dry or moist, hard or soft. Sharks probably do not have such a detailed sense of touch—they have their lateral lines, and they make physical contact with few animals and objects. But their skin can feel a certain amount of basic contact, larger-scale changes in temperature, noxious or corrosive chemicals in the water and physical damage. These are detected by the bare endings of sensory nerves, called free nerve endings, embedded in the skin. In particular, the mouth and jaws and the teeth themselves have detailed touch sensation, and many sharks "mouth" an object to know more about it.

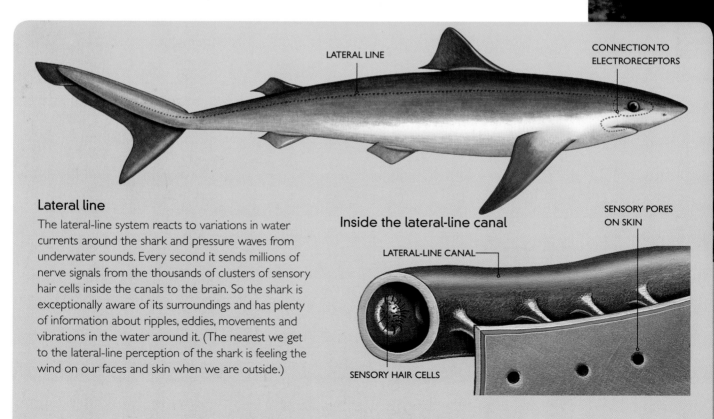

Lateral line

The lateral-line system reacts to variations in water currents around the shark and pressure waves from underwater sounds. Every second it sends millions of nerve signals from the thousands of clusters of sensory hair cells inside the canals to the brain. So the shark is exceptionally aware of its surroundings and has plenty of information about ripples, eddies, movements and vibrations in the water around it. (The nearest we get to the lateral-line perception of the shark is feeling the wind on our faces and skin when we are outside.)

LATERAL LINE

CONNECTION TO ELECTRORECEPTORS

Inside the lateral-line canal

SENSORY PORES ON SKIN

LATERAL-LINE CANAL

SENSORY HAIR CELLS

Although their skin is not as sensitive as ours, this gray reef shark will certainly be able to feel the touch of this diver. Some researchers have even stroked the snouts of great white sharks attracted to a boat and suggest the sharks enjoy the experience. In general, wild ocean animals should not be touched.

Inner sense

Like other animals, sharks need information about their internal body organs and processes. This ranges from knowing when to stop eating because the stomach is full or when urine must be expelled to whether the muscles are pulling the tail to the left or right for a smooth, coordinated swimming motion. Microscopic sensory cells called proprioceptors are scattered throughout the muscles, joints, digestive system, blood vessels and other inner body parts. They can detect when these parts are being bent, stretched or squashed. This is the shark's inner sense of position and posture, called the proprioceptive sense.

Sixth sense

Any muscle activity of a living creature creates fields of electricity. (We can detect these pulses from our own hearts and can see them as an electrocardiogram trace.) On land, electricity cannot travel away from busy muscles since air is a very poor electrical conductor. But water is a very good electrical conductor, and several groups of animals, including sharks and rays, can detect the tiny electrical pulses in the water around them, generated by the muscle movements of other creatures.

Even a prey creature that keeps still, hiding in weeds or mud, gives off these electrical pulses, since its heart and other inner muscles are active.

Electricity sensors

The shark's electricity-sensing devices are clusters of tiny pores or cavities in the skin around its head and front end. They are called ampullae of Lorenzini. Actively hunting sharks have 1,500 or more ampullae; sluggish bottom-dwellers have only a few hundred.

Each ampulla consists of a pore in the skin's surface, leading into an almost microscopic bottle-shaped pit filled with jelly. The bottom portion of the pit is lined with sensory cells, similar to the hair cells of the ear and lateral line, but adapted to produce nerve signals when they are stimulated by electrical pulses in the water. They also react, to a lesser degree, to changes in water pressure and temperature.

The ampullae of Lorenzini of this blue shark are situated mainly on the underside of its long, pointed snout. The snout also contains the eyes and the olfactory organs.

A detailed sense

The ampullae are remarkably sensitive. They can detect a change in voltage with distance—a voltage gradient—of just 10 millionths of a volt per half-inch (1 cm). This would be equivalent to attaching two wires to a single 1.5-volt AA-type battery and dipping the ends of the wires into the sea more than 1,000 miles (1,600 km) apart. The breathing movements and heartbeat of a resting flatfish, such as a plaice, give off voltages 100,000 times stronger. Some sharks can pick up the minute voltages of nerve signals inside an animal's body.

The head shapes of some sharks may have evolved to increase their sensitivity even further. A hammerhead shark uses its flattened head like a metal detector, sweeping it to and fro over the seabed, to detect electrical signals from buried prey. Its nostrils are also farther apart than normal, which improves their directional perception of scents.

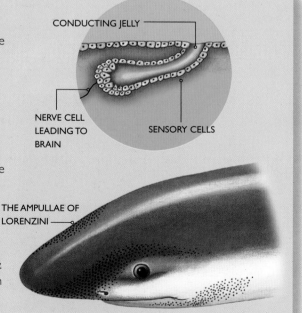

CONDUCTING JELLY

NERVE CELL LEADING TO BRAIN

SENSORY CELLS

THE AMPULLAE OF LORENZINI

Tricking shark senses

- A shark may attack a metal electrode (rod) dipped into the water, which is emitting electrical pulses. Presumably it mistakes this for a prey animal.
- In fact, the shark may prefer biting the electrode to attacking a real prey animal. It seems that electricity detection is the main sense, rather than sight or hearing, when a shark is close to prey.
- The salts and minerals in the leaking body fluids of an injured animal or person create a certain type of electrical signal. This could explain why sharks keep attacking the original victim and ignore uninjured rescuers.

The struggles of an injured or speared reef fish will soon be picked up by the sensors on the snout and lower jaw of this silvertip shark. Spearfishers sometimes have to discard their catch when they attract the unwanted attention of sharks.

A guide to shark body language

Face to face with a shark, most of us would run a mile. Some brave scientists, however, have stayed around sharks long enough to study the threat displays of 23 different species of shark.

The interest is not purely academic. The popularity of water sports and growing populations of humans near water means that humans are now in closer contact with sharks than ever before, and the experts hope that an ability to recognize warning signals in sharks' body language could help to prevent accidents.

Some of the signals are universal in almost all the sharks studied so far. A relaxed shark will swim with its body fairly horizontal against the seawater, propelling itself with its tail, but a shark under a high degree of stress will hunch its back and point its pectoral fins down. The shape of the signal is popular among many species, but the duration does vary. If you are near a great white shark you'd better be watching pretty carefully, as this signal can last as little as four seconds. With the gray reef shark its much more obvious, and you may have up to 40 seconds to get away.

Another signal that is common across all shark species and well known among divers is the shark pointing its pectoral fins down, and this can also suggest an imminent attack.

A prolonged display of the shark's flank is also common among many species of shark—the shark turns sideways and swims past the target very slowly.

Other signals, however, are more specific to individual species, such as the "long shiver" in which the silvertip shark lies still in the water, shuddering. The great white shark is also known to exhibit a couple of individual signals, including a wide grin that bares all of its teeth and a dart, aimed toward its target, that it deflects away at the last minute. Some signals also include the production of sound, such as the shotgun sound the sand tiger shark makes when it bangs its tail loudly in the water in the face of a threat.

Scientists have noted that many of the sharks mostly exhibited the displays when they were approached by one of the researchers, but not when they were feeding. This suggests the displays are more common when the sharks felt themselves under attack, rather than when they wanted to protect their own resources from theft.

A relaxed shark swims with its body horizontal to the water's surface (left). If it hunches its back, however, you know that it is feeling under threat, and it is best to retreat rapidly.

Aidan Martin from the University of British Columbia, Canada, found that most sharks only exhibited stress when they felt themselves to be in danger and not when they felt their food resources were being threatened.

A friendly smile or something far more menacing? It doesn't take an expert in shark body language to realize that you'd better get away if you see a shark with this expression on its face.

Shark design

Sharks are adapted to different environments through variations in body, fin and tail shape and color over the basic shark design.

A pointed head and streamlined, smooth body indicate that this silvertip shark is a fast-swimming, predatory fish.

Shark shapes

The shape of the typical shark, especially a streamlined member of the mackerel or requiem families, is quite unmistakable. The shark's body is basically torpedo-shaped, or fusiform, with a wider and taller middle, and tapering ends.

Most sharks have two back or dorsal fins that stick up from the upper surface. There are also two pairs of fins that project at an angle, out and downward from the underside. These are the pectoral fins in front and the pelvic fins behind. There is usually also a smaller, single anal fin at the rear of the underside and a large caudal fin—better known as the tail.

Head to tail

The front end of a fast-swimming shark, like the mako or blue shark, has a pointed wedge shape. This offers minimal resistance to the water, while still housing the eyes and other sense organs and an effective mouth. The head may be flattened slightly to act as a hydrofoil and counteract the shark's natural tendency to sink.

The rear of the shark's body narrows to the tail stem, or peduncle, to reduce the resistance when moving through water. It is also flattened from side to side to increase the effectiveness of the tail's propulsive swimming movements. There are sometimes ridges, or keels, along the peduncle, like tiny vertical fins, as on the whale shark or porbeagle. These help to stabilize the body and stop it rolling from side to side.

Flat bottoms

Sharks that live on the seabed, such as the carpet shark and angel sharks, have little need for swift movement and streamlining. They rely more on camouflage and

The basic body shape of this Atlantic spotted dolphin is very similar to that of a fast-swimming shark, such as the blue shark. This design produces minimal water resistance.

concealment. The head and body are wide and flat with large, rounded fins attached to the sides rather than to the underside. The dorsal fins are small and near the rear, toward the tail. The anal fin is also small, as is the caudal fin or tail, since powerful tail-flicks are used little.

Copycat designs

Human designers and engineers have come up with the same basic shape for moving through the water as sharks and similar sea creatures like dolphins and bony fish. Submarines, boat hulls, and torpedoes have a similar outline to the typical shark, with a wide middle that tapers at both ends. This shape maximizes energy use and minimizes drag.

A submarine has the general slim shape typical of sharks and other fast fish. The positions of its "fins," or hydroplanes, mirror those of sharks, with two vertical and two horizontal at its rear end, to control direction and diving, and two lateral hydroplanes.

Shapes and sizes

There are many other shapes of sharks between the two extremes of fast swimmer (like the blue shark, right) and seabed dweller. Species that live near rather than on the bottom, for example the dogfish, are more snakelike. They wriggle among the weeds with long, narrow, eel-like bodies, wide and rounded pairs of side fins and small back fins. Their heads are large and blunt snouted.

Sharks that live in very deep water, e.g the sleeper, tend to have rounded, flabby, floppy bodies as an adaptation to the immense pressures in the depths.

Sharks on the move

The ease and grace of a shark belies the difficulty of moving through water. Anyone who walks in water or swims regularly knows the hard work required to push through this relatively dense medium.

Water is viscous, thick and glutinous. It is more than 1,000 times heavier and denser than an equal volume of our own usual medium, air. Water strongly opposes being pushed aside, producing a force against motion, called resistance. And it clings to anything trying to move through it, holding on like glue, with a force called drag.

S-shaped waves

The shark has not only overcome these problems but uses them to advantage. Its streamlined shape is designed to minimize both resistance and drag by a forward force—thrust. This comes from the shark's swishing body and tail. As a shark swims its body undulates from side to side with S-like curves. These press on the water around, which pushes back with equal and opposite force. The sideways motions cancel each other out. The rearward force pushes the water back, and the water forces the shark forward.

Swimming muscles

The shark's main swimming muscles along the flanks are arranged in zigzag blocks called myomeres. The ends of the muscle fibers in each myomere attach to a tendon called a myosepta, which then connects to the cartilage of the skeleton. There are the same number of myomeres as vertebrae in the spinal column but their zigzag shapes extend their effect over several vertebrae. This gives more pull for less energy use.

Each myomere attaches at two points along the spinal column. When they contract, they pull these two points of the column toward each other, bending the column into a wave. Along the row of myomeres, each contracts after the one in front of it and then relaxes as the one behind it contracts. This sequence produces a curve, or wave, that travels along the shark from head to tail.

The curviness, or amplitude, of each wave gets larger as it passes along the shark's body. This has the effect of increasing the push on the water. The final thrust is given by the tail, or caudal fin, which traces a spiral figure eight through the water—just as a rower with a single rear paddle gyrates it in figure eights to propel the boat.

Almost weightless

One advantage of living in water is that it provides support and buoyancy. Its density buffers the effects of gravity. Sharks and other water dwellers do not have to use as much energy as land animals, who need to stay upright and overcome gravity as they run and leap. Also, a shark may use warm, rising ocean currents to achieve greater height above the seabed, as birds soar upward in the rising air of thermals or above mountains.

A typical shark moves by rhythmically bending its body sideways, forming an S-shape, first one way then the other. The head and especially the tail move the furthest to each side, while the trunk, where the pectoral fins attach, moves the least. The diagram of a dogfish (below) shows how the S-shaped curves pass along its body, increasing in size as they reach the tail.

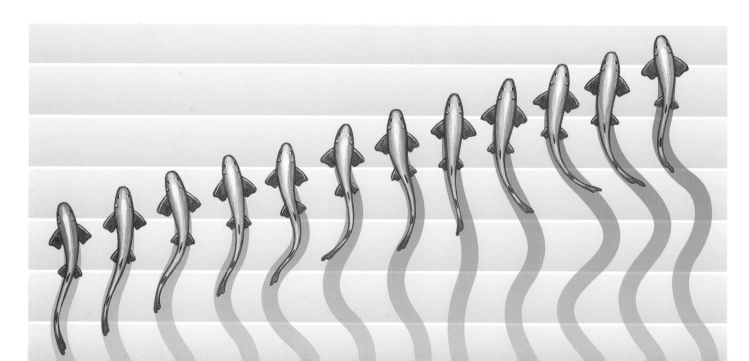

The flexible cartilage backbone of this blue shark allows it to twist and turn with great agility. Its powerful tail provides a strong thrust as the shark bends its body from side to side. Its stiff fins provide stability and steerage but not precision swimming.

Fins as legs

The zebra shark spends a lot of its time resting on the seabed. It swims in a similar manner to more mobile sharks, but its swimming is much less efficient as its body does not have the ideal height-to-length ratio of a great white shark or a tuna. The tuna has the ideal streamlined shape for fast swimming. The top lobe of the zebra sharks' tail is much more developed than the bottom lobe, which is characteristic of bottom-living sharks. This shark also uses its strong pectoral fins to prop itself up when looking out for prey.

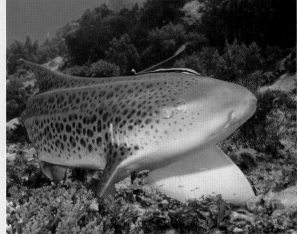

Tails and fins

In bony fish, the fins and tail can be fanned out, bent and tilted at different angles. Most sharks do not have this flexibility. Their vertical fins, in particular, are relatively stiff and rigid and fixed in shape and angle. This places limitations on the shark's maneuverability and fine control when moving through the water.

Caudal fin (tail)

The two-lobed caudal fin is supported by cartilaginous rods within and by dermal (skin) filaments. The spinal column projects into the upper lobe of the tail, which is called the heterocercal design. It differs radically from most bony fish, in which the spinal column ends before the tail starts, and the two tail lobes are equal—called the homocercal design.

In some sharks the spinal column has a kink and turns upward into the tail's upper lobe. In others it is straight, and the tail is kinked down slightly to fit onto it. Great white sharks, makos and porbeagles have a tail whose upper and lower lobes are outwardly almost symmetrical, like the homocercal tails of most bony fish, but their inner structure is still heterocercal.

Dorsal (back) fins

The dorsal fins of sharks cannot be folded flat against the back to reduce drag, like the fins of swordfish, tuna and similar speedy bony fish. But sharks use the turbulence created by the dorsal fins as pivot points to help push themselves through the water. In some species the swirling eddy, or vortex, created by the first dorsal fin is in just the right place—as the shark moves forward and its body undulates—for the second dorsal fin to push against when it arrives there. As the shark continues forward, the next undulation along the body brings the tail to the same place, again to make use of the vortex.

Side (paired) fins

The pectoral and pelvic fins of most sharks are tilted slightly, with the front, or leading, edge aiming up. This tends to lift the front end of the shark as it swims forward, counteracting the sinking effects of the heavy body and the heterocercal tail. Most sharks can adjust these fins, to an extent, to control rising and descending, as described on the following page. Bottom-living epaulette and horn sharks have developed another use for their side fins: they "crawl" on them along the seabed.

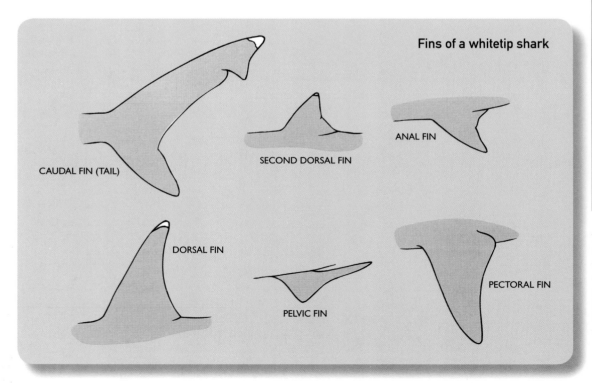

Fins of a whitetip shark

CAUDAL FIN (TAIL)

SECOND DORSAL FIN

ANAL FIN

DORSAL FIN

PELVIC FIN

PECTORAL FIN

The tall dorsal fin of a whitetip reef shark, situated almost in the middle of its back, helps to counterbalance the powerful sideways thrust of its tail and keep it upright—rather like the keel of a boat only the other way up.

This silky shark has a typical shark's tail, with the upper lobe slightly longer than the lower. This provides good thrust but also helps to give the shark lift, preventing it from sinking. The tails of really fast sharks, for instance the mako, have almost identical lobes.

Extreme tails

The great white's tail (left) has relatively equal lobes, but a thresher shark's tail is extremely unequal, or heterocercal. The upper lobe is much longer than the lower one—even longer than the rest of the body.

Sink or swim

It was once thought that sharks needed to swim constantly to stay alive. In fact, they must swim to stay off the bottom—but not all sharks need to stay off the bottom.

A shark's body tissues are slightly denser and heavier than water, so the natural tendency is for a shark to sink slowly. To counteract this inconvenience, the shark has various buoyancy aids. One is the cartilaginous skeleton, which is lighter than the equivalent bone version. Another is a large, oily liver, which may take up as much as one-fifth of the body volume. It contains a fatty substance called squalene (see page 24). Like most oils, it is lighter than water. Squalene has a relative density of 0.86, compared with seawater at 1.026 and the rest of the shark's body at about 1.1 (the density of pure water is 1.0). Just as oil floats on water, the shark's oily liver helps to keep it afloat. Whale and basking sharks have particularly huge livers to help them maintain their optimum feeding position near the water's surface.

No swim bladder

Bony fish control their buoyancy using a swim bladder. This is a saclike extension of the gut, and bubbles of gases can be introduced into it from the blood or withdrawn from it. More bubbles make the whole fish lighter and less dense, and so it rises. Thus the bony fish can swim level and even "hang" in mid-water.

Sharks do not have a true swim bladder, probably as a chance vagary of evolution. So this precise control of buoyancy is not available. An associated problem is that a shark's heterocercal tail, with unequal lobes—the upper larger than the lower (see page 102)—tends to drive the shark's nose down as it swishes.

Counteracting the dive

These sinking tendencies are counteracted by the side fins, especially the pectorals. They are angled upward like hydrofoils and are also wing shaped, with a curved upper surface and flatter lower surface (known as the aerofoil or hydrofoil section) to provide lift. The shark can tilt its pectorals to alter their "angle of attack" and also bend and curve them to a degree, and so adjust their upward lifting force. The wedge-shaped snout has an effect too, forcing the nose up. If one pectoral fin is dipped slightly its lifting force lessens, and so the shark veers around to that side as part of its steering mechanism.

But all of these hydrodynamic effects work only while the shark is moving. When it stops swimming it tends to sink.

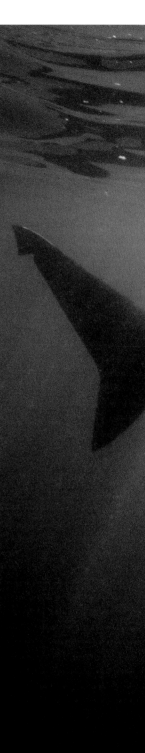

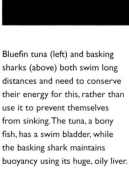

Bluefin tuna (left) and basking sharks (above) both swim long distances and need to conserve their energy for this, rather than use it to prevent themselves from sinking. The tuna, a bony fish, has a swim bladder, while the basking shark maintains buoyancy using its huge, oily liver.

Gulping air

Not to be outdone by the lack of a swim bladder, a few sharks can use air to help them maintain buoyancy, by gulping it into the gut. Captive sand tiger sharks do this at their tank surface. They can then "hang" motionless and without effort for some time. The more conventional buoyancy devices of three marine creatures are shown on the right: the oil-filled liver of a shark, the low-density cuttlebone of a cuttlefish and the gas-filled swimbladder of a bony fish.

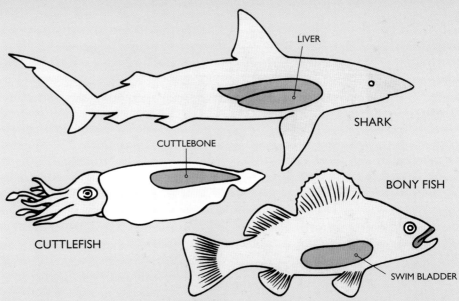

LIVER

SHARK

CUTTLEBONE

BONY FISH

CUTTLEFISH

SWIM BLADDER

Spines or spikes

Larger predatory sharks have few enemies and need little in the way of specialized defense. Their size, power and formidable teeth are more than adequate. But many smaller sharks—half of all shark species average less than 5 feet (1.5 m) long when mature—need strategies to deter attacks from predators, especially bigger sharks.

Most prehistoric sharks had a tall spine or blade standing in front of each of the two dorsal fins. These may have evolved originally to support the fins, in the way that a sailing ship's masts support its sails. The tough, smooth spines were often flattened from side to side, as in *Cladoselache*, or elaborately ridged and lumped. Gradually, internal supports took over, as cartilage rods and dermal rays within the fins. The spines disappeared. But in some sharks the spines stayed and assumed a new role—defense.

Fierce protection

Most living sharks that possess dorsal fin spines are small bottom-dwellers who use them as protection against attacks from above. The majority of species are in the dogfish family, *Squalidae*. The spiny dogfish or spurdog, *Squalus acanthias*, is caught commercially; its spines do not protect it from fishing nets, but they can inflict painful wounds on fish-handlers. Each spine bears a groove containing a mild poison. The shark can inject this poison by flicking its body into a curve around the assailant.

The rough sharks, *Oxynotus*, are sometimes called prickly dogfish. They not only have large spines on the back but also skin like barbed wire. Horn sharks of the family Heterodontidae, such as the Port Jackson or bullhead shark, also have a spine in front of each dorsal fin, which is mildly venomous.

The goblin shark

The grotesque-looking goblin shark, *Mitsukurina owstoni*, has a flattened extension like the peak of a cap protruding from its forehead. It looks like a menacing weapon, but it may simply be a support for extrasensory organs in the skin to detect prey. The goblin shark was first caught and described for science in the 1880s. Eventually it was recognized as a "living fossil," belonging to a group of sharks that were thought to have died out 100 million years ago (see also page 50).

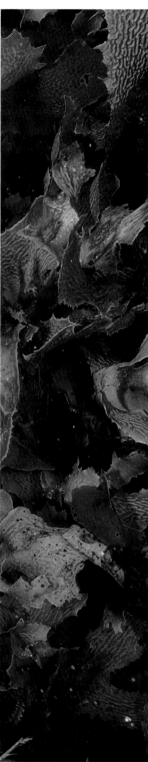

The Port Jackson's main dorsal fin has a defensive spine, which contains a mild poison. A close up of the spine can be seen on the left.

Surprise defense

The swell shark (page 64) is named for its surprising method of self-defense. If threatened it suddenly inflates its body to twice its normal size by swallowing air or water. This shark normally hides by day in a crevice, and if it performs its trick there it wedges itself in. Held even tighter by its rough skin, it is almost impossible to dislodge. Away from its shelter the swell shark must rely on startling its attacker by its sudden increase in size, thereby buying enough time to swim away. However, some swell sharks have been seen floating at the surface for several days, so on some occasions when they inflate themselves the letdown may be difficult.

Colors and camouflage

Most sharks hunt by stealth. The colors and patterns on their bodies are mainly for camouflage and disguise. But vision is more limited in the dim underwater world than in air. Also, seawater absorbs some colors of the light spectrum more than others, dulling reds and yellows especially.

So shark coloration may not seem incredibly effective to our own eyes. But it must work for the shark. Coloring substances, or pigments, are produced in the shark's skin by microscopic star-shaped cells that are known as chromatophores.

Changing colors

Most sharks develop and keep the same colors through life. In some species the young start life in the shallows and have beautiful markings to camouflage and protect them there. As they grow large enough to venture into deeper water they become duller. For example, the leopard shark starts life with the spots of its big-cat namesake but loses them as it gets older. Likewise the zebra shark has stripes when young, but these change with age to spots.

Some horn sharks wear dramatic zebralike stripes or giraffelike blotches in the early years, but these fade with age. The sand tiger lives in sandy shallows all its life. Despite its stripe-suggesting name, it has golden spots for disguise.

Blending in

Sharks must see their surroundings, since when they have a choice they select patches of seabed that suit their camouflage. The small-spotted cat shark, *Scyliorhinus canicula*, has dark yellowish-gray spots and prefers the sandy seabed. The nursehound, *Scyliorhinus stellaris*, on the other hand, has reddish spots and selects a more pebbly bottom.

Many sharks of open water have darker backs and lighter undersides. This is called countershading, and it is common among surface-dwelling fish of all kinds, from tuna and marlin to mackerel and herring. It counteracts the effect of sunlight from above.

Vision is very poor in cloudy water. So sharks that lurk in murky, muddy offshore areas, like nurse and bull sharks, are generally blue-gray. In the sea's depths there is no light at all. Sharks who dwell there, such as the lantern shark, are mostly allover dark gray or black.

The blacktip reef shark shows typical countershading camouflage. When viewed from above its dark back blends with the dark seabed. When viewed from below its white belly is hidden against the bright surface of the water. Black fin tips may help break up its outline.

Named from their colors

• The leopard shark, *Triakis semifasciata* (pictured), has distinctive spots to provide camouflage against dappled ground.
• The patterns of the coral cat shark, *Atelomycterus marmoratus*, and the marbled cat shark, *Galeus arae*, resemble swirling patterns in marble rock.
• The blue shark, *Prionace glauca*, is indeed blue, varying from deep blue on the back to lighter blue along the sides, and paling to white on the belly.
• The bronze whaler or copper shark, *Carcharhinus brachyurus*, is usually a shade of that color on its back and sides.
• Curiously, the great white, *Carcharodon carcharias*, has only a pale or white underside, its back and upper flanks being gray, gray-blue or gray-brown.

The mottled pattern of a whale shark provides camouflage in the sunlit, shadowy surface waters. White spots and blotches blend in with the sunlit dappled patterns of dancing waves and ripples. The pattern of spots is unique to each individual.

Cunning disguises

Apart from basic skin colors and camouflage, some sharks have extra tricks to deceive their victims or enemies. These involve flaps, frills and fronds of skin and even alluring lights in the dark water.

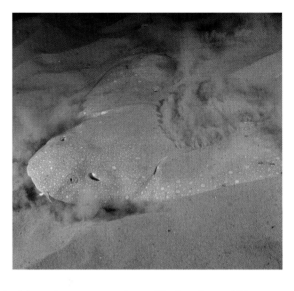

Carpet sharks, the group that includes the wobbegongs, have an excellent skin disguise, with patterns of colorful splotches and spots. These blend in perfectly with the sand, pebbles and seaweeds on the seafloor. But these sharks also disguise their body outline and sharklike shape. They have frills and fringes of skin around the head and mouth. They resemble seaweeds and corals not only in color, but also in shape—and even in movement, as the frondlike skin flaps waft in the current, like real seaweed.

There are about eight species of wobbegong (family *Orectolobidae*) living mainly in the seas around Australia and Japan. They include the descriptively named ornate wobbegong and tasseled wobbegong. Largest is the spotted wobbegong, *Orectolobus maculatus*, which can grow to a length of 10 feet (4.3 m); (see page 65).

As a wobbegong lies perfectly still on the seabed, the only sign of life is its spiracle holes as they open and close. The shark may even ripple its fronds gently to catch the attention of a curious crab or fish. As a potential meal approaches to investigate, the "wobby" opens its huge mouth. The influx of water sucks in the hapless victim. As the shark's jaws close it is trapped within a cage of long, fanglike teeth.

Light meals

Deep-sea fish live in a vast and sparsely populated world, where encounters with other creatures are rare and brief. Searching for a meal could take weeks. Many deep-sea species, including some sharks, use glowing lures of light to tempt prey out of the gloom.

The ability of living things to emit light is called bioluminescence. The glow is produced by special cup-shaped glands, called photophores, in the skin. The cells in the gland contain a substance known as luciferase. This alters a body protein, luciferin, by adding oxygen to it. During the reaction chemical energy is changed into light energy.

The photophore gland is surrounded by transparent microscopic cells that together form a glassy lens to focus the light. One of the "brightest" sharks is the cookiecutter, *Isistius brasiliensis*. It lives in mid-ocean and grows to 19 inches (51 cm) long. In the dark, its lower surfaces glow with an eerie green sheen. Its curious method of biting lumps out of victims is described on page 157.

This Australian angel fish is busy wriggling downwards and flicking its fins to cast sand over itself. In a few seconds it will be almost buried and hardly noticeable—an innocent patch of seabed.

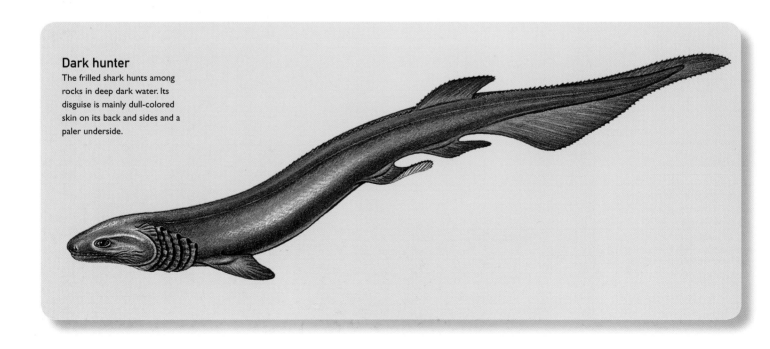

Dark hunter
The frilled shark hunts among rocks in deep dark water. Its disguise is mainly dull-colored skin on its back and sides and a paler underside.

Wobbegongs are so varied in their individual coloration that they can be difficult to identify. The banded wobbegong shown above was once thought to be a form of the ornate wobbegong, but is now recognized as a separate species.

Bright and dark

"Wobbies" like the tasseled wobbegong (left) need good camouflage in their shallow, brightly lit waters. Much deeper and darker, the lantern sharks, *Etmopterus virens*, disguise themselves with luminous organs scattered over the skin. The green lantern shark (dogfish) is less than one foot (30 cm) in length.

Do sharks sleep?

Sleep is a phenomenon that baffles scientists studying all animals. Mammals, birds, reptiles and some species of fish all need periods of rest in which their brainwave patterns change dramatically; but the biological reasons for spending hours of each day unconscious remain unclear.

Sharks are more of a mystery than most other species: no one has even been able to establish whether they actually do sleep, let alone the purpose this inactivity might serve. Marine biologists have reported seeing sharks resting motionless in caves in Australia, Mexico and Japan but they also note that the sharks' eyes continue to follow divers moving around in the caves—so they are not asleep in the way we usually understand the term.

It once seemed that sharks needed to swim constantly in order to breathe, as the oxygen-rich water needed to sustain life flows through their gills only during movement. Biologists assumed that if a shark stopped swimming for more than a few minutes it could not breathe correctly. However, this theory—that a few snatched minutes of sleep was all a shark could afford—has been disproved. Some species of shark have spiracles—small openings behind their eyes—that force water across their gills even when they are not moving, allowing them to rest motionless. The nurse shark is one such species. This shark hunts at night and returns to solitary spots, hidden in crevices on the seabed, to sleep during the day. Other species, such as the spiny dogfish, do not use their brains to control movement but rather their spinal cord. This means that during periods of sleepy brain activity the shark can continue to swim and therefore to breathe.

Some scientists have also conjectured that sharks sleep in the same way as dolphins, which close down half the brain for rest while the other half coordinates continued motion and consciousness. It's possible that sharks close down their fore, mid and hind brains in sequence to sleep while remaining semiconscious.

When do sharks sleep?

Sharks that have been tagged and tracked have revealed to scientists that several species, including the tiger shark and the whitetip reef shark, are most active at night, with more restful periods during the day. This tracking technology has overturned many previous assumptions, for instance that the great white shark was most active in daylight hours. It now seems that this theory arose purely from the fact that great whites had been most often observed during the day—without sophisticated sonic tracking, it's very difficult to observe creatures swimming at great depth. Recent research has suggested that the species mentioned above, at least, do not sleep at night. In fact, the great white is very active and feeding on the seabed at night.

Tracking sharks

Tagging sharks is a specialist skill that requires a lot of care. A misplaced tag could injure the shark, stunt its growth or even kill it. It's not just scientists who do this work—fishermen are also helping scientific studies by tagging sharks accidentally caught in their nets to help researchers build up a larger volume of data on shark movements. The tags can vary from plastic chords containing the contact information of the researchers to high-tech radio tags that continuously transmit information about the shark's movements.

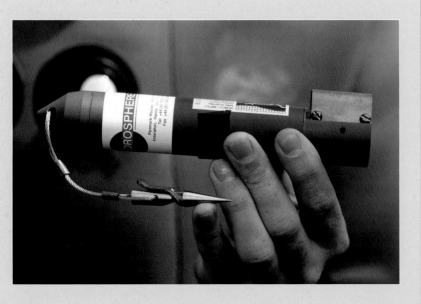

It is not obvious whether sharks, such as this Galapagos horn shark sleep at all in the sense that we generally understand the word. Scientists believe that sharks may just rest one area of their brain at a time, leading to periods of semiconscious activity.

It is not possible to tell whether a shark, like this zebra shark (left) is asleep just by looking at it. Many sharks appear to be resting, semiconscious, on the ocean floor, yet their eyes still follow divers' movements.

How sharks live

Sharks are found throughout the world's oceans in many different habitats and adopt very varied and sometimes unusual lifestyles.

Silvertip sharks live in relatively shallow water over continental shelves, near rocks, coral reefs, islands and offshore banks.

The world of the shark

Sharks are an integral part of the biggest natural system on the planet—the marine ecosystem. This is the largest and oldest of all Earth's environments, covering more than two-thirds of the world's surface.

On land, we are used to many different conditions and habitats—mountains, valleys, woods, grassland, hot desert, steamy rainforest, icy tundra. The ocean is also far from uniform. It is divided into many different kinds of habitats, each with vastly different characteristics.

On the bottom

The seabed is the benthic habitat—that is, the home of benthos, the flora and fauna that live on the bottom of the sea. Its topography varies enormously, from flat plains and gentle hills and valleys to towering seamounts, sheer cliffs and plunging submarine canyons. Seabed material also varies, from bare rock, pebbles and gravels to sparkling sand and thick, gooey mud. If the sea is shallow and light can penetrate, algal plants (seaweeds) thrive.

The ocean floor is subjected to a constant "rain" of material from above, such as dead bodies, animal wastes and detritus. Worms, shellfish, flatfish and similar benthic creatures live there, forming their own food chains and food webs. Sharks have adapted to all of these benthic conditions.

Open waters

The pelagic habitat—open water—can be categorized in several ways. One is by latitude, from equator to pole, and another is vertically, into three main layers of depth.

• The uppermost layer, to an average depth of 330 feet (100 m), is relatively bright and sunlit. Algae thrive and are the basic food for all ocean creatures. This surface water is also under the influence of global weather patterns and temperatures fluctuate greatly. Most of the well-known sharks live in this uppermost layer.

• The middle layer ranges from about 330 to 3,300 feet (100–1,006 m). It is a twilight zone, too dark for most plants to grow, and occupied mainly by fish, squid and other creatures with huge eyes, including sharks, who hunt each other in the gloom.

• Below about 3,300 feet (1,006 m) it is pitch-black. The pressure of the water is gigantic. Temperatures and currents are less varied. It is a world we have hardly explored, yet it is the biggest part of the marine environment. New animal species are regularly discovered here, including the occasional previously unknown shark.

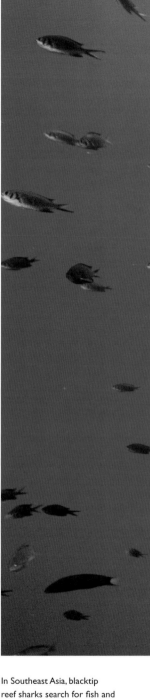

In Southeast Asia, blacktip reef sharks search for fish and invertebrates in very shallow water on coral reefs. People wading over reef flats are sometimes surprised to find these 3-foot (0.9 m) long fish brushing around their legs, often at depths so shallow that the dorsal fin breaks the surface.

Coral reefs are home to a variety of reef sharks, attracted by the wealth of fish life. Steep drop-offs, such as this one in the Red Sea, are regularly patrolled by sharks, especially at dusk when day-hunting fish are streaming home to the safety of the reef top.

Known and unknown

The tawny nurse shark (left) is a well-known shallow-water species. A species from a very different habitat was discovered in 1976, as a U.S. Navy ship trailed its parachute anchor 450 feet (137 m) deep, near Hawaii. When winched in, a huge shark was entangled in the line. New to science, it was nearly 15 feet (4.6 m) long, weighed 1,650 pounds (748 kg) and had a colossal mouth. Nicknamed "megamouth," after intensive study it received the scientific name *Megachasma pelagios* (see page 54).

Where sharks live

This world map shows the areas frequented by
some of the better-known sharks. Most live in
warmer coastal waters, but some species prefer
cooler oceans (see page 120).

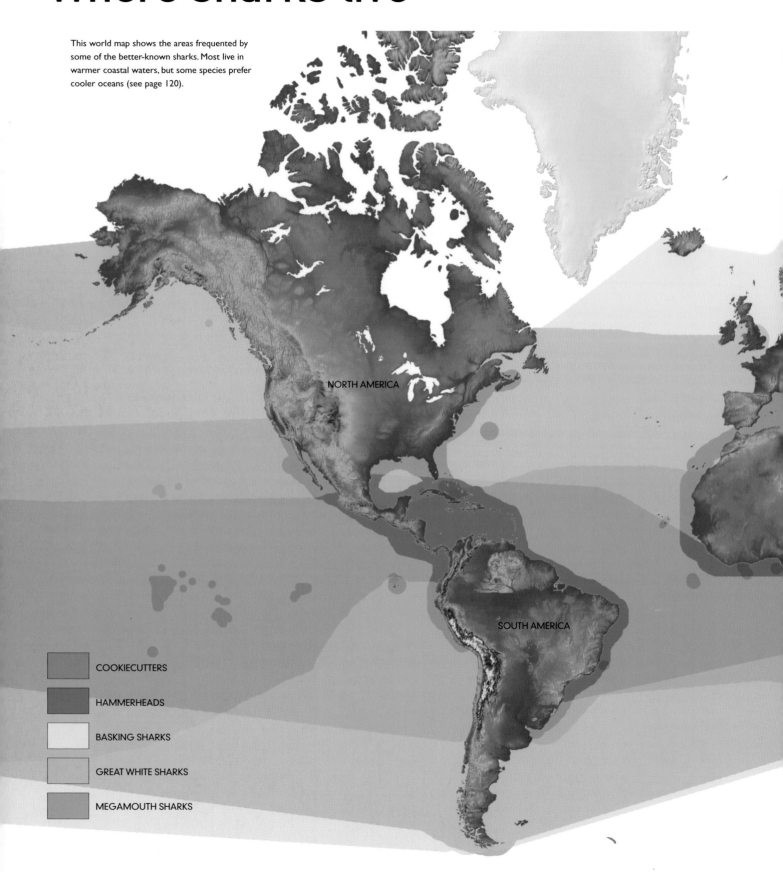

NORTH AMERICA

SOUTH AMERICA

COOKIECUTTERS

HAMMERHEADS

BASKING SHARKS

GREAT WHITE SHARKS

MEGAMOUTH SHARKS

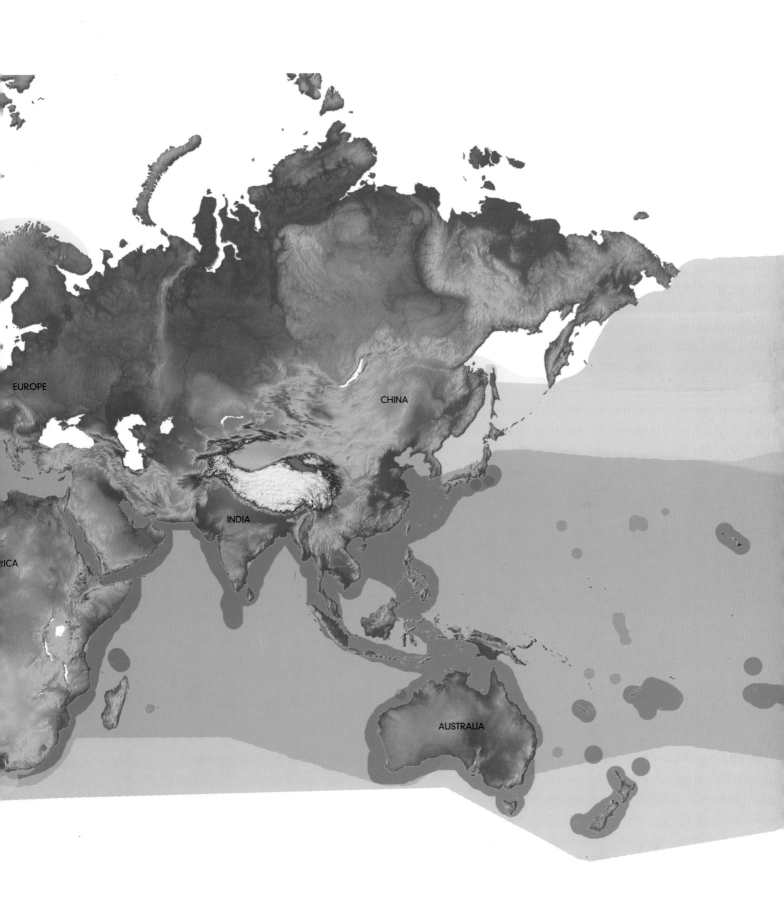

EUROPE

CHINA

INDIA

RICA

AUSTRALIA

Tropics to poles

Sharks are found throughout the world's oceans. However, there are relatively fewer species and individuals in cold polar seas and more in temperate waters. Most species, especially the larger meat-eaters, prefer temperate or warm tropical conditions.

Warm-water sharks

Most of the sleek predatory sharks thrive in the tropics, the seas on either side of the Equator, where the water is warmer than 70°F (21°C). The oceanic whitetip is probably the most common in all tropical oceans—Atlantic, Indian and Pacific. The blue shark is also found in tropical and subtropical seas around the world.

There are several species of hammerhead shark, each occupying its own particular region of open ocean. The scalloped hammerhead is found in all tropical waters. The winged hammerhead is found mainly in the subtropical Pacific and Indian oceans. Their close cousins, the bonnethead sharks, live in the east Pacific and west Atlantic.

Temperate sharks

Some shark species frequent temperate waters, at temperatures of about 50–70°F (10–21°C). One is the great white, found off the coasts of North and South America, Europe, southern Africa, the Mediterranean, eastern and Southeast Asia and Australasia.

The basking shark is found in a wide variety of waters, from the tropics almost to the polar seas. Mako sharks live in temperate regions and some tropical ones. Thresher sharks once had a wide distribution, as far north as Norway, but overfishing has reduced their numbers in cooler seas. They are still found in the English Channel between Britain and continental Europe, but most are found in warmer temperate and subtropical areas.

Lemon sharks move into the relative safety of shallow sandy areas, such as Bimini Lagoon in the Bahamas, to give birth to their young.

Cold-water sharks

Where the water temperature averages less than 50°F (10°C), sharks are less numerous and more sluggish, such as the smooth hound and spiny dogfish. These regions include the North Atlantic and north Pacific and the Arctic Ocean—plus the great depths of all the oceans, far away from the warming sun.

Well-known cold-water sharks are the porbeagle and the sleeper sharks. The Greenland sleeper shark, or gurry, has been found in waters within the Arctic Circle. The Pacific sleeper shark, *Somniosus pacificus*, is more temperate and frequents waters from about 70°N to 47°S, with sightings near sub-Antarctic islands.

Cold killer

The porbeagle, *Lamna nasus*, is a large, powerful member of the mackerel shark group, Lamnidae. Reaching 12 feet (3.7 m) and 500 pounds (249 kg) it has a wide distribution in the North Atlantic, from Greenland south to the coasts of New Jersey in the west and eastward to Morocco. It is also seen in water of similar temperatures, 40–50°F (4–10°C) in the Southern Hemisphere, and occasionally down to 35°F (2°C, close to freezing). Far from being slow and sluggish, the porbeagle chases herring and mackerel near the surface.

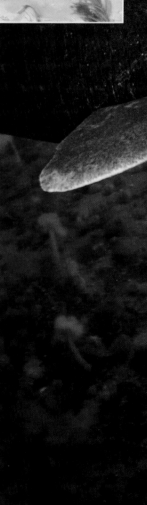

Living in the frigid waters under the Arctic ice, the Greenland sleeper shark is a sluggish hunter and is easily caught through ice holes. Like many cold-water animals, this shark is long-lived, grows slowly and reaches a large size—possibly 20-plus feet (6+ m) long.

Shallows to the deep

Sharks are found at all depths of the seas. Some bask in the warm sunlit water or chase prey just below the surface. Others seemingly doze at the bottom on the sea bed, waiting for food to come to them. A shark's coloration, body shape and swimming skill indicate its preferred water depth, lifestyle and food source.

Shallow-water sharks

The majority of sharks live in warm, shallow waters, down to about 650 feet (198 m). Most other sea creatures live there too and provide the sharks' diet. Spiny dogfish form huge single-sex schools just offshore. Whitetip reef sharks and nurse sharks laze sluggishly on the bottom by day but become swift, fierce hunters at night.

Angel sharks, saw sharks and carpet sharks spend almost all their time on the shallow seabed. They have unstreamlined bodies and appropriate camouflage—carpet sharks look like weedy, knobbly rocks, while angel sharks resemble the smoothness of the sandy bottom. Swell sharks are also shallow-water fish.

Open-ocean sharks

The great predatory groups, the mackerel and requiem sharks, cruise the sunlit upper layers of the open oceans. They can find food by sight as well as by scent. Their streamlined bodies are countershaded, being darker on the upper surface and lighter on the underside. Viewed from below, the pale belly merges with the lighter surface waters. Seen from above, the darker back blends with the dimmer depths. And from the side, countershading offsets the sun's lightening of the upper side and shadowing effect on the belly.

Deep-water sharks

The diminutive dwarf shark is found mainly in gloomy waters 1,000–3,000 feet (305–915 m) deep. Its luminous (light-emitting) organs help it to find food in such deep water. The velvet belly shark, which also has light-producing organs, dwells between 2,300 and 6,550 feet (700–1,995 m) down. Various species of *Centrophorus*, the gulper sharks, are found at similar depths in all tropical and temperate seas. Cat sharks and false cat sharks swim in mid-water blackness below 3,300 feet (1,005 m).

The inky blackness of the deep benthic habitat is home to the strangest sharks, chiefly spiny-finned species from the dogfish group. In some regions, where food is plentiful, they form the largest component of the biomass in that habitat. Bramble sharks dwell below 1,600 feet (488 m) as do frilled sharks, sixgill and sevengill sharks. They feed on carrion floating down from above or on bottom-dwelling creatures such as shellfish and worms.

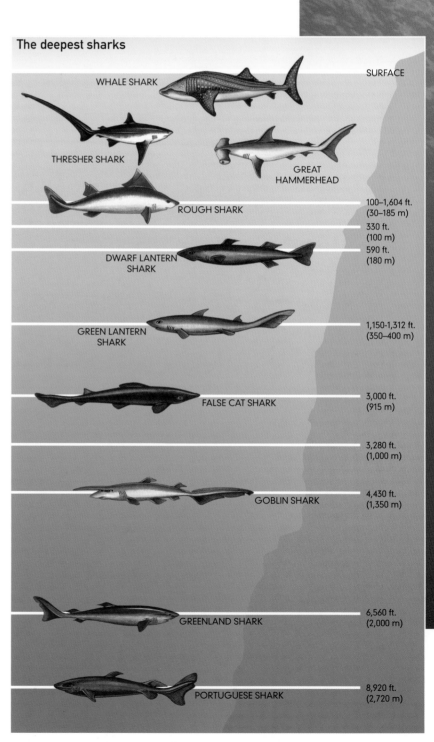

The deepest sharks

WHALE SHARK

SURFACE

THRESHER SHARK

GREAT HAMMERHEAD

ROUGH SHARK

100–1,604 ft. (30–185 m)

330 ft. (100 m)

DWARF LANTERN SHARK

590 ft. (180 m)

GREEN LANTERN SHARK

1,150–1,312 ft. (350–400 m)

FALSE CAT SHARK

3,000 ft. (915 m)

3,280 ft. (1,000 m)

GOBLIN SHARK

4,430 ft. (1,350 m)

GREENLAND SHARK

6,560 ft. (2,000 m)

PORTUGUESE SHARK

8,920 ft. (2,720 m)

Up in the shallow sunlit waters near the surface, tiger sharks scan the surface for seabirds, turtles and marine mammals. They will also eat almost anything else they find.

Shallow to deep

Sharks such as the tawny nurse (left) rarely venture to depths beyond 200 feet. One of the deepest shark records was a Portuguese shark (Portuguese dogfish), *Centroscymnus coelolepis*, a type of sleeper shark. It was caught by line in the Atlantic southwest of Ireland, in the 1970s from a depth of about 12,000 feet (3,658 m).

Friends and enemies

It seems unlikely that other creatures would willingly come near a large and hungry shark. But several types of fish are often found with sharks, and others make regular visits—for reasons of hygiene.

The various species of shark-suckers, also called remoras, are slim fish varying from about 8 inches to just over 3 feet (20–90 cm) in length. They have bold markings and dorsal fins modified into large oval suckers. The two halves of the fin form louverlike ridges with a raised rim around the outside. When the rim is put against a surface and the louvers are lowered this creates a vacuum inside, and the surrounding water pressure forces the sucker against the surface. Remoras suck onto sharks, other large fish, turtles, whales and even ships, saving energy as they hitch a ride.

Other fish that often accompany sharks are pilotfish. About 4 feet (70cm) long, they swim alongside sharks, whales and other large creatures and ships, too, sometimes for many days. They save energy by keeping close to the bigger animal, "slipstreaming" within the water it drags. Using another animal for transport in this way is called phoresy.

Keeping clean

Sharks and other fish who live around coral reefs often visit a particular site called a cleaning station. The cleaners are fish, usually small, finger-sized wrasse or perhaps cleaner shrimps. Huge sharks, barracudas, groupers and other fearsome giants allow the little cleaners to enter their mouths and gill slits and pick off dead skin and scales, small parasitic animals like lice, barnacles, fungi, growths and other debris. The cleaners have distinct patterns and dances that inhibit the "killer instinct" of the larger fish, but how is not clear.

Threats to sharks

The main natural threats to a shark are larger sharks and big hunting mammals such as porpoises, dolphins, killer whales and sperm whales. Porpoises are known to attack a large shark in self-defense. They surround it and ram it in turn from the sides until it retreats. Dolphins are also known to ram sharks, especially on their sensitive gills or cloacal region.

The killer whale (or orca), bigger than a great white, is an intelligent, fearsome, powerful, pack-hunting predator. Most animals in the sea avoid it, including sharks—an average-sized shark species would make a nice-sized snack for the orca. Playing the recorded sounds of killer whales to a bull shark causes the shark great agitation.

Striped marlin are one of the fastest fish in the ocean and are unlikely prey for most sharks. However, their rapierlike bill is very strong, and they can inflict a nasty wound on any attacker.

Gigantic, slow-moving whale sharks are often accompanied by shark suckers also called remoras. These small fish hitch a ride using a powerful sucker on the top of their heads. They jump ship to catch small fish or leftover scraps.

Megamouth menaced

In 1998 biologists witnessed an "interaction" between three sperm whales and a 16-foot (4.9 m) shark near North Sulawesi, Indonesia. The commotion ceased as their boat approached and the sperm whales swam away. The shark turned out to be a megamouth, only the thirteenth on record. It showed signs of being bitten on the gills and dorsal fin. Whether the sperm whales were curious, playful or aggressive was not clear.

Pests and parasites

Threatening animals do not have to be big and fierce. Like other living things, sharks are unwilling hosts to parasites that live on and inside them, feeding on their tissues.

Sleeper sharks often have parasitic copepods, known generally as sea lice or fish lice, attached to their eyes. These are not true lice, which are insects, but small crustaceans, distant cousins of crabs and shrimps. They resemble woodlice or water fleas and vary in size from smaller than this "o" to larger than a human hand.

Eyes and gills

These copepod parasites do considerable damage to the cornea (the domed, transparent front of the eye). Sharks can have scar tissue on the cornea from past parasitic attack. This must impede vision. But sleeper sharks are slow-swimming bottom-dwellers in dark waters, so they probably do not depend on eyesight to any great degree.

New parasites of this type are discovered routinely. An example is the sea louse *Caligus oculicola* discovered in 2004 attached to the eyes of tiger sharks. A great white captured off California in 2003 had five kinds of copepod parasites on its skin alone, apart from those in its mouth, gills, eyes and internal organs.

The monogenea are types of worm usually known as flatworms or platyhelminthes, a group that includes tapeworms and liver flukes. Most are leaflike and live on the skin or in the mouth or gills. Like the copepods, they extract nourishment from the shark, and a heavy infestation can cause severe malnutrition and increase susceptibility to disease.

Skin

Big sharks may be dotted with firmly fixed skin parasites such as barnacles, lice and copepods. Barnacles are crustaceans, cousins of crabs and prawns. They fix

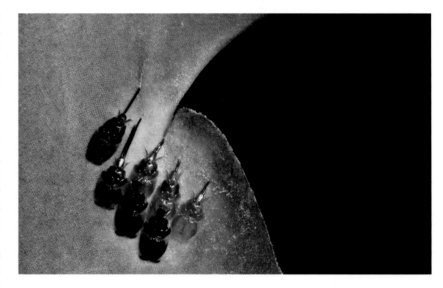

themselves to any firm surface as tiny larvae (immature young) and grow a cone-shaped set of hard plates for protection. The animal pokes its feathery-looking limbs out of a hole at the top of the cone and "kicks" to draw in water bearing tiny food particles.

Once adhered, barnacles are extremely difficult to shift. Although they do not draw any nourishment from the shark, they can slow swimming and be a route for infection. Whale sharks may rub against boats, apparently itching to get rid of the unwelcome guests.

Some sharks have more than a dozen species of copepod parasites on their skin (seen here on the tail fin), such as the widespread genus *Pandarus*. There may be hundreds of individual animals. A whole branch of biologic science is devoted to them—parasitologic copepodology.

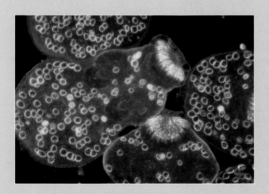

Gut worms

Sharks are hosts to several kinds of internal parasites, including tapeworms in their digestive system. The worm hangs onto the lining of the gut with its tiny hooked head and absorbs the nutrients all around it, through its thin, moist skin. Tapeworms produce bags of eggs at their rear ends, which detach and pass out with the shark's feces. Like tapeworms on land, they have complicated life cycles that involve other hosts in addition to the shark.

A shortfin mako trails "banners" from its first dorsal fin—they are formed from the egg strings of small copepod parasites. The parasites themselves are the lighter spots near the trailing edge of the fin. Copepods are crustaceans, related to crabs, krill and barnacles.

Finding the way

To us the open ocean seems featureless. But sharks and other oceanic creatures know that the oceans are far from uniform. The water itself varies in its speed and direction of movement, its physical and chemical makeup, and its temperature.

Different currents of water flow horizontally, vertically and diagonally cross each other or flow over underwater cliffs and along deep-sea valleys. Sharks are highly tuned to this world of motion, scents, chemicals, salt concentrations, temperatures and pressures, and they may use the currents as guides when navigating.

Magnetic sense

The Earth has a weak natural magnetic field, which we detect with our magnetic compasses and use in navigation. In recent years, several experiments have shown that sharks can sense magnetic fields. In one study, scalloped hammerhead and sandbar sharks in a large tank were provided with food in a particular area. At the time of feeding an artificial magnetic field was switched on, produced by a copper wire coil around the tank. The sharks learned to swim quickly to the feeding zone. After a time, the magnetic field was switched on but no food was provided. Even so, the sharks quickly converged at the food area, as usual. This demonstrated that they could detect the magnetic field, which they had learned to associate with food.

Another study involved a lemon shark that swam along a regular daily route. Scientists set up electromagnets in the water there. When this magnetic field altered the Earth's natural field, the shark altered its swimming direction. Also, observations of long-distance shark journeys in the wild suggest that they use the Earth's natural lines of magnetic force. These lines bend and dip in specific places, influenced by the types of rock under the surface. As the sharks swim they follow these bends and dips.

Magnetic electricity

Other animals known to have a magnetic sense have particles of the naturally magnetic mineral magnetite their tissues. There is no evidence for magnetite in

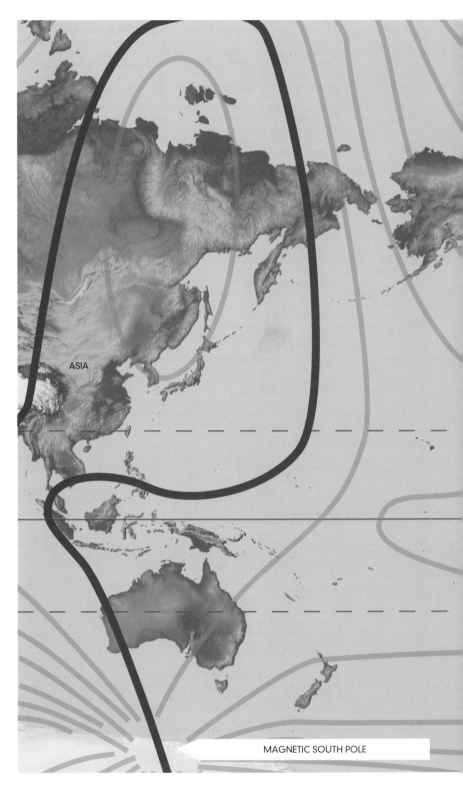

ASIA

MAGNETIC SOUTH POLE

sharks, but they do have electrosenses. When electrically charged particles move through a magnetic field they generate electricity. Shark tissue contains electrically charged natural salts. As the shark moves through the Earth's magnetic fields it generates miniscule electrical currents, which it can detect with its electrosense. From this electrical signal the shark could deduce the size and direction of the Earth's magnetic field.

MAGNETIC NORTH POLE

EUROPE

NORTH AMERICA

ASIA

AFRICA

SOUTH AMERICA

Clues from sounds

Sounds in the sea may be a clue to location and direction. The oceans are full of background noise from turbulent water, animals and other sources. This background of "wet noise" may form a type of detailed sound image. The shark's lateral-line system and ears would help it to form "sound pictures" of its surroundings.

The Earth is a giant magnet and has a magnetic field, which our compass needles detect. However, because of the composition of rocks, the field is not constant. The contours of this map show where the main magnetic variations occur.

Shark migrations

Some sharks have no home base or territory. A proportion of these are lone wanderers, turning up almost anywhere at random. However, other sharks regularly move long distances, or migrate, for various reasons—to exploit new food sources, to avoid danger or to breed.

Seasonal patterns

Many animals, from butterflies to whales, migrate to find food. Sharks are no exception. Numerous species, like salmon sharks in the north Pacific, move seasonally to follow the migrations of their food items such as fish, squid, small whales and seals. These creatures, in turn, are often following their own smaller food, traced back through oceanic food webs to the plankton.

Plankton grows fast, or "blooms," in the nutrient-rich polar seas during the short summer. As a result, in spring marine animals such as fish and whales head from tropical and temperate regions to the far north and south. In fall the polar waters become cold and dark with little plankton. So the migrants head back to the tropics, where the waters support less plankton growth, but at least there is a supply (and it's warm). Thresher sharks follow this pattern in the Atlantic. They are found in warmer waters in winter and migrate north as far as the North Sea in summer.

Champion migrant

The most proficient shark migrant is the blue shark. Tagging studies, ranging from simple numbered plastic labels to complex radio beacons in contact with satellites, reveal a fascinating cycle of movement in this species. In the eastern North Atlantic mating takes place during the spring until about June. Then some blues set off eastward, riding the prevailing currents, such as the North Atlantic Current and Gulf Stream. They turn up off the coasts of Europe, where they produce their offspring. But not all blues do this. The migrants are principally females, while most males stay near North America.

In the western North Atlantic the females give birth to their young, or pups. Because of the length of the journey, they had to store sperm from their mating for some time before allowing fertilization to occur so pup development could begin (see pages 174–179).

It's thought that the females then travel south along the coasts of Europe and North Africa and west, back across the Atlantic. Again they utilize natural flows, such as the Canaries and North Equatorial currents, to reach the Caribbean or North American coasts. It is an epic journey of some 10,000 miles (around 16,000 km).

Spinner sharks, seen here schooling in a shallow lagoon, migrate inshore in the Gulf of Mexico as the water warms up in spring. Here they find plenty of food and they breed. As winter approaches they move offshore again and may also travel further south.

In contrast to many ocean-living sharks, reef sharks such as these blacktips do not generally make long migrations. They are, however, strong swimmers, wandering in search of food and have been known to move into the Mediterranean Sea through the Suez Canal.

Following food

The bronze whaler or narrowtooth shark, *Carcharhinus brachyurus*, feeds on various prey such as mullets, sardines and similar fish, as well as squid and octopus. In winter in southern Africa, groups of "bronzies" track large sardine schools as these travel along the coast of KwaZulu-Natal province. Here, several bronze whalers herd a baitball (very tightly packed school) of small hardyheads into shallow water, where the prey has little chance of escape.

Social sharks

Some sharks gather in large single-species groups, called schools, but their reasons are not yet clear. In many cases the groups probably provide protection for their members, since predators are less likely to attack such a massed gathering. However, most of the larger sharks have very few enemies—apart from other larger sharks.

Whitetip reef sharks rest by day in large groups in caves or under rock overhangs. With their collective awareness, using many pairs of eyes, lateral lines and other senses, they may be able to detect danger or prey more effectively. On the other hand, they may simply congregate at the site because it is the most suitable resting place.

When nurse sharks rest on the bottom they may lie one on another, like puppies in a heap. Tactile communication may play a part in these gatherings.

Finding mates

A second possible reason for schooling behavior is to increase reproductive success. Compared with a solitary life, gathering in groups allows individuals to be more aware of the maturity and sexual condition of potential mates, and it provides opportunities for breeding (see page 172). However, some species, like spiny dogfish and lemon sharks, live in single-sex schools outside the breeding season. Mating cannot be their aim.

Scalloped hammerhead sharks are nocturnal hunters. By day they rest, swimming lazily in schools of many hundreds. They move and turn in coordinated fashion, like schools of other fish. But the females, who may outnumber the males by four to one, jostle and head-butt each other to stay in the center.

Hunting together

A third reason for schooling could be to hunt as a pack and increase food-catching success. Many sharks feed in large groups. However, this is often simply because food is abundant at a particular site. Each shark has no complex interactions with fellow members of its species, and when the feeding is done they go their separate ways. In the North Atlantic in summer, the second-largest shark species, the basking shark, has been seen in groups of 50 or more where ocean currents concentrate its planktonic food items.

Observations of great white sharks suggest that they may cooperate while hunting, as each individual responds to the movements of others in its group.

Huge schools of scalloped hammerhead sharks swirl lazily around the tops of oceanic seamounts during the day. At dusk they disperse to hunt for food. Strong upwelling currents around the seamounts carry nutrients and plankton that attract large numbers of prey fish.

Who's boss in the shark school?

In many single-species groups of animals, from lions to crocodiles, there is a dominance hierarchy, or pecking order. The chiefs get first choice of food, rest sites and mates, while others are submissive to them. The dominants maintain their position by displays of health and strength, threats and—rarely—physical combat. Sharks in large groups have been seen to head-butt each other with open jaws, their teeth leaving minor wounds on the opponent. These actions do not seem to be full attacks. Perhaps they are ways of settling dominance disputes within a school.

During the day, whitetip reef sharks rest singly or in groups in suitable gullies or swim slowly around. At night they often hunt in packs, jostling each other, nosing and banging into the coral. Groups of sharks may have more success than individuals in flushing out sleeping fish.

Territorial sharks

Do sharks have territories—their own "patch" of seabed, reef or similar habitat, where they stay to feed and breed?

For now the answer is not clear. The difficulties of identifying and observing individual sharks in the wild, given their speed, tendency to roam and often elusive nature, makes this area of shark science particularly awkward and sometimes dangerous. It is also an accepted fact that simply being present to watch sharks, or any wild animals, can alter their actions in unnatural ways, so that we do not receive a true reflection of their uninhibited behavior.

In the natural sciences, an animal's territory is an area that it frequents, which may well provide its living space, food, shelter and other resources, and which—importantly—it defends against intruders, especially those of its own kind. Territories are held by many kinds of creatures, especially birds. In some cases the territory is far too small to provide food or shelter, but its possession is necessary as a symbolic token to attract a partner for breeding purposes. In contrast, an area where an animal habitually roams and feeds, but which it does not actively defend by chasing others of its species away, is generally known as a home range rather than a territory.

Get away

Possible forms of territorial behaviour are known in the gray reef shark, *Carcharhinus amblyrhynchos*. Some divers suggest that if challenged near to a particular marker on the reef, such as coral outcrop or sandy patch, this shark demonstrates its assertiveness by arching or hunching its back, and angling its pectoral fins so they point almost straight down. This is a sign that the shark is ready to attack (see pages 94–95).

Another species suspected of aggressive defense of a territory is the bull shark. Normally slow and sluggish, it can put on a surprising burst of speed if it wishes to investigate or repel any creature than encroaches. Well known for its attacks on animals and humans, the bull shark may be driven by instinct to defend the immediate area of "personal space" around it (see panel), rather than by hunger or by the defense of a particular area of water or patch of seabed.

Shark space

Humans may feel uncomfortable, even aggressive, if other individuals approach too close, especially face to face. This concept of "personal space" has also been suggested for certain types of shark. If another creature enters this area around the shark it will react. This is not so much the traditional view of an animal territory as a fixed geographical location, but a "traveling territory," like an invisible bubble that moves with the shark. If the shark is being defensive, then the nearer the intruder gets, the greater the shark's aggression as a warning to keep out. However, if the shark takes the initiative and decides to approach an animal or human, then the personal space is much more flexible.

If approached too closely a gray reef shark will either swim away or show its displeasure by lowering its pectoral fins, arching its back and exaggerating its head and tail movements. This shark is showing a little agitation, as it has lowered its pectoral fins slightly.

Gray reef sharks are a social species, often congregating during the day in quiet lagoons or in channels between coral reefs. These sharks tend to prefer home sites that they know. At nighttime the groups break up as individuals go off to hunt for reef fish, squid and small invertebrates.

Intelligence and learning

Sharks were long thought to function like unthinking robotic eating machines, with almost no intelligence in the way we normally conceive of this attribute. But recent studies show that this is far from true. Experiments and observations of both wild and captive sharks are slowly dispelling the myth of the shark as an unthinking, unintelligent automaton.

Studies have revealed that these creatures remember, learn from experience, communicate and interact with others of their own kind and with other animals in the sea.

Instinct and learning

Types of behavior based on in-built patterns are called instinctive responses. They usually happen as reactions to certain specific stimulations, and they are usually relatively simple and predictable. In many animals, including sharks, instinctive responses can be modified to some degree by decisions based on experience. The animal confronts a situation, behaves in an instinctive way, assesses the results of this behavior and forms a memory. Next time it meets the same situation it recalls its previous experience, and perhaps it modifies or changes its behavior in a trial-and-error fashion. This is the basis of simple learning. Sharks can do all of this and more.

In captivity

Experiments with captive sharks have shown that they are as capable of learning and modifying their behavior as small mammals such as mice and shrews. In aquaria, species such as lemon and nurse sharks are shown to learn well and quickly. After fewer than 10 "training sessions" they come to associate certain sounds or movements with food. They can be trained to take food from a certain place or even a particular person. They learn to navigate a simple maze as quickly as a rat or mouse. They can discriminate by sight between shapes so that they know, for example, a circle signifies food but a square does not.

In the wild

Sharks in the wild learn by themselves to harass spear-fishing humans, who avoid attack by giving up their catches, which the shark then consumes. Sharks fed regularly for the benefit of tourists rapidly get to know the routine, such as hearing the sound of the boat approaching—and if another boat with a different noise arrives they may well not respond. There are also many well-studied instances of sharks turning up at a particular site at the right time to exploit abundant seasonal prey, such as young seabirds or seals.

A Caribbean reef shark eats a dead fish fed to it by a diver. Although large and capable of attacking people, these sharks are generally peaceable as long as they are treated with respect. These are the most common sharks on the Caribbean reefs.

Experienced tour leaders feed Caribbean reef sharks by hand. Local sharks soon learn that diving groups mean they will be fed and gather quickly when the divers arrive. Some biologists worry that shark-feeding may lead to sharks associating people with food and thereby increase attacks on humans.

Curiosity

There are many records of sharks approaching unfamiliar objects and nudging, bumping or perhaps nipping them lightly with their teeth. Divers are sometimes subjected to this unnerving process. The behavior is usually interpreted as curiosity. The shark is investigating a strange and unknown item, presumably to find out if it has any relevance, such as presenting a threat or being good to eat.

Sharks in captivity

The natural habitats of sharks are the world's oceans, where they are free to hunt wherever and whenever they please. Many scientists and conservationists wish to hold sharks in captivity in order to study their behavior and to educate the public about these fascinating creatures.

Unfortunately, keeping a large and powerful animal like a shark presents some unique challenges that have made this very difficult to achieve.

One of the key difficulties in keeping sharks in captivity is simply keeping the shark alive in an artificial environment. When the freedom to roam the wide ocean is taken away from them, many sharks (notably the great white shark) simply refuse to eat, making it difficult to hold them in a tank over long periods. This has made it very difficult for scientists to study the behavior of these species, meaning that their knowledge is limited to studies made in the ocean. Luckily some sharks, such as the tiger shark and the lemon shark, respond more positively to captivity, meaning that we generally know more about these species.

This situation is now improving, albeit slowly, as scientists begin to understand what sharks need to feel at home in an aquarium. A great white shark held in the Monterey Bay Aquarium in California in 2005 lived for 198 days in captivity, a huge improvement on the previous record for that species of 16 days.

The shark was eventually released back into the ocean when it grew too big to live comfortably in the tank. The aquarium staff believe that the shark's young age contributed to their success—at just a year old, she was young enough to adapt readily to a new environment away from the ocean. Similar results have also been achieved with the gigantic whale shark, and in 2007 the first ever angel shark pup to be born in captivity was born at the Aquarium of the Bay in San Francisco.

Once a shark has been captured and transferred to its tank, shark handlers need to exploit different tricks to control the shark without getting hurt. A common trick is to paralyze a shark temporarily by turning it upside down or by placing the hands on either side of the shark's snout around its eyes. During this state, called tonic immobility, the shark is awake but unable to move or attack the handler, during which time he or she can study its anatomy. Scientists have recently used this technique to test different chemical and electrical shark repellents—a successful repellent would typically awaken the shark from its paralysis.

Sharks are happiest in their natural habitat, roaming the oceans with total freedom. When they lose this freedom in an aquarium tank they can become very unhappy and starve themselves to death.

Capturing and handling a large shark in an aquarium is a difficult procedure that requires highly skilled staff.

Many aquariums try to replicate the sharks' ocean environment to help them feel more at home.

Bertha

One of the most successful examples of sharks being held in captivity was Bertha, a 43-year-old female sand tiger shark who lived in the New York Aquarium until her death in 2008.

Bertha was originally delivered to the aquarium in 1965, making this the longest-known time a shark has survived in captivity. She lived in a round 90,000-gallon (340,687 L) tank with five other sand tiger sharks, two nurse sharks and a whitetip reef shark. Although sand tiger sharks are known for being dangerous predators, Bertha had an unusually docile personality.

Hunters and killers

Sharks include some of the most efficient and terrifying predators in the world, capable of killing large mammals, turtles and even people.

One of the largest sharks, the great white, is a highly effective predator with massive jaws and triangular, serrated, interlocking teeth.

Food webs and chains

Living things depend on each other for nourishment, in complex and interlinked patterns of food chains, food webs, nutrient cycles and population pyramids. To appreciate how and why sharks fit into these natural systems, it helps to understand something of marine ecology and feeding relationships.

The basic food in almost any habitat is plants or plant-like organisms that trap the sun's light energy; they do this by the process of photosynthesis. On land they are familiar as flowers, grasses and trees. In the open ocean they are much less obvious. They are drifting microscopic, single-celled algal organisms called phytoplankton. At the coasts and in shallow waters are much larger algae—seaweeds such as wracks, oarweeds, dulse, carrageen and sea lettuce.

Herbivores

Animals that eat only plants or plantlike organisms are called herbivores. Near the seashore, they include mollusks such as limpets and winkles grazing on seaweeds. In the open ocean, the herbivores are mainly zooplankton—tiny animals and animal-like organisms that consume phytoplankton. Some are miniature developing larvae (immature stages) of larger creatures such as crabs, shellfish, worms, jellyfish, starfish, squid and fish. Others spend all their lives as small drifters and include microscopic foraminifers, tiny copepods mostly less than one-tenth of an inch (0.25 cm) long and krill up to the size of a human finger.

Carnivores

Animals that eat other animals are called carnivores. In the sea, the tiny animals of the zooplankton are eaten by small fish, shrimps and similar creatures.

These, in turn, are eaten by bigger fish, squid and other predators. And so the food chain builds up, and in general, the carnivores get bigger. Most sharks are carnivorous. Their position is near or at the end of the food chain. So they are known as top carnivores or apex predators.

Detritivores

Nature wastes nothing and recycles everything it can. The dead and dying bodies of animals and plants, carrion, animal excrement and any other nutritious bits and pieces are eaten by detritus-feeders or detritivores. These include shellfish, such as mussels, and crustaceans, such as crabs. Some sharks, for instance the Greenland shark, are notorious carrion-eaters. They play a significant part in ridding the ocean of rotting carcasses.

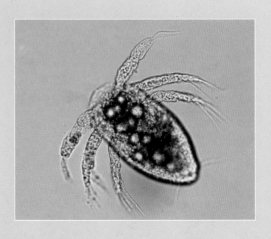

Chains into webs

The distinctions between herbivores and carnivores are often blurred. Over the course of a week or two, a Port Jackson shark may eat plant matter, animal flesh and carrion. This is how food chains become interwoven into food webs, as individuals consume a range of foodstuffs.

Also, some food chains are short, and others are lengthy. A shark consumes a dugong that ate sea grass—a three-link chain. Then the same shark eats a seal, which consumed a fish that hunted a squid, which feasted on larval crustaceans (left), and so on—a chain of more than 10 links.

Bluefin tuna are fast, open-ocean predators that catch smaller schooling fish such as herring and sprat, as well as squid. In their turn, they are eaten by large, fast, oceanic sharks, including great whites and oceanic whitetip sharks. They are also heavily overfished by humans.

Small, shrimplike krill are a vital link in ocean food chains, especially the krill in the Southern Ocean around Antarctica. They are eaten directly by baleen whales, penguins and seals, as well as by many fish—all potential prey for sharks. The krill feed on tiny floating algae.

Food for sharks

Feeding is one of the most basic built-in motivational drives. Sharks eat to stay alive, to provide their muscles with energy, to grow, to maintain, repair and replace damaged tissues and, ultimately, to reproduce.

The oceans provide a wide variety of foods, and sharks have responded by evolving an equally varied set of tastes and food-catching methods. An ecologist would call a shark a heterotroph. Like nearly all animals it cannot make its own food, as plants do (autotrophs). It must feed on food made by other living organisms, those farther back along the food chains and webs.

More accurately, sharks are carnivorous heterotrophs. Their food is meat—the flesh of other animals. There are no truly herbivorous or plant-eating sharks. The nearest are the filter-feeders, such as the whale, basking and megamouth sharks. They consume the rich "soup" of plankton, which contains a complex mix of tiny floating animals and algae. Most other sharks are predators—hunters who pursue prey.

Feed and fast

The carnivore's food of meat usually comes in nutritious packages, which take some time to digest. Carnivores consume food relatively infrequently compared with many herbivores, who must regularly eat large quantities of nutrient-poor plant food. So after a shark has had a big feed it fasts while its digestive system breaks down and absorbs the nutrients. Ten percent of the nutrients go to make more shark, in the form of growth and maintenance of body tissues. The rest of the food is broken down to provide energy for the vital processes of life, including reproduction.

A typical shark takes in, on average, food weighing between 0.5 and 3 percent of its own body weight daily. This is usually in the form of a large meal every two or three days. But a shark can survive a fast of many weeks, even months, using up the food reserves stored in its relatively huge liver.

As sharks hunt they don't only feed themselves. They help to keep their prey, such as fish, seals and squid, in peak condition by weeding out the old, diseased and poorly adapted individuals. Sharks are a potent force in ensuring the survival of the fittest, and thereby driving the process of evolution.

A wide variety of animals is on the menu for sharks. Bottom-living and bottom-feeding sharks often eat invertebrates such as these slow-moving spider crabs (left). Yellowfin goatfish (above) and many other reef fish are hunted by resident reef sharks and other sharks visiting the reef.

Food for thought

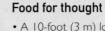

- A 10-foot (3 m) long captive lemon shark ate an average of 0.5 percent of its total body weight of food every day in the form of two or three large meals each week.

- A very large great white shark, weighing around 1 ton (0.9 metric tons), probably consumes about 10 tons (9 metric tons) of meat in one year. (The great white is at the higher end of the shark consumption range to fuel its active lifestyle and ability to raise body temperature.)

- A typical human weighing around 150 pounds (68 kg) consumes half a ton (0.5 metric tons) of food yearly. (If the human weighed a ton, its annual consumption would be 8 tons/7 metric tons.)

Great killers

Most killer sharks are large because a big body can swim faster than a small one. Most fish in the sea are bony fish less than 3 feet (0.9 m) long, but the big killer sharks are several feet long, with the advantage of both size and speed.

When hunting, the shark instinctively assesses the value of a prey item, in terms of nourishment, against the energy and risks needed to chase and catch it. This is why most sharks ignore healthy, mature prey animals, which have a good chance of escape. They tend toward easier meat—immature, ill, injured or even dead creatures.

Favored foods

The shortfin mako, *Isurus oxyrinchus*, is perhaps the fastest shark and one of the speediest fish in the ocean. It has been timed on a "sprint" of 31 miles per hour (50 km/h) and moving over an appreciable distance at 22–25 miles per hour (35–40 km/h). It needs such speed because it feeds on other very swift swimmers, such as tuna, mackerel and swordfish. The mako's premier technique is to chase and outswim its prey in a short burst, bite it hard and swallow it whole. Failing this, it bites off the victim's tail and then has a much easier target. One 740-pound (336 kg) mako swallowed a swordfish of 120 pounds (54 kg)—one-sixth of the mako's body weight.

The largest killer shark, the great white, takes the largest prey. It may eat other big fish, such as tuna and sharks, but it specializes in sea mammals—seals, sea lions, dolphins and porpoises. Tiger sharks also target large prey such as porpoises, turtles and other sharks, although they are famed for their unfussy tastes.

Dusky diet

The powerful, 14-foot (4.3 m) dusky shark, *Carcharhinus obscurus*, is widespread in coastal waters. Its wide diet of fish includes other sharks, skates and rays, schooling species such as anchovies and sardines, larger tuna, eels, grouper and flatfish, as well as squid and octopus, crabs, starfish and even mollusks such as clams. It also has been seen attacking or scavenging on dolphins.

The lemon shark, *Negaprion brevirostris*, can reach 12 feet (3.6 m) in length. In its range of tropical shallow waters it feeds on or near the bottom on a range of fish such as mullet, jacks, catfish, cowfish, guitarfish and rays. It also munches up crabs and other crustaceans.

Sting-tailed snack

The hammerhead shark specializes in stingray prey. It finds them buried in the sand by sweeping its "metal-detector" hammer-shaped head from side to side over the seabed to pick up electrical signals, scents and sounds. When it locates a stingray it swallows the meal whole, seemingly unbothered by the poisonous spine on the stingray's tail. Sometimes the spine sticks permanently in the hammerhead's throat, with apparently no adverse effect.

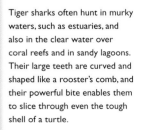

Tiger sharks often hunt in murky waters, such as estuaries, and also in the clear water over coral reefs and in sandy lagoons. Their large teeth are curved and shaped like a rooster's comb, and their powerful bite enables them to slice through even the tough shell of a turtle.

When a great white shark attacks a seal it swims beneath the animal and then lunges upward to grab its prey. The momentum of its attack often carries it above the water surface in a spectacular leap. It may drop its captured prey and then return to eat it.

Junk food

Tiger sharks are extremely successful large predators because they will eat almost anything. As well as being great killers capable of catching small whales, seals, turtles, marine iguanas and seabirds at the surface and fish below, they are also lowly scavengers and will readily eat carcasses from land and sea.

Pack hunters

Mention animal "packs" and thoughts turn to wolves, lions, wild dogs and killer whales, which sometimes hunt in same-species packs or teams. They cooperate with each other to varying degrees to maximize the chances of catching prey. The idea is that they each obtain more food by teamwork than they could by hunting alone.

Recent observations of shark behavior are revealing evidence that sharks can also organize themselves, at least to some degree, and cooperate as group predators. This is different from sharks congregating to feed because food is there, when there is little interaction apart from minor squabbles when two sharks try to eat the same food item.

Sweep of death

Spiny dogfish, or spurdogs, sometimes gather in huge schools and sweep along the seabed, driving all living things before them, like the shark version of army ants. Any animal that cannot escape is consumed. Each of the sharks constantly watches its fellows, as well as looking out for its own food. When one finds something edible others notice its behavior and rapidly congregate at the site to see if there is more. Many types of birds feed in this way, as flocks hopping across a field, all searching for a meal but also watching each other.

Hunting schools

It is very difficult to unravel the behavior of sharks in big, fast-moving groups, but a few species may, at times, hunt cooperatively. Sharks such as smooth hounds and dogfish are often found prowling in large bands, like wild dogs. This has the advantage of enabling smaller sharks to catch and feed on larger prey with less expenditure of effort. However, the behavior seems to be based more on sets of instinctive responses than on intelligent planning.

Some sharks may spread out around their intended prey, such as a school of fish. The sharks then swim inward from several different directions, herding the fish into a tight knot and perhaps maneuvering them to shallower water to reduce the chance of escape. Species showing this behavior include the silky, dusky, bronze whaler, whitetip reef and sand tiger sharks. Thresher sharks work in pairs, thrashing the fish together with their long tails. In such cases, as the fish school is kept together in a dense mass by the circling pack, one shark at a time comes in for a mouthful. This behavior can continue for several minutes, until the school of fish becomes too small and is no longer worth the effort.

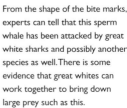

From the shape of the bite marks, experts can tell that this sperm whale has been attacked by great white sharks and possibly another species as well. There is some evidence that great whites can work together to bring down large prey such as this.

Spiny dogfish are unusual among sharks because they often form immense feeding schools in areas where there is plenty of food. Where food is scarce they are more likely to be solitary hunters. This species is very heavily fished and endangered in many areas.

Making friends

Some observers have suggested that two or three great white sharks seem to form "friendships" or coalitions. Male cheetahs also do this, being the only cats apart from lions that hunt together. Not only do the great whites seem to hunt cooperatively when the opportunity arises, they may also feed at each other's catches as though sharing food and even travel together to seasonal feeding grounds.

The feeding frenzy

Some sharks seem to go completely out of control at feeding time. The presence of food drives them into a frenzy of whirling, thrashing bodies, during which the sharks tear chunks out of their victim and consume it in minutes.

Yet sharks do not seem to feed in response to pangs of hunger, when there is no food in the stomach, as we try to do. There are many examples of sharks eagerly swallowing bait when their digestive systems are already stuffed full of food. Other sharks in aquaria remain uninterested in a suitable meal for days, possibly even weeks.

If a shark is in a generally unaroused state, cruising gently on "autopilot," it may make a half-hearted effort to grab a passing injured fish or to investigate a possible meal by nudging it with its snout. However, when a shark detects food using its supertuned senses or detects other sharks feeding, then its casual, low-level behavior changes into a heightened state of arousal. The shark swims more actively and is now more likely to bite earnestly at anything around. Perhaps it knows instinctively that any moments lost in exploratory nudges or lethargic test bites could mean another shark might steal the food.

Escalating excitement

As more sharks are attracted to a feeding scene, tension mounts and excitement levels escalate. The sharks are highly aroused, yet they do not attack each other. In an extraordinary high-speed ballet, they avoid contact or collision, and contrary to popular belief, they rarely slash or bite one another, except when a dominant shark fights over food with a smaller individual.

Such frenzies are observed most often when sharks are fed artificially with bait or in situations such as near a fishing boat when the catch is hauled in. However, a dense concentration of injured and struggling fish trapped in a net is hardly natural. And the results are devastating for the fishing crew. Even more horrendous are reports of shark feeding frenzies at shipwrecks, where people are consumed. Again, a group of humans in mid-ocean is hardly a natural occurrence.

In these cases, perhaps the sharks are responding to what biologists call a "supernormal stimulus." This is an unnatural situation that they have not encountered in their millions of years of evolution but that triggers off sets of instincts and motivations to a highly abnormal level. Put simply, they have never seen anything like it, and they "overreact."

A sperm whale carcass like this will soon attract numerous sharks, and, as they start to tear the carcass apart, the massive amount of food available may start a feeding frenzy. Whatever is left of the carcass will sink to the seabed and form a useful food source for scavengers.

Caribbean reef sharks make short work of a school of fish they have managed to isolate. Although there is a lot of action and all the sharks are feeding as hard as they can, this is not really a true frenzy, which is generally stimulated by unusual amounts of blood in the water.

Plenty for all

Apart from human encouragement to feed, sharks show a certain level of natural frenzy in shallow waters when large quantities of nourishment suddenly become available. Examples are when many young seabirds, seals or sea lions enter the water for the first time. Many sharks gather, thrash around and eat until almost bursting.

Shark teeth

The shark's ultimate lethal weapons for attack, feeding and defense are its teeth. They constantly grow and replace themselves, so they are always brand new and ready for action.

The typical shark's teeth are enlarged versions of the dermal denticles that cover its body. Each tooth is made of the hard but slightly pliable, shock-absorbing substance called dentine. This is covered by an outer layer of even harder enamel. In the tooth's center is the pulp chamber, or cavity, with blood vessels and nerves. Some sharks have thousands of teeth, others only a few dozen.

In a typical shark the bases of the teeth, called the roots or feet, are not anchored in the jaw cartilages. They sit in a fibrous mass, the tooth bed, which in turn sits on the jaw cartilage and is held in place by the fleshy gum. The teeth are arranged in rows, which move slowly forward, like a conveyor-belt system, from the rear inside df the jaw along to the jaw rim at the front. Usually only the front one or two rows are functional in biting. As they wear and fall out or break off, a new row moves from behind and tilts into place. This replacement happens every few weeks or months depending on the shark species and conditions.

The tooth-replacement process starts even as a shark develops in its egg case or mother. And it continues until death. So a shark may get through as many as 20,000 teeth in its lifetime.

Variations on the dental theme

The shapes of a shark's teeth reflect the types of food it eats. They vary from long, thin, pointed awls for catching fast, slippery fish and squid to serrated or fluted triangular blades for cutting through and sawing off chunks of flesh to flat millstones for grinding shellfish and crabs out of their shells.

Some sharks have different shapes of teeth in different parts of the mouth to cope with a variety of foods. Also, tooth shape may change throughout life. The young shark takes smaller, easy-to-catch prey and then moves on to larger, more difficult food items. In the lined cat shark, *Halaelurus lineatus*, teeth vary between the sexes. The males use their small front teeth to nibble the females during courtship.

Shark's jaw

Sharks have several to many rows of teeth. In the tiger shark, the rearmost teeth are laid almost flat and are covered by a fold of tissue that lines the mouth. The front teeth are easily lost as, unlike mammalian teeth, they do not have roots, and they fall out after some use. The back teeth gradually move forward and straighten up through tension, breaking through their covering. Some sharks can lose and replace teeth in as little as eight days.

TOOTH IN USE

TOOTH ERUPTING

GUM TISSUE

JAW CARTILAGE

TOOTH READY TO BE DISCARDED

Teeth and diet

- Bull shark: steak-knife teeth with serrated edges for catching almost any prey.
- Porbeagle: three or four rows of slender awl-like teeth with small, sharp cusps at the bases.
- Smooth hound, nurse shark: a "sidewalk" of flat, slablike, crushing teeth for shellfish.
- Goblin shark: long, fanglike teeth at the front, smaller, shorter teeth at the back.
- Swell shark: tiny, sharp teeth for small fish prey.
- Hooktooth dogfish: curved, or hook-shaped, teeth in both the upper and lower jaws.

(See also tooth descriptions in the individual shark profiles, pages 34 to 67.)

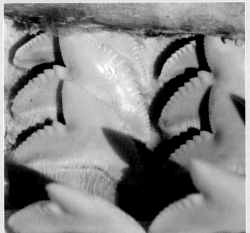

The large, triangular teeth of a great white shark are designed such that the teeth in the top jaw fit into the spaces between the teeth in the lower jaw. When the shark closes its bite the teeth act like a razor-sharp knife that can slice through tough skin and flesh.

Jaws!

At first sight, the jaws of an open-ocean predatory shark, a mako or great white for example, do not appear to be ideally positioned for hunting. They are slung awkwardly underneath the protruding snout, rather than being at the front of a more flattened face, as in land predators such as lions and tigers.

In fact, both the lower and upper jaws of the typical shark can move separately from its skull, attached only by elastic ligaments and stretchy muscles. When it bites, the great white shark tilts its head up and back and pushes or protrudes both jaws forward. As it opens its mouth it strikes with the lower jaw first, stabbing the victim with the longer, narrower teeth there. Then the upper jaw bites downward onto the victim, so that its wider, bladelike teeth can shear off a slice of flesh. The rest of the shark's head and body are protected from the power of the impact by an elaborate system of shock-absorbing joints around the skull and spinal column.

Biting techniques

The bite strengths of sharks and other animals have been measured or estimated scientifically using a device called a gnathodynamometer—*gnatho* meaning "related to jaws" (see panel).

Sharks like the great white sometimes feed on prey that is too big to swallow whole and need to slice off chunks. Their teeth are effective blades that mesh and lock together almost perfectly when the jaws close. But this means the shark cannot shear and slide its jaws from side to side to complete the cut. So the shark shakes its whole head rapidly from side to side. The teeth work like saw blades, slicing sideways through the flesh.

Some shark species do not need a powerful cutting bite. They grind up crabs, clams and other similar small, hard-shelled items. The upper jaw of the Port Jackson shark is held to the skull by tough ligaments, while the bottom jaw is supported by a separate structure, the hyomandibular cartilage. This arrangement allows the jaws to move against each other, forward, backward and also sideways. The flat teeth inside form a powerful grinding mill.

Bite strengths compared

Using scientific means, biologists have measured the bite pressure of different animals. Although the bite force of a shark has a different impact than the bite of a human—the shark's teeth are sharp and the human's are blunt—the figures, measured in pounds of pressure per square inch, make for interesting comparisons.

ANIMAL	RELATIVE BITE STRENGTH
Tyrannosaurus	3,300 (estimated)
Alligator	2,125
Hyena	1,000
Snapping turtle	1,000
Lion	940
Great white shark	600
Wolf	400
Hyacinth macaw	375
Dusky shark	300
Labrador dog	125
Human	120

A shark's jaws at full gape can be an impressive size. In life this jaw of a mako shark would not open as wide as this, but the mako still achieves a large gape. Sharks' jaws are often sold as souvenirs, a practice that should be discouraged to help conserve sharks.

The gape of a great white shark is immense. Some of the largest jaws held by natural history museums will frame the head and torso of an adult human. A seal or sea lion can easily be bitten in half by such a large shark. Chunks sliced out of hard surfboards show the strength of the bite.

The long, thin, slightly curved teeth found in the lower jaw of a mako shark are ideal for catching and holding slippery, moving fish before they are swallowed. They spill out from the shark's mouth so as to snag any fish within reach, giving the shark a toothy grin.

Shark scavengers

Few sharks, even the highly tuned killers, refuse a free lunch. Given the opportunity, they scavenge and take carrion. It's usually an easy option, being just as nutritious as living prey but requiring much less energy to catch—and with less risk of fight back and injury.

Several sharks, such as the Greenland shark, are avid scavengers. This natural tendency has probably led to the catalog of strange human-made objects found inside shark stomachs. The stomachs may be opened by curious sports anglers or as part of butchering the shark's carcass for food and materials or by marine biologists and scientific researchers. Or the shark regurgitates its gut contents on being caught because of stress and as a defense reaction. The list of objects reflects the types of refuse found in the sea, rather than the tastes of sharks. Perhaps the most notorious underwater scavengers are tiger sharks (as described on page 56).

The murder suspect

In 1935 in Sydney, Australia, a tattooed human arm was regurgitated by a captured tiger shark. Detailed examination showed that the arm had been cut not by the shark's teeth but with a blade of some sort—a murder had been committed. A suspect was arrested for killing and dismembering the victim, who was identified from the tattoo, in a case that became known as the "Shark Arm Murder." The tiger shark was acquitted as merely an innocent accomplice.

Blue sharks, among others, follow ships at sea. Like the seagulls in the air above them, the sharks undoubtedly anticipate a free meal when the ship jettisons its garbage, leftovers and out-of-condition food supplies.

One gray shark, 10 feet (3 m) long, was found to have eaten eight legs of mutton, half a ham, the back end of a pig, the front half of a dog—complete with collar and lead—about 300 pounds (136 kg) of horse meat, a barnacle-scraper for the ship's hull and a piece of sacking!

The tiger shark (main right) is notorious for the odd and inedible items it swallows, which are found when it regurgitates them or when the shark is caught and opened. Its natural diet is vast, from live fish and seabirds to dead whales, sharks, turtles and even poisonous sea snakes.

The smalltooth sandtiger shark is found near the bottom of continental and insular shelves, and near coral reef dropoffs. It lacks specialized teeth for cutting and crushing and therefore feeds on smaller prey such as squid, crustaceans, and small bony fish.

Parasite shark

A parasite gains food, shelter or some other need at the expense of another living thing, the host, causing it harm in the process. The cookiecutter shark, *Isistius brasiliensis*, is only about 19 inches (48 cm) long, very brightly bioluminescent and feeds on small squid and similar prey. However, it is also a parasite on much larger animals, including seals, whales, dolphins and fish. The cookiecutter sneaks close, opens its mouth wide, sucks itself onto the host skin and then employs its teeth. These are small and curved in the upper jaw and in a continuous sawlike row in the lower (resembling a cookiecutter as used in the kitchen). The shark closes its lower jaw, twists its body around and slices out a conelike "plug" of flesh, similar to half a scoop of ice-cream. The host is not killed but is probably left feeling very sore, with a distinctive wound open to infection.

Filter feeders

No sharks are herbivorous. All eat animal matter of some kind, typically fish. But not all sharks are deadly hunters or pursuit killers. In fact, the largest sharks consume the smallest prey, filtering seawater for tiny food items.

Even the clearest seawater is a "soup" of small suspended particles, including the microscopic plants and animals that make up plankton. There are also the eggs and larvae of crabs, starfish, shellfish and countless other tiny sea creatures. Moving up the size scale, from as small as a grain of rice to as large as a human thumb, are the young of fish and squid and shrimplike crustaceans such as copepods—which vaguely resemble the water flea daphnia, commonly found in ponds—and the krill and euphausiids. This "sea soup" provides food for the two largest shark species, the whale and basking sharks, as well as the very sizeable megamouth.

Whale shark

Each of the three main filter-feeding sharks has a different method of consuming its food, although in all of these species it is based on the gills. The whale shark has horizontal plates, or strips, made of relatively soft brownish-pink tissue that span the spaces between adjacent gill bars (the structures supporting the gill arches.) The gill bars are very long, so that the left and right sets encircle much of the head and neck region. Also the whale shark's mouth and throat muscles are powerful, enabling it to open its cavernous jaws very wide.

These features mean the whale shark is a versatile filter-feeder. It may swim along with mouth open, allowing its forward motion to pass water bearing food items through the plates, which work like a strainer or sieve. It can open its mouth while almost stationary and with its body at any angle draw in water by bellowslike suction. Or it can "bob" up and down vertically at the surface, using its sinking motion to encourage water to pour in through its open mouth. In this way whale sharks capture sizeable food items, up to the size of anchovies and sardines.

Basking shark

Like the whale shark, the basking shark's teeth are small and degenerate. But in contrast to the whale shark, the basking shark is a ram-jet feeder, relying on its forward swimming motion to force water and food into its mouth and out through the gill slits. The filtering mechanism consists of comblike gill structures called rakers, reminiscent of the prongs of a garden rake. These are quite stiff and coarse, made of modified versions of the skin denticles (placoid scales). In a typical basking shark the rakers are about 2 to 3 inches (5–8 cm) long and arranged around the gill arch at a density of 10 to 12 per inch (4–5 cm).

The basking shark swims through schools of its staple food, the copepod *Calanus*, which are trapped by the "combs." Every few minutes the shark trembles or flutters its gills to dislodge and swallow the food.

During the cold season, copepods and similar food items decline drastically in abundance. The basking shark is thought to shed its gill rakers and rest or "hibernate" in deeper waters, or perhaps bottom feed, until the rakers grow again for renewed feeding activity in the spring. (Gill rakers are used for filter feeding in other kinds of fish too, such as herring and mackerel.)

Unlike most sharks, which have underslung mouths, whale sharks (main right) have their mouth at the end of their snout. This is much more efficient for a filter feeder. As well as plankton, whale sharks eat small fish, ploughing through schools and vacuuming them up.

What do filter feeders actually eat?

Even fairly clear seawater contains suspended edible tidbits for sharks, including the tiny plants and animals known as plankton, eggs, the immature larvae of fish and crabs (left) and other creatures and bits of floating debris and detritus. The concentration of plankton in water varies enormously, but on average is around 1 fluid ounce per 7,800 gallons (around 1 ml per 6,000 L)—meaning the filter-feeder must sift huge volumes of water to gather any appreciable amount of food.

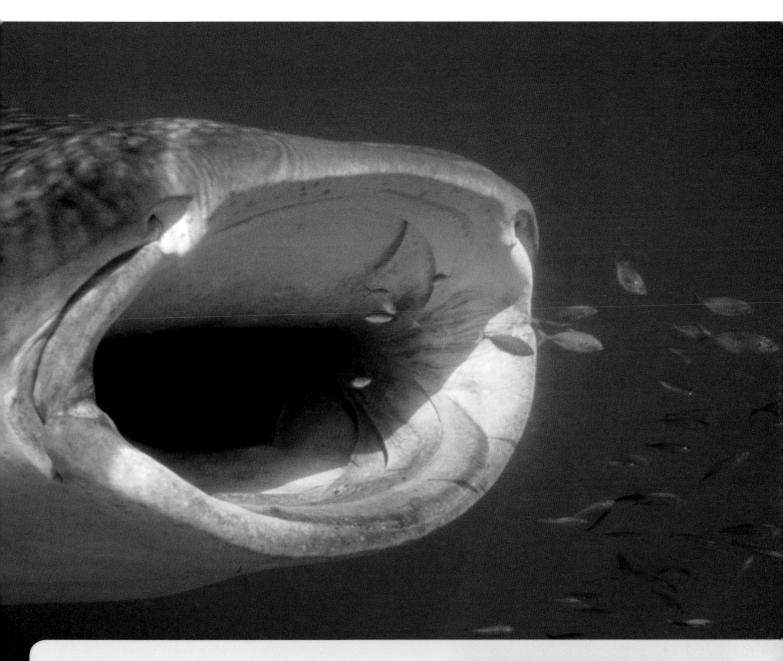

Megamouth

Like the basking shark pictured, the megamouth probably uses modified gill rakers, rather than its teeth, to gather food. Its rakers are finger shaped with cartilage cores, up to 6 inches (15 cm) long, and in four rows along each gill arch. The mouth and throat regions of this shark are highly flexible, suggesting that the megamouth opens its enormous mouth—possibly protruding its jaws—to suck in water and prey. As the mouth closes the water passes out through the gill slits, and the rakers strain out the food, such as small shrimps, copepods, jellyfish and similar creatures. Tagging has shown that these sharks dive to deeper waters by day, 300 to 600 feet (92–183 m) down, then come nearer to the surface at night, at depths of 30 to 60 feet (9.1–18 m)—the same vertical daily migrations made by their mainly planktonic prey. The reflective, but not actively glowing or bioluminescent (although this is debated), tissues around the megamouth's inner lips may serve to attract food items.

Shark guts

Most sharks cannot chew and soften their food to begin its physical breakdown or digestion. So the shark needs a strong, effective digestive system.

The shark's digestive tract is basically a long tube from mouth to cloaca. The jaws and throat muscles push the food back for swallowing into the short, narrow, muscular gullet, or esophagus. This leads into a U-shaped stomach. The first arm of the U is called the cardiac limb (since it is near the heart.) The second arm is the pyloric limb, leading onward to the intestine.

The typical shark stomach is loose-walled and very stretchy, so the creature can take advantage of a plentiful meal. Stomach lining glands produce gastric juices, which contain strong hydrochloric acid and enzymes to begin the chemical breakdown of food.

Unpleasant trick

The shark's stomach has a trick to get rid of unsuitable, indigestible or unwanted items. It can evert, or push itself almost inside out, back into the throat. In this way, troublesome stomach contents can be forcibly regurgitated out of the mouth. (We have a similar mechanism in our bodies—vomiting.) Sharks also regurgitate as a means of self-defense to distract or repel any creature threatening them. Although for some predators the ejected stomach contents offer an alternative meal.

In the intestines

After many hours, even days, in the stomach, the semidigested food dribbles into the intestines. It is propelled by waves of muscular contractions, called peristalsis, along the intestinal walls. More digestive juices are added by the liver and the pancreas gland. In the intestine, absorption of digested products takes place. This is enhanced by a structure unique to their group—the spiral valve (see panel.) Next is the rectum, or hind gut. It is short and wide and has an adjacent gland, the rectal gland, sometimes called the "third kidney." This filters wastes from the blood and empties them into the rectum. The rectum in turn empties all the digestive wastes into the cloaca, which opens to the outside via a slit in the shark's rear underside, usually just behind the pelvic fins, called the vent.

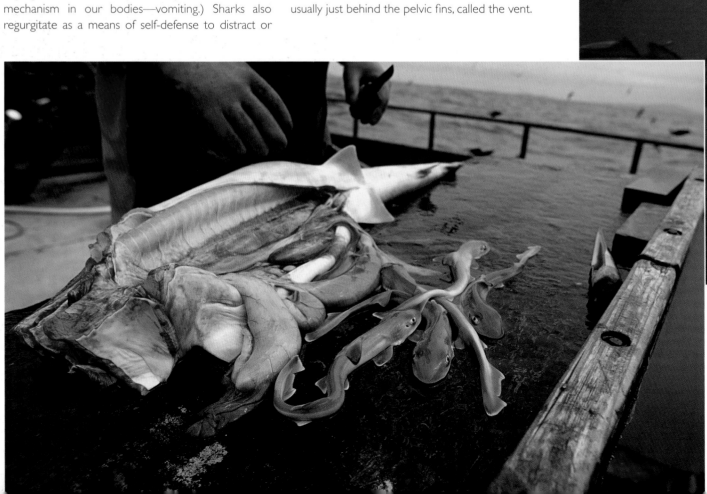

As a bronze whaler cruises through a school of yellowtail scad, its drive to hunt is affected by the easy availability of prey, as well as food already in its gut. The stomach contents of a recently gorging shark can be one-quarter of its whole body weight

Sharks often feed on other sharks in the same way that any fish might eat a smaller fish. This shark's stomach (left) contained several smaller cat sharks. It's not cannibalism unless they eat their own species.

FROM THE DUODENUM

INTESTINAL WALL

TO THE COLON

SPIRAL VALVE

The spiral valve

Actually a helix shape, more like a screw, the spiral valve in the shark's intestine is composed of a shelflike outfold of the intestinal wall twisted round and round as many as 40 times. This increases the surface area of the lining within the intestine for better absorption of digested nutrients.

The spiral valve varies in different shark species. In the hammerhead, it looks more like a scroll, or roll of paper. In the dogfish, it resembles a series of stacked cones, with the point of one inside the wide base of the next. In the megamouth shark, it looks like a wide "spiral" (helical) staircase.

Shark invasions

While global warming may not in itself contribute to the dwindling of shark populations, the warming of the seas could have a dramatic effect on their behavior and migration patterns.

As the temperature of the water rises, some species of shark will be able to survive in areas they had never before populated. This could completely disrupt oceanic ecology, as the sharks feed on species that had never before been threatened by them.

Scientists are particularly worried about sharks invading the water around Antarctica. Sharks haven't lived in the Antarctic Ocean for 40 million years, meaning that many species, such as giant sea spiders and floppy ribbon worms, have evolved to live without any significant predators. Because of this they are typically slow moving and soft bodied—easy targets for sharks. These species are unique to the coldest oceans, with interesting features such as antifreeze proteins in their blood that scientists may wish to study in the future; an invasion of sharks would change the food chain and could cause a mass extinction.

Global warming

The temperature of the Antarctic has risen by up to 36°F (2°C) over the last 50 years, and researchers fear that it could take less than 100 years for the Southern Ocean to become hospitable to sharks. Scientists are now calling for urgent action to reduce fossil fuel emissions—the primary cause of global warming—before more damage is done.

The effects of this climate change have already been observed in Alaska in the Arctic (near the North Pole), where scientists have reported greater numbers of salmon sharks, which are damaging the local fishing industry. The researchers also found declining numbers

of sea lions and seals, which they have blamed on the shark invasion. While scientists believe that this may be the result of a natural shift in the local climate, which oscillates every 20–30 years, they think that global warming may also be an important factor.

Global warming is not limited to extremely cold climates, and the consequences of changing shark migration could also have important ramifications for human safety in more temperate regions. In the late 1990s a great white shark attacked a cabin cruiser in the Adriatic Sea next to Italy. This was the first ever sighting of a great white shark in the Adriatic, and experts believe that global warming may be the cause of its changing migration. Experts fear that other shores, such as the coastline of Britain, that have previously been free from dangerous sharks could be invaded within the next few years.

Salmon sharks have spread their range in recent years from the north Pacific toward Arctic waters. They grow to 10 feet (3 m) in length and can cause considerable damage to fishing gear, as well as consuming fish stocks in this new area.

As the polar ice floes and icebergs shrink because of global warming, whole marine communities are disrupted. Polar bears, walruses and seals have fewer haul-out resting places and face extra danger from sharks ranging into their region.

Giant at risk

The giant sea spider of the deep, cold Southern Ocean near Antartica can grow to the size of a dinner plate. Its future may be threatened not only by the warming water, but also by bottom-dwelling sharks that it has never previously encountered.

Making more sharks

How some shark species breed is known in vivid detail, but the reproduction of others is still very much a mystery to us.

A male shark seizes the pectoral fin of a female in his teeth, which is a common mating action in many shark species.

Breeding patterns

Sharks have a reputation as being the creatures that time forgot. Of course this is far from true. Evolution keeps them as modern as any other living thing, in all respects, including their reproduction.

The way that sharks breed shows features far more advanced than reproduction in, for example, bony fish.

Weight of numbers

Biologists recognize a spectrum of strategies for survival and reproduction. At one end are animals that put their energies and resources into producing huge numbers of eggs, so great that any form of parental care is impossible. The eggs are left to hatch, and the young develop at the mercy of the environment. The chances of any single youngster surviving are very poor. This method is known as the "R strategy" and is followed by many sea creatures, including most bony fish. A mature female cod, about 3 feet (0.9 m) long for example, produces around four to six million eggs. The male partners simply cast their sperm into the sea near the eggs. Fertilization of the eggs by sperm is external (outside the female's body) and is also an incredibly chance-ridden process. But by sheer weight of numbers, a few offspring make it to maturity.

A good start

At the other end of the spectrum is the "K strategy." The animal puts its reproductive energies and resources into producing relatively few young but gives them a very high chance of survival with a good start in life. Most mammals are K-selected, with just a few young developing in the female's uterus (womb). Humans are one of the ultimate K types.

Many creatures' strategies lie somewhere between these extremes. In general, sharks tend toward the

The goatsbeard brotula or bearded brotula is a bony fish whose numerous eggs are laid in a gelatinous mass. This floats at the ocean surface, exposed to many hungry creatures, with only a jellylike coating.

K end of the spectrum. Rather than casting millions of eggs and sperm into the sea, the female produces relatively few eggs. There is mating and internal fertilization, where sperm join with the eggs inside the female's body, not outside in the water.

In egg-laying sharks, the eggs have thick, protective cases and large reserves of yolk, so the young are well-developed before hatching. In live-bearing sharks, the eggs are retained inside the mother's body and hatch there. The young sharks develop further and are born well formed and equipped for independent existence.

The ling, or ling cod, demonstrates the typical reproductive strategy of most bony fish: a female 3 feet (0.9 m) long contains an estimated 300,000 eggs. In an equivalent-sized shark that would be less than 100, maybe fewer than 10.

Slow-breeding problems

The K strategy contributes to a species' success especially in stable environments. But it is less able to cope with dramatic change. Sharks mature only after several years and then breed only every two or more years, producing only a few young each time. When conditions alter rapidly the slow reproductive rate means that numbers have trouble responding. Increased fishing, pollution and general persecution of sharks by humans are incredibly rapid changes in terms of the evolutionary timescale. Many sharks are having huge problems with this, as explained on pages 206–207.

Piked spurdogs are heavily fished around the southern coasts of Australia. Recent information indicates this commercial pressure may be affecting stocks, which would take many years to recover.

The male shark

Inside the male shark's body are two long reproductive glands, the testes. In most species they are in the upper middle body, just below and in front of the main dorsal fin. Besides making the microscopic sperm, the testes are also part of the hormonal system.

The testes secrete hormones that control the development of male bodily features and characteristics, such as the growth of the claspers. Hormones also control the shark's yearly breeding cycle and initiate the urge to mate.

The sperm cells produced in the testes pass along a tube toward the common opening for digestive, excretory and reproductive materials—the cloaca. The first part of the tube is called the vas efferentia, and the second part is the vas deferens. Glands in its lining make a sticky, mucuslike substance that binds millions of the tiny sperm into bundles, or packets, known as spermatophores. These then pass into a storage bag, the seminal vesicle, until the shark mates.

Claspers

The main external difference between a male and female shark, apart from the female's usually greater body size, is that the male has claspers. These appendages are formed from the inner sides of the pelvic fins, which are rolled around in a scroll-like fashion. They were named by the ancient Greek "father of natural history," Aristotle, who assumed that the male shark used them to grasp and hold the female during copulation. But Aristotle was mistaken. Like a male mammal's penis, they are intromittent organs—conduits or channels for placing the sperm into the female's body.

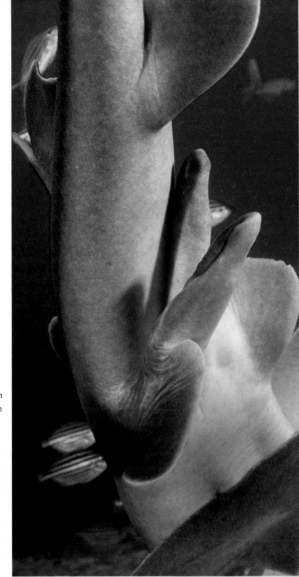

The claspers on this Port Jackson shark (right) are clearly seen as it feeds on a reef. A groove runs down the center of each clasper; sperm travels down this groove when the clasper is inserted into the female's reproductive tract.

Known scientifically as myxopterygia or pterygopodia, the two claspers are stiffened by cartilaginous rods. They contain erectile tissue which enlarges and stiffens when it is engorged with blood for mating. Each clasper has a mechanism for pumping the sperm in their spermatophore packages, through the channel at the center of the scroll. There is also a hole in each clasper near the cloaca, called the apopyle, and two siphon sacs lying under the skin nearby, in the anal region. These sacs are believed to secrete lubricating fluid into the apopyle and over the claspers to reduce friction during copulation. The sacs also contain seawater, which is used to help wash the sperm into the female's body.

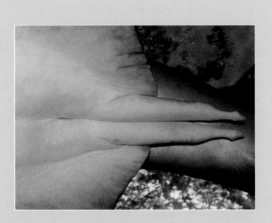

Variety of claspers

The claspers of male sharks have a range of sizes and shapes, according to the species. They may be flat, round, smooth or covered with hook- or spurlike denticles (tiny skin scales). They are small in juveniles, reaching their full size only at maturity. However, from this stage they do not get any bigger, although the rest of the shark's body does continue to grow slowly. So older, larger males have proportionally smaller claspers.

Male sharks can be recognized by the paired claspers, which lie swept back along the body just inside of and behind the pelvic fins on each side of the body, as in the male gray nurse shark (above and right).

The female shark

The female shark's main reproductive parts are her two sex glands, the ovaries. These make eggs, which are fertilized inside her body by the male's sperm. In some species, once the eggs are fertilized, they are coated with tough shells and laid outside the body. In others, the eggs remain inside the female's body until the babies have developed.

Most female sharks have a pair of ovaries in roughly the same part of the body as the male shark's testes. But in some species the female has only one functional ovary. This is adequate, because the shark's low reproductive rate means that only a few eggs, comparatively speaking, are needed through life.

Female features

Ovaries, like testes, are part of the hormonal, or endocrine, system. They produce sex hormones that stimulate the development of female bodily features. Most obvious externally, in most types of sharks, is the female's larger body size compared with males of her species. She may weigh one-quarter more than he does. Females also have skin up to three times as thick as the males, perhaps to prevent injuries during the very physical process of mating. The ovarian sex hormones also control mating behavior and either eggshell production and egg-laying or the maintenance of pregnancies.

Parts of the egg

During the breeding season, the ovaries ripen and release several eggs. These are wafted by microscopic hairlike cilia into the funnel-shaped openings of the two egg tubes, or oviducts. As the eggs move along their oviduct they pass a gland that makes the egg's "white," an albuminlike substance that coats the egg and is mainly a reserve of food. Next, the eggs pass

the shell gland, which wraps them in a soft, filmy case, sometimes called a candle.

If mating has been successful, at some stage during the eggs' passage along the oviduct they meet sperm coming in the other direction, and they are fertilized. The sperm may have just been introduced by a recent mating, or the female may have stored them from a mating some time ago—even over a year before. What happens next depends on whether the shark is an egg-layer or live-bearer, as described on the following pages.

It was recently discovered that sharks of the hammerhead family can give birth without the need to mate with a male. This phenomenon has been observed in a captive bonnethead shark.

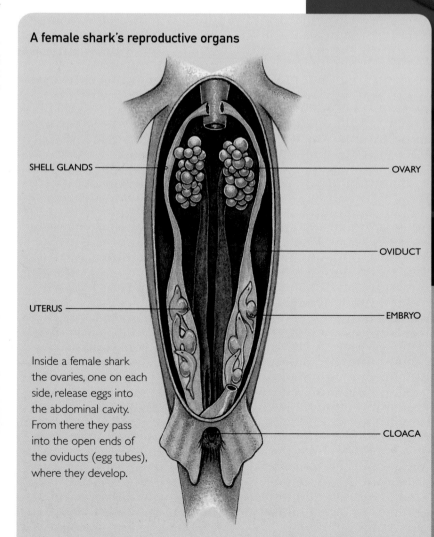

A female shark's reproductive organs

SHELL GLANDS

OVARY

OVIDUCT

UTERUS

EMBRYO

CLOACA

Inside a female shark the ovaries, one on each side, release eggs into the abdominal cavity. From there they pass into the open ends of the oviducts (egg tubes), where they develop.

In most species the female sharks—like this great white—are larger than the males of their kind. This may be linked to breeding and the need to produce large eggs or harbor growing embryos inside the body.

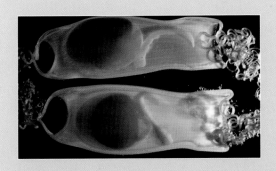

Big eggs

Compared with their cousins in the animal kingdom, female sharks lay relatively large eggs compared to their body size. For a fairly standard shark, about 6 feet (1.8 m) long, the egg in its case may be 2 to 4 inches (5–10 cm) in length. Biggest are the cased eggs of the whale shark—as much as a foot (30 cm) long. In contrast, the eggs of many bony fish are the size of rice grains, pinheads or even smaller.

Courting sharks

Sharks do not show any parental behavior, care for or protect their young—indeed, they are just as likely to eat their offspring. A female and male shark come together only to mate, with courtship as a prelude.

Courtship in animals, as far as we know, does not have the human connotations of love and romance. It is simply a way of ensuring that animals of the same species and maturity, but different sexes, come together in the same place at the right time. It serves to stimulate the reproductive organs, so eggs and sperm are ripe and available. It also allows each shark to assess and select a fit, strong, healthy partner, thereby increasing the chances of fit, strong, healthy offspring.

In most shark species, courting behavior begins with a seasonal migration to the breeding area. Since sharks tend to live alone or in single-sex groups, the first stage is getting both sexes together, rather than relying on a very rare, chance encounter in the open ocean.

Forbidden feeding

When sharks arrive at the traditional mating grounds the males begin a fast that can last days, even weeks. This may help to prevent the male's aggressive mating behavior from turning into a feeding frenzy—where the female is the main course! The males' fast, together with the excesses of courtship and mating, leave them somewhat weakened, with severely depleted reserves of oil in their livers.

Courtship probably involves all the shark's sensory equipment—especially smell, sight and touch. As females arrive and reach a state of sexual readiness, they probably release substances called pheromones into the water. These are chemical messengers, and they stimulate males, who rapidly congregate around the females, chasing and touching and prodding them with increasing force. This stage may last from an hour in some species to days in others.

The most aroused male sharks begin to mouth and nibble the females. Gradually a male gains the attention of one particular partner and inflicts skin wounds, or "love bites," on her with his teeth. The female may initially resist these attentions, but she then becomes subdued and has a generally passive role in the mating procedure.

The male continues to shove and bite and writhe around the female with greater violence. He grabs one of her pectoral fins in his teeth and arches his body around her. This is the usual position for actual copulation to commence.

"Love bites" are part of the courtship ritual in many large sharks, including these Port Jackson sharks. As a result, female sharks are often seen with bite marks on their bodies and fins, despite often having thicker skins than males.

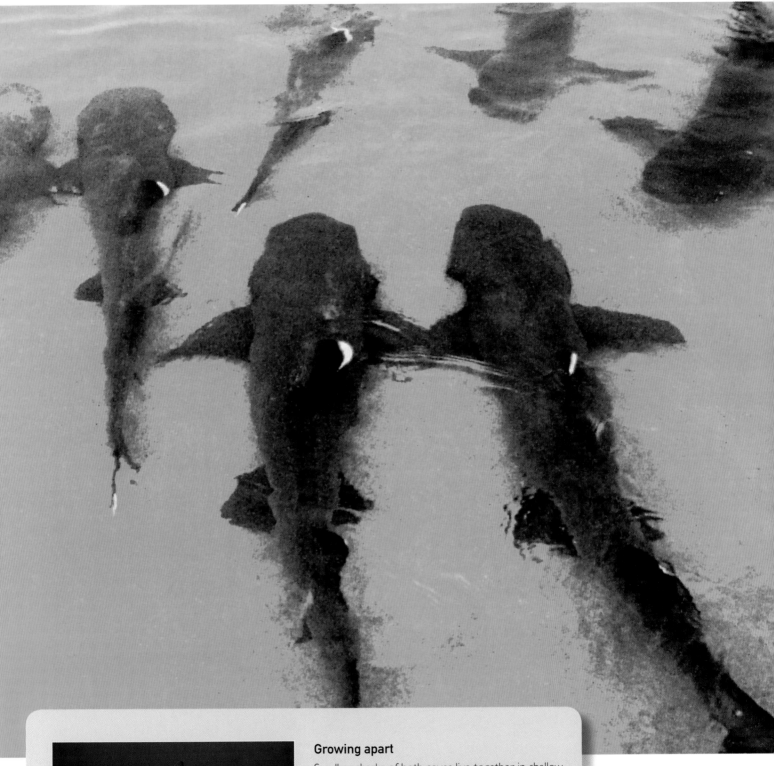

Growing apart

Sandbar sharks of both sexes live together in shallow coastal waters when young, but they live increasingly solitary lives as they reach sexual maturity. Adults are separated from young—perhaps to reduce the incidence of cannibalism—and the sexes separate except for the spring and summer mating season.

Whitetip reef sharks gather in their traditional mating place—a lagoon in the Galapagos Islands.

The mating game

Fertilization occurs when a male's sperm joins with the female's egg, to begin the development of a new shark. In all sharks fertilization is internal, taking place in the egg tubes or oviducts of the female, rather than external, in the seawater, as with most other fish and invertebrates. Internal fertilization requires mating, during which the male places his sperm into the female's body.

Once the male shark has a hold of a female he must maneuver his body into a position which enables him to introduce one of his claspers, along which the sperm pass, into her vent (the slit that opens into the cloaca.) In some species the male may use both claspers, either at the same time or one after the other.

Seawater flush

Once the pair have achieved their mating position the male releases his packets of sperm—spermatophores—from their storage chambers (the two seminal vesicles), into his cloaca. From there they pass into the apopyle (front opening) of the clasper. Seawater is sucked into his siphon sacs, under the skin nearby, and then pumped through the groove along the middle of the clasper. This washes and flushes the spermatophores

along the clasper, out the rear end and directly into the female's cloaca. From there, the sperm pass into the oviducts to fertilize the eggs or are stored by the female for fertilization in the future.

Shark matings that have been fully observed generally take 15 to 30 minutes. During this time, the male's rear body moves rhythmically against the female. She stays passive until the male withdraws his clasper and then, without ceremony, the pair separates. In many cases it is not clear if a female mates with more than one male, or if a male copulates with more than one female. Many males are thin and weak after mating, with their genital areas swollen and bleeding. They leave the area quickly to avoid becoming prey to any of their fellows.

Mating positions

Different shark species adopt differing positions when they copulate. These can be modified by circumstances, such as other males attempting to take over from a male who is already in position with a female.
- A small and flexible male shark, such as a dogfish, gets into position by wrapping his body right around the rear end of the female.
- The male horn shark grasps the pectoral fin of his partner and twists his tail over her back, pressing onto the second dorsal fin, to bring his claspers into position.
- Larger, more rigid-bodied species, such as whitetip reef sharks, may swim head down with undersides together or side by side.
- Lemon sharks mate while they are slowly swimming, with the rear parts of their bodies touching but their heads apart.

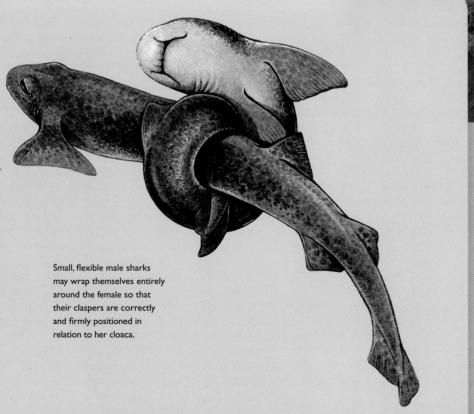

Small, flexible male sharks may wrap themselves entirely around the female so that their claspers are correctly and firmly positioned in relation to her cloaca.

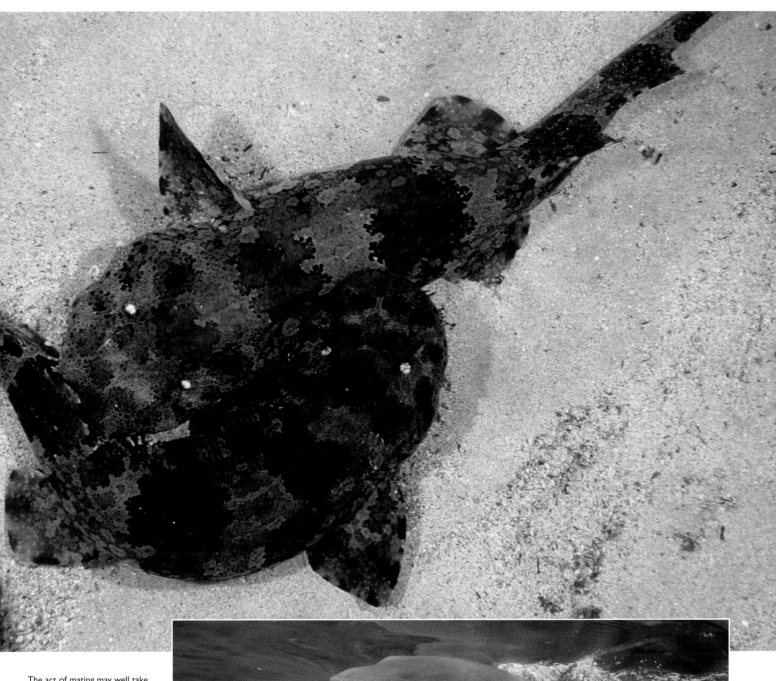

The act of mating may well take place on the seabed, as with these Ornate wobbegong sharks (above), where they have a surface to rest and push against. Nurse sharks may temporarily come into very shallow water (right), where the male bites and shoves the female. These sharks do not mate until about they are 18–22 years old. At sites such as the Florida Keys the individuals are known to return to the same place each year to mate.

Egg-laying sharks

Among the sharks that lay eggs are dogfish, horn sharks, cat sharks, carpet sharks and swell sharks. The egg-laying method of breeding is called oviparity. The eggs pass out of the female shark's body via the cloaca and vent.

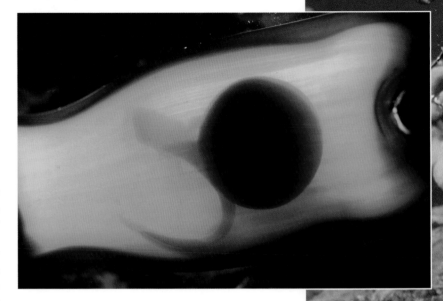

On contact with seawater the shell material hardens into a tough protective coat. Inside their egg cases, the developing embryo sharks have ample food in the form of the yolk store.

Female sharks do not always lay their eggs directly after they mate. Horn sharks, for example, produce their eggs two at a time, every week or two, for up to four months. Small spotted cat shark females mate in the fall then take the following winter and spring to develop and lay just 20 or so eggs.

Carefully laid

Shark mothers lay their eggs very carefully. It takes as long as two hours for a horn shark to twist each of her eggs out through her vent. Each egg case has a conical, double-helix thread that causes it to spiral and twist into sand or between rocks. Cat sharks lay oblong or pillow-shaped eggs with long, curly tendrils at each corner. These tangle around seaweed when freshly laid, and as they harden the tendrils contract and pull the egg to greater concealment within the fronds. The tendrils hold the egg while the embryo develops inside. Such empty egg cases are often washed up on beaches after hatching and are popularly known as "mermaids' purses." Zebra shark eggs are similarly equipped with tufts of stiff hairs for anchorage among weeds and rocks.

Shark eggs must be securely fixed and safe because the young take between six and 10 months to develop before hatching. The time period depends partly on water temperature. In tropical seas, horn shark eggs grow fairly quickly and hatch seven months after laying. In cooler Northern European waters, small-spotted cat shark eggs take nine months to mature and hatch.

The egg of the swell shark (top left) has four corner tendrils that catch onto seaweed and rock. The embryo and yolk sac can be seen inside this egg. The Port Jackson shark (left) will take her spiral egg and wedge it into a crack in a rock.

Growing and hatching

1 The fertilized egg develops into the embryo, which begins as a microscopic speck on the surface of the yolk.

2 The embryo develops its main organs and systems, such as the brain, heart and guts and grows larger.

3 The embryo is attached to the membrane of the yolk sac by an umbilical cord containing blood vessels, through which it obtains sustenance from the thick, nutrient-rich yolk.

4 Oxygen passes in through the egg case from the surrounding water, and body waste seeps out.

5 The baby shark, known as a pup, takes on the skin pattern that will best camouflage it when hatched.

6 The pup begins to wriggle and rotate.

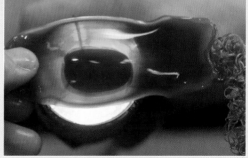

7 Eventually the egg case bursts at one end, and the pup pushes itself out.

8 Most shark hatchlings are 8–12 inches (20–30 cm) long. They swim off, fully independent and ready to hunt.

Unlike the Port Jackson shark, the closely related crested bulhead shark simply releases her eggs into the sea. Their spiral shape helps them roll in the current until their tendrils catch onto something, for example these sea squirts (above).

Having babies

Most species of shark are live-bearers, but there are two distinct methods.

One is to retain the eggs inside the female's body until they hatch and then give birth to the babies. This is ovoviviparity, shown by frilled sharks, sand sharks, threshers, tigers, nurse sharks, makos, basking sharks and most spiny sharks. The eggs are retained in the oviducts and have their flimsy membranelike coverings, but these never thicken and toughen into proper egg cases, as they do on eggs laid externally.

The embryonic sharks live on food supplies in the eggs, and they are in a carefully maintained environment, with controlled temperature, plenty of oxygen and little danger from predators. When their yolky food supply is gone, they finally hatch from their soft membranous cases and are born.

Some sharks take ovoviviparity a stage further. After hatching, the pups stay for hours, even days, within a specialized region of the oviduct, called the uterus. Here, they are provided with extra sustenance. In porbeagles, threshers and mako sharks, this sustenance takes the form of unfertilized eggs, which the mother continues to produce from her ovaries. Feeding on other eggs within the mother's body is called oogeny.

Pregnant sharks

The second, more specialized, version of live-bearing is viviparity. The embryo sharks develop inside the mother, but not within egg cases or nourished by yolk. They develop within the uterus, or "womb" area, where the mother provides nourishment via a specialized nutrient-exchange system, an adaptation of the yolk sac known as the placenta. In this system, the mother shark, like a mother mammal, can be called "pregnant." Viviparity is shown by smoothhounds, bull sharks, hammerheads and the typical open-ocean, streamlined sharks of the requiem group.

Most shark pregnancies, for instance that of the sand tiger shark, last up to about 12 months. In the spiny dogfish it is up to 24 months, and in the frilled shark it may be as long as three and a half years.

As birth approaches, the pups move from the uterus, along to the end of the oviduct, then into the cloacal chamber and finally out through the vent slit. In viviparous birth they thrash strongly, breaking the umbilical cord that still links them to the placenta, which emerges from the mother too, as the afterbirth.

Most shark pups are born tail first but some, like sand tigers, emerge head first. Baby hammerheads are born head first, with their hammerlike flanges folded back.

Sharp "teeth"

Saw sharks have a long snout or rostrum studded with rows of sharp "teeth". Being ovoviviparous, also known as aplacental viviparity, the mother gives birth after the eggs hatch inside her (pups are shown here with their yolk). At birth the rostral teeth are angled back, presumably to avoid injuring her. Over the next few hours these teeth assume their normal position.

Both whiskery sharks (above left) and gray nurse sharks (above right) are ovoviviparous. These whiskery sharks are embryos, taken from their mother's uterus, with the yolk sacs from which they get their nourishment still attached.

The spots on this gray nurse shark (passing a spotted wobbegong, right) show that it is a youngster. It hatched from an egg inside its mother's uterus, where it ate the developing embryos around it, then emerged after six to nine months.

The Virgin Birth, 2001 C.E.

Despite the limitations in our knowledge of the reproductive process of many species of shark (see page 174), scientists used to think they could at least rely on one basic fact—it needed both a mother and a father.

Imagine the confusion, then, when in 2001 a female hammerhead shark, held in a tank in Omaha's Henry Doorly Zoo aquarium with only three other female hammerheads (and a host of other species) for company for more than three years, gave birth to a pup. The case baffled scientists, whose search for explanations lasted for more than five years.

The virgin phenomenon

The three female hammerheads had come into contact with males of other species of shark, so the researchers wondered whether the pup could have been the result of interspecies mating, but this is very rare. They also wondered if she had mated with a male hammerhead before she was captured and stored the male's sperm until she ovulated. Female sharks are capable of holding and maintaining sperm in this way, but to store it for more than three years (the length of her captivity) is unheard of. In addition, sex between sharks is very rough, and she had none of the bite marks associated with shark courtship.

After extensive genetic testing, the researchers finally knew the answer: the female hammerhead had not mated with anyone. It was a virgin birth—a phenomenon never before observed in a shark.

To come to this conclusion, the researchers sequenced the DNA of both the pup and its mother. They expected to find that half of its DNA came from its mother, and half from the unknown father (which they hoped to identify.) Instead, when comparing the two sequences they found that the pup had received all of its genes from its mother.

The researchers believe the shark reproduced using automictic parthenogenesis, in which an unfertilized egg merges with another cell from the mother—called the "sister polar body"— to form a fetus. This process may be an automatic response by female sharks when faced with few encounters with male sharks, in an attempt to rebuild their population.

However, because the two merged cells contain exactly the same genetic material, there is very little genetic diversity in the resulting pup.

Because of this, a virgin birth would be undesirable in the wild, where populations need to be as varied as possible to have the best chances of growing and surviving the tough conditions of the sea, and it could actually contribute to a more rapid decline in numbers. With some species nearing extinction, experts fear that this phenomenon may be common in the wild among these populations, exacerbating the problem.

A female shark is capable of storing sperm after mating until she ovulates. However, the hammerhead at Omaha's Henry Doorly Zoo aquarium gave birth after having not seen a male shark in three years, which would have been an unprecedented length of time to store sperm. Here, a newborn Lemon shark pup swims away from its mother.

These hammerhead sharks have no shortage of potential mates, but left in the loneliness of an aquarium with only her girlfriends for company, a broody female shark has to impregnate herself.

Growing up and old

Shark mothers usually lay their eggs or give birth to their pups in shallow-water nursery areas such as coasts, bays and mangrove swamps. There the young are relatively safe from predators and have ample small food, such as worms, shellfish and small fish.

The pups are slimmer and more snakelike in shape than their parents. As they grow, they shift to new prey suited to their size and stay in the cover of the weedy or pebbly seabed, well camouflaged from predators.

As the pups grow typically they move, by stages, away from the shore into deeper waters. Their teeth alter to feed on bigger meals. Their skin coloration changes, adapting to camouflage in the new surroundings. And their body shape takes on the form of the adult. For example, lemon sharks spend their first two years hiding among seaweed, then graduate to slightly deeper water between the ages of three and five years, then to deep-water reefs as they reach adulthood.

Not all shark pups begin life in sheltered nursery areas. Big ocean-going sharks such as makos produce youngsters who are already large and strong enough to withstand the perils of the sea and begin hunting right after birth.

Slow growers

Compared with other similar-sized animals, sharks take a long time to reach sexual maturity. Small-spotted cat shark are ready to mate after about 10 years, when they are around 3 feet (0.9 m) long. Thresher sharks mature at about 14 years, while the spiny dogfish takes approximately 20 years. Also, animals such as mammals and birds grow to adult size then stop. Sharks, on the other hand, keep growing, although the rate lessens with age. Growth is also slower in cold conditions and when food is scarce.

Assessing lifespans for wild animals is famously difficult. Accurate measurements for sharks kept in aquaria are one method, but this is hardly a natural habitat. In the wild, catch-and-release and tagging projects can give clues, as can the study of the vertebrae of the spinal column, which may show growth rings like those in a tree trunk.

In aquaria, young healthy sharks with plentiful food grow about 6 inches (15 cm) longer each year. This is much slower than comparable bony fish. In the wild, sharks probably grow more slowly. One tagged great white lengthened less than half an inch (1.3 cm) each year. A re-caught Greenland shark had grown only a fifth of an inch (0.5 cm) per year. The fastest-growing species are the large ocean hunters when food is abundant. Blues and makos may lengthen by 8 inches (20 cm) or more yearly in favorable conditions.

It takes seven to 10 months before a swell shark hatches from its greenish-colored egg case, depending on water temperature. The hatchling has two rows of toothlike projections to help it cut its way out of its egg case.

Young sharks, such as this Japanese bullhead shark (main photo), remain in shallow water for several years to avoid being eaten by other sharks. When this Port Jackson shark (inset) hatches from its egg, it too will move into a shallow-water nursery area.

Some ripe old ages

Results of shark tagging experiments, observations, and estimates include:

- Australian school shark—at least 34 years.
- Porbeagle—estimated at 45 years.
- Sand tiger—43 years for an aquarium specimen.
- Great white—mature at around 15 years, lives at least 25 years, possibly exceeds 60 years.
- Spiny dogfish—recorded at 75 years.
- Whale shark—possibly over 100 years.

Sharks and us

Our relationships with sharks have come a long way, from disdain and kill-at-all-costs to respect, admiration and awe.

A young snorkeler takes the plunge with a blue shark.

Sizes and numbers

More than half of all shark species are less than 6 feet (1.8 m) long when mature adults. In fact, the "average" shark is less than 4 feet (1.2 m) long. Only about 10 species regularly exceed 12–13 feet (3.7–4 m) in length.

Stories of shark size abound with exaggeration. But certainly the largest shark, and the biggest fish, is the whale shark. One authenticated record stands at 41 feet (12.5 m) and 22 tons (20 metric tons) for a whale shark measured off the coast of Pakistan. A commonly quoted upper estimate is about 55 feet (17 m) and 30-plus tons (27 metric tons) for a specimen near Thailand. The second biggest shark is another filter-feeder, the basking shark. One specimen was estimated at just over 40 feet (12 m) long, weighing 19 tons (17 metric tons). (See species profiles, from page 34, for average sizes of all the sharks discussed here.)

Largest and smallest

The largest predatory shark, and the biggest of all hunting fish, is the legendary great white. The largest reliably measured specimen was 21 feet (6.4 m) and maximum weights are in the order of 2 tons (1.8 metric tons). A great white landed in the Azores was reputed to be 30 feet (9.1 m) long, but stories of such huge individuals have no scientific authentication. (The great white, however, would easily be beaten by its extinct cousin, *C. Megalodon*—see page 14.)

The next-biggest hunting sharks are probably the tiger, Greenland and sixgill sharks, which may all exceed 20 feet (6 m). There are several contenders for the title of smallest shark, in the 6–8 inch (15–20 cm) bracket. They include the dwarf lantern shark, *Etmopterus perryi*, the spined pygmy shark, *Squaliolus laticaudus*, the pygmy ribbontail cat shark, *Eridacnis radcliffei*, and the Caribbean lantern shark, *Etmopterus hillianus*.

Shark numbers

The great white shark, despite its fame and image, is a rare fish. Its world population—probably measured in four figures—is declining. Indeed, most big sharks are relatively uncommon, reflecting their role as apex predators and top carnivores. The megamouth and frilled shark are rarely seen, so it is not known how many of them exist. Only a couple of handfuls of specimens have ever been studied. Whale sharks are also rarely sighted, although their habit of cruising just below the surface makes their sightings proportionally more frequent. In general, smaller sharks are more common. Dogfish abound along many rocky coasts, probably numbering millions. One of the world's more abundant large sharks, and large fish was the oceanic whitetip, *Carcharhinus longimanus*, but like many sharks its numbers are reducing at an alarming rate.

The slendertail or Molleri's lantern shark (left) is among the smallest sharks, growing to only around 18 inches (46 cm) long. It lives near the bottom of deep water. In contrast, the surface-living whale shark (above) is the largest fish in the ocean—its size at birth is larger than an adult lantern shark.

Sharks in perspective

- The only animals in the ocean larger than the biggest sharks are great whales. The blue whale (pictured) can be three times longer and seven times heavier than a whale shark.
- Bony fish are small in comparison to sharks. Heaviest is the ocean sunfish (*Mola mola*)—up to 2.3 tonnes (1.8 metric tons). Longest is the oarfish or ribbonfish, (*Agrostichthys parkeri*) exceeding 30 feet (9.1 m), but its slim form means it weighs comparatively little, perhaps 600 pounds (272 kg).

How dangerous are sharks?

Many people are killed or injured every year by all manner of animals, including rogue elephants, hippos, tigers, lions, bears, pet dogs, snakes, spiders, scorpions and bees.

Away from land and into saltwater, marine dangers include certain jellyfish, box-jellies and sea-wasps, blue-ringed octopuses, stonefish, lionfish, sea snakes and saltwater crocodiles. In terms of numbers of people suffering or dying, sharks are very near the bottom of these lists. In an average year in Australia, box jellyfish, *Chironex fleckeri*, kill more people than stonefish, crocodiles and sharks added together. And to put things into perspective, malaria—carried by mosquitos—kills more than one million humans every year.

How we perceive the threat

The reasons why people believe that sharks are so dangerous lie more in our perceptions than in the threat itself. Many people seem to have an innate fear of sharks, as of spiders and snakes. But why?

• For most people, sharks are beyond their experience and understanding. Few of us ever encounter a real shark at close quarters, other than perhaps safely behind aquarium glass. Our fear and terror of sharks probably stems from several roots based in our primeval psyche, unhindered by factual information or realistic common sense.

• Sharks have received bad press from the beginnings of our storytelling and written history. Around ancient seaside campfires, people retold and embellished tales of shark attacks. They knew only about the sharks that inflicted terrible wounds on sailors, fishermen and divers. The vast majority of sharks went about their business unseen and innocently harmless.

• Dread of sharks may come from our subconscious fears of the unknown and the unexpected. Many people, and animals, have an instinctive fear of water, especially deeper water. Who knows what might be hiding there? If there is a shark, it may well strike swiftly and without warning. The victim can rarely see it coming.

• The appearance of a shark may be very worrying to us. People communicate by facial expressions and bodily gestures, showing intelligence and emotions. But to the uninitiated, a shark seems to move mechanically, like a robot. It has hard and rough skin, an expressionless face and glassy, staring eyes. It is apparently without feelings or reason. This lack of responsive psychology is profoundly unsettling for most people.

The box jellyfish, found around northern Australia and in nearby waters, is one of the most dangerous animals in the world. Almost invisible in the water, a severe sting from its 3-foot (0.9 m) long tentacles can kill a person within just a few minutes if adequate first aid is not readily available.

The olive sea snake, along with most other sea snakes, is highly venomous. It forages over coral reefs in search of small fish. Sea snakes have very small mouths and cannot easily bite a person. Most are nonaggressive, but like many land snakes, their bite can be fatal.

Relative risks

Data for Western industrialized nations such as the U.S. show that overall, the relative risk of death is:

- Heart disease: 1 in 5
- Influenza and complications: 1 in 70
- Road traffic accident: 1 in 100
- Train accident: 1 in 150,000
- Lightning: 1 in 80,000
- Shark attack: 1 in 3 million

The risks of attack

Around the world each year, there are some 70–100 recorded shark attacks. Of these, an average of 8–12 are fatal. Considering how many people swim in the sea, the risk of attack is very tiny indeed.

Comparisons help to shed light on the true risk of being a shark attack victim. For example:

- The chance of a citizen in one of the U.S. coastal states being struck by lightning is twice that of being attacked by a shark and 80 times that of being killed by a shark.
- Globally, the risk of drowning at sea is 1,000 times that of suffering a shark attack.
- In Australia, where sharks often swim relatively close to popular beaches, drownings outnumber shark attacks by 50 to one.
- Compared to other animals, sharks injure or kill far fewer people than dogs, big cats, crocodiles and alligators, snakes or stinging bees and wasps.
- For an average individual, the risk of being in a road traffic accident or suffering injury at home is thousands of times greater than running into a problem with a shark.

Which sharks attack?

More than 30 species of shark are on record as attacking humans. Most attacks are carried out by the "big three"—great white, tiger shark and bull shark. These species are also ahead on the proportion of attacks that are fatal, ranging from one in five to one in three. However, reports of sharks attacking are always treated with caution because, in the heat of the moment, it is all too easy to misidentify the species responsible.

Shark attacks by species	
Great white	33%
Tiger	12%
Bull	8%
Sand tiger	6%
Unidentified requiem species	5%
Nurse	4%
Mako	4%
Hammerhead	3%
Blue	3%
Blacktip	3%

For the reasons why sharks attack people, and how to deter them, see pages 196–200.

Single-strike attacks

More than nine out of 10 shark encounters are single strikes, which rarely result in significant injury to the human (or the shark). Some are simple bumps with the snout. Others are quick passes where the abrasive shark skin, or perhaps the teeth in the part-open jaws, cause superficial abrasions, cuts and damage.

In some of these cases the shark may be investigating whether the strange creature presented to it might be a useful source of food. This is part of the natural exploratory suite of instincts common to a vast range of wild animals.

In other single-strike cases the shark may be doing something else that all creatures do, to a greater or lesser extent—defending itself. The human body is relatively large compared to many kinds of sea life, and it moves in ways that are unfamiliar and unpredictable to sharks and other fish. This can present an apparent threat to the shark, which responds by signaling that it is ready to defend itself, and to do this by attack if necessary. The shark's intention is shown by its body position and swimming motions, known by various terms such as threat posture and agonistic display. If the human causing the threat recognizes this and withdraws, it is likely that the shark will do so, too.

The most feared attacker, a great white shark opens its jaws in readiness for an attack in the Neptune Islands in South Australia. Big sharks feed on correspondingly big prey, such as seals, turtles and sea lions. Humans on surfboards can resemble turtles from underneath (the shark's viewpoint), which may explain the relatively high rate of great white attacks on surfers (see page 193).

Bull sharks in a river—unlike most other marine sharks, this species can tolerate freshwater and often travels far upriver. Bull sharks usually dwell in shallow water, making them very dangerous to humans.

Threat postures

Different types of shark have a range of behaviors that warn other creatures, including those of their own kind, that all is not well and an attack is possible. The shark may be defending its territory, protecting its kill or feeling at risk in some other way. These threat postures vary from species to species, but there are certain elements common to most. The behavior has been especially well documented in the gray reef shark, partly due to ease of observation.

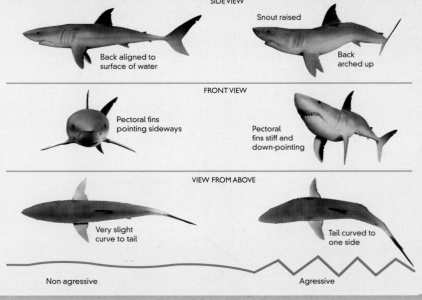

SIDE VIEW

Back aligned to surface of water

Snout raised

Back arched up

FRONT VIEW

Pectoral fins pointing sideways

Pectoral fins stiff and down-pointing

VIEW FROM ABOVE

Very slight curve to tail

Tail curved to one side

Non agressive

Agressive

How attacks happen

Like most wild creatures in their natural habitats, sharks are usually on the lookout for food. How does a typical attack by a big shark happen—on a human or a more conventional prey animal?

Observations of actual shark attacks—for example, by great whites on baits, as well as attacks by other species—combine with studies on captive sharks in more controlled conditions and our increasing knowledge of shark sensory biology to produce an informed account of a "typical" attack.

Coundown to the bite

The shark's longest-distance sense is usually smell. The scent of blood or body fluid substances in the water may well first alert it to the possibility of a meal from many hundreds of feet away. Sharks can discriminate between various bodily chemicals, such as amino acids and fatty acids, from different animals.

Approaching the scene, the shark's hearing also comes into play at considerable distance. It can detect various frequencies of sound vibrations, which travel much faster and farther in water than they do when we usually hear them, in air.

Closing in

As the shark approaches, its lateral line system begins to feel ripples and currents in the water produced by movements of its potential victim. These sensations, like the other sensory inputs, could be compared with those from previous encounters in the shark's brain memory banks.

In fairly clear daylight water, eyesight also now begins to discern the shape and movements of the target. Tank experiments have shown that sharks have reasonable visual acuity and discrimination, although, as far as we can tell, they tend to be farsighted.

If all these sensory cues fit together to indicate a possible meal, the shark comes closer still, with the decision to attack. Just a few feet away, its electrical sense picks up the fields made by the active muscles of the victim. At this stage the shark may well be traveling fast, mouth ready to open and, in some species, eyes rolled up into their sockets for protection, so physical touch and the electrosense play vital roles. Finally comes the bite, and the sensations of touch and taste in the mouth. The shark's next reactions depend on what it has found.

Once the shark has identified its victim, it may charge at them at great speed with its mouth open. Only once it has taken its first bite and tasted its flesh will it decide whether to feast on the victim.

Surfer and seal

A famous depiction compares the shark's eye view of a human paddling a surfboard and a favorite prey of big sharks, a seal. The similarities may seem striking to us. But we are predominantly visual creatures looking through air at a clear static image on paper. We have no real idea of how a shark perceives this type of view in its brain. Also, the shark is in an entirely different world, where vision may well be limited by dim, cloudy water. As it swims, all kinds of scents, currents, temperature changes, waterborne sound vibrations and electrical energy continually update its brain about its environment in a way we can hardly imagine.

A forest of human arms and legs presents a very unusual experience for a shark. We have no way of knowing how many passing sharks decide to avoid what, as far as they know, could be a dangerous encounter for them.

Where attacks happen

A map plotting shark attacks on humans around the world shows clusters of events along certain coasts. These include eastern North America and the Caribbean, subtropical and tropical western North America (mainly north of the Equator), tropical Pacific islands, Australia and Southeast Asia and southeast and southern Africa.

Less frequently there are attacks around Japan, New Zealand, northwest South America, West Africa and the Middle East.

These distributions reflect several factors. One is the range of the main sharks involved, chiefly the "big three" of great white, tiger shark and bull shark. A second is the likelihood of humans going into the ocean. Many of the map's blank areas are unpopulated coastlines.

A third factor is whether news of an attack makes it into the official statistics, as compiled for the International Shark Attack File (ISAF). Some attacks on poorer people along the coasts of poorer countries may go unrecorded. Fourthly, there may be debate over whether a shark was to blame, rather than another large fish such as a barracuda and if so, which type of shark.

Overall, most reported shark attacks occur in the warm, calm, shallow waters of vacation resorts. They happen more frequently during weekends and usually in the afternoon. The victims tend to be affluent Westerners. These statistics reflect people's vacation habits and global tourism, rather than the behavior of sharks (as discussed on page 190).

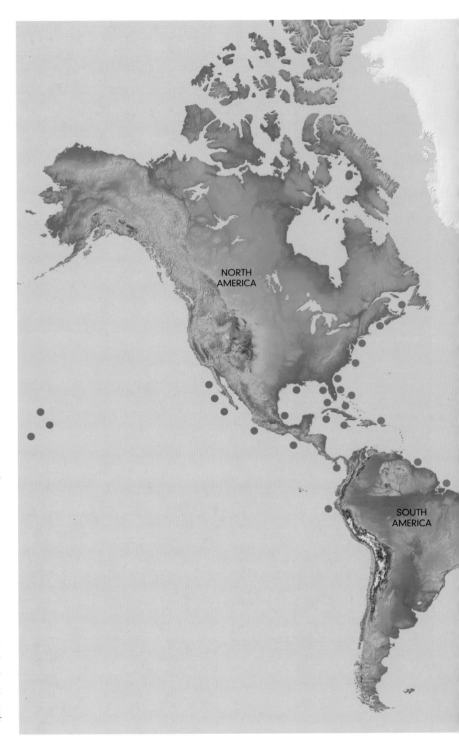

Multiple attacks

• In 1942 during the Second World War, a German U-boat holed the Allied steamer *Nova Scotia* off South Africa. The ship sank in minutes, leaving 900 men in the water. By the time a rescue ship arrived 60 hours later, there were only 192 survivors, owing to a gathering of sharks.

• In 1945 the *USS Indianapolis* was returning to the U.S. from the Tinian air base in the Pacific, after delivering parts of the atomic bomb to be dropped on Hiroshima.

Torpedoed by a Japanese submarine, it left more than 900 men in life jackets or clinging to wreckage. Owing to the mission's secrecy, the rescuers did not arrive for almost four days and found only 300 survivors—many of the rest killed by sharks (see page 26).

• In 1916 at Matawan Creek, on the U.S.'s New Jersey Atlantic coast, there were five attacks in 10 days, with four fatalities. This may have been a great white or perhaps a bull shark.

This map shows the main sites of recorded fatal shark attacks around the world. Others probably go unrecorded in official statistics, while some "blank" areas are simply unpopulated coastlines.

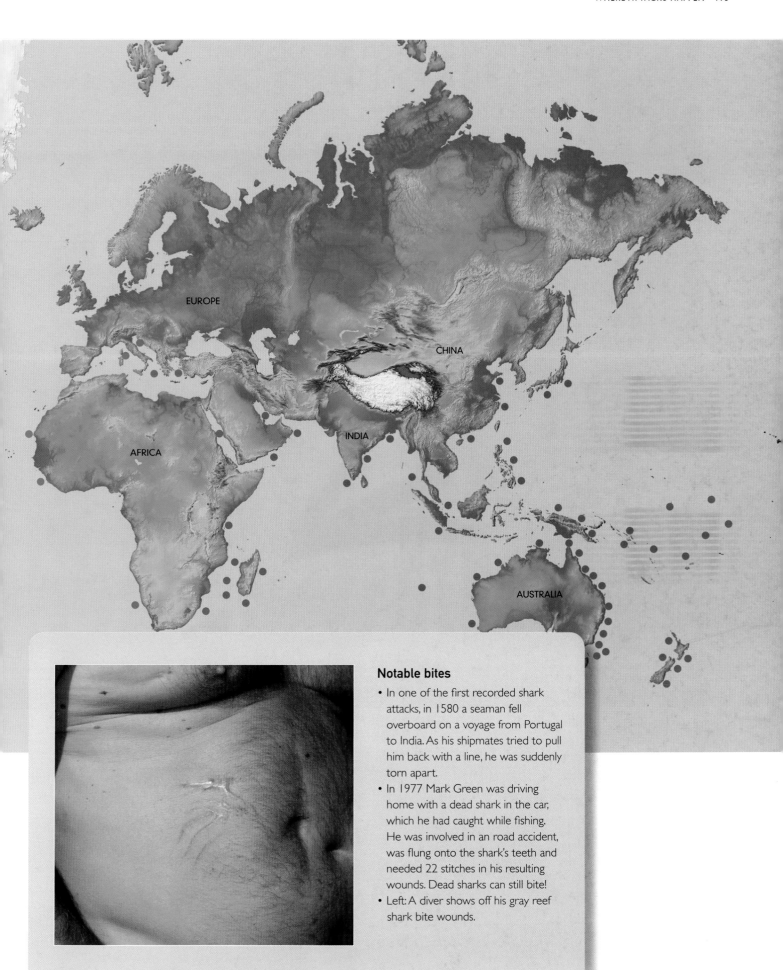

EUROPE

CHINA

INDIA

AFRICA

AUSTRALIA

Notable bites

- In one of the first recorded shark attacks, in 1580 a seaman fell overboard on a voyage from Portugal to India. As his shipmates tried to pull him back with a line, he was suddenly torn apart.
- In 1977 Mark Green was driving home with a dead shark in the car, which he had caught while fishing. He was involved in an road accident, was flung onto the shark's teeth and needed 22 stitches in his resulting wounds. Dead sharks can still bite!
- Left: A diver shows off his gray reef shark bite wounds.

Shark deterrents

Many scientific studies of sharks aim to make ocean bathing and swimming safer by somehow repelling or deterring them—hopefully in a humane and enlightened fashion.

Menaced by a shark?

- Avoid risky locations—swim within a shark protection zone.
- If a shark appears then swim quickly, quietly, powerfully and smoothly away from the area.
- Avoid splashing and erratic or uncoordinated movements.
- Remain under the surface for as long as possible.
- If a shark does attack, a punch to its snout, eyes or gills may be effective. (Then again, it may not.)

During the Second World War, the U.S. Navy commissioned shark biologists for the first full-scale study of shark-repelling methods. Their "guinea pig" sharks were dogfish in tanks. Sounds of various pitches, poisons, chemical irritants, nasty waterborne scents and even toxic gases were tried. Only one chemical seemed to have any effect—copper acetate. Bottled as "Shark Chaser," it was issued to military personnel at sea. It may have boosted morale, but tales of its success are scarce.

Understanding the deterrent

To find a shark deterrent, we need to understand sharks better. After more than 50 years of research, today's range of repellents or deterrents could be viewed as less than impressive and rarely proven. They include large, floating, black plastic bags to disguise the potential victim's shape and prevent body fluids from leaking into the sea and oddly colored or striped wetsuits to baffle the shark's vision. Some of the more popular types of shark deterrents use electrical currents to confuse or upset a shark's senses. These devices can be worn on a belt or suit and send out an "electric shield" that affects the shark's electricity-detecting sense but causes no lasting harm. Another line of research involves the group of substances known as seriochemicals, such as pheromones. These are the natural "messengers" made by certain living things to affect the behavior or actions of others. Seriochemicals have been tested on sharks to try and switch their intentions from feeding to flight and dispersal. Some of these chemicals are being isolated from the shark's own tissues, others from different fish. In nature, they warn sharks to stay away. An important feature is that the seriochemical should not be toxic to the shark, just alter its behavior. A successful slow-release version could be incorporated into a bracelet, anklet, swimsuit, wetsuit or even sunscreen.

Physical protection

To protect people from sharks, resort beaches depend on physical barriers made of bars or chain-link fencing, plus lookouts on towers or headlands or in patrol boats or spotter planes. Individual divers may tour the area carrying electric stun-prods. Should a shark approach too close, the prod is switched on and interferes with the electroreception system in the shark's snout. Divers use many kinds of metal cages, studying and photographing sharks from within.

Shark deterrents such as the shark pod (left) send out electromagnetic waves to scares sharks away. These special devices can allow divers to get closer to sharks than they would otherwise feel comfortable, although caution is always important.

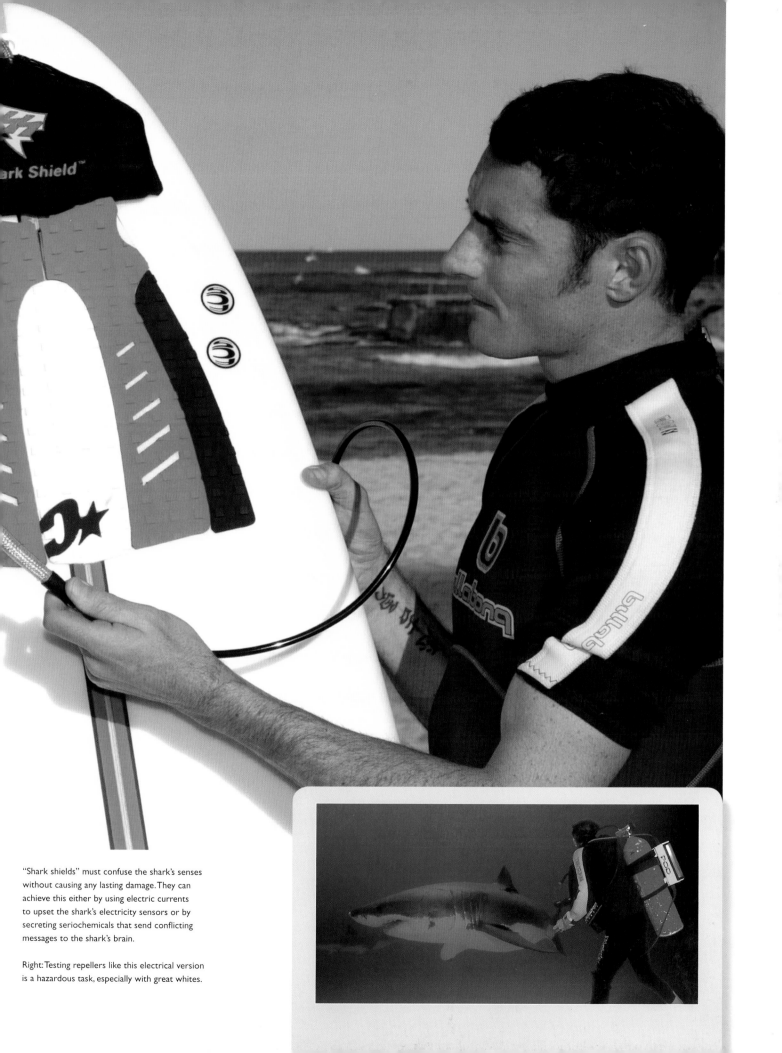

"Shark shields" must confuse the shark's senses without causing any lasting damage. They can achieve this either by using electric currents to upset the shark's electricity sensors or by secreting seriochemicals that send conflicting messages to the shark's brain.

Right: Testing repellers like this electrical version is a hazardous task, especially with great whites.

Sharks in science

Serious science eats up money, and serious money is usually available more easily for research that might lead to useful applications and profits.

A juvenile hammerhead shark is force-fed a tracking device that will beam out radio signals, allowing researchers to track it for several days.

Shark scientists work in several overlapping and potentially profitable fields. These include unraveling the biology and ecology of commercially fished sharks—at the same time to help conserve them and to advance our understanding of the marine ecosystem—and developing useful shark-derived products, particularly in the fields of health and medicine.

Natural cures

Eastern systems of medicine have long looked to animals, including sharks, as sources of preparations to cure many kinds of ailments. Important here is the long-established observation that sharks seem astonishingly free of usual forms of illness and disease. Very few of the countless sharks caught and studied appear to suffer from cancer, bacterial infections or other disorders. Many traditional shark-derived substances remain untested by Western scientific medicine. Some have been investigated and proved ineffective, while others remain a "don't know."

Possible shark remedies

Shark cartilage extracts have a long reputation for treating or even curing cancer. The scientific evidence is complex, and mainstream medical opinion is unimpressed. Rigorous recent trials of shark cartilage on lung cancer patients, organized by the American Society for Clinical Oncology, showed no clear positive benefits. A group of natural chemicals called aminosterols, including squalamine, are being extracted from dogfish and other sharks and investigated in several areas. These include an antibacterial action to treat certain infectious diseases; killing body cells that have become infected with disease-causing viruses; and as an antiangiogenic, which prevents abnormal tissues and growths from developing their own blood supply. The angiogenic process occurs in some tumors (brain, lung, ovary) and in forms of the eye condition known as macular degeneration.

The gall bladder is part of the digestive system, linked to the liver, which produces bile fluid as part of digestion and excretion. A substance from shark bile has been extracted and purified as sodium scymnol sulfate, or isolutrol, and marketed as a treatment for acne and pimples. Other shark parts and products that have been tested include an anticoagulant or antiarthritis preparations for joint problems, the cornea for possible transplant to human and various shark extracts as burns treatments. Much of this work is controversial, is in its early stages or has yet to be embraced by the scientific and medical establishment.

Contributions to education

The small sharks called dogfish, such as the spiny dogfish pictured, have taught generations of young scientists about fish biology. Easy to keep and breed in cold-water aquaria, they are an ideal sea-fish version of the laboratory rat, for dissection and study. Dogfish research has also produced significant information about the finely tuned senses of sharks, their swimming prowess, their physiology (body chemistry and functions), and the way they breed.

Observing the behaviors and actions of living sharks are vital in biological and ecological research, but may put scientists at risk. This lightweight armor is very similar to the chain mail worn by medieval soldiers. Although it is flexible, it is also very strong, as this whitetip reef shark found when it put the armor to the test.

How to survive a shark attack

The risk of attack by a shark is slim, and your chances of surviving an attack are impressive. You can be even safer by taking a few precautions.

Avoid swimming alone, as sharks will always choose vulnerable prey, especially individuals far from the shoreline, and avoid swimming at night, when many species of shark are feeding and therefore at their most active. Try to stay in areas with good underwater visibility—murky water is a haven for sharks as their prey will rarely see them before it is too late. Never enter the water if you are bleeding from an open wound or menstruating—the shark's sense of smell is astonishingly acute, and it can detect the scent of blood from great distances. Be aware of a shark's visual acuity, too. They are particularly sensitive to contrasting colors, such as the difference between a bright swimsuit and muted flesh tones. Shiny jewelry glinting through the water is thought to resemble the silvery sheen of fish scales, so you would be ill-advised to keep rings on when you go into the water. If, while swimming in a stretch of open water, you become concerned that a shark is present, swim swiftly back toward the shoreline without splashing violently or calling to attract attention. Erratic movement and splashing on the surface will only draw the shark's attention to you.

Being aware of the other marine life in an area will also help you avoid becoming a shark victim. Look out for signs of small bait fish, which normally swim together in schools, making a dark cloud in the water to which sharks and other predators will be attracted. Bait fish can also be detected by raising your head above water—look out for seabirds swooping down into the ocean to eat the remains of previously killed fish or hunting for live bait fish. Where seabirds are hunting, more dangerous predators are also likely to be gathering.

Underwater terrain is another thing to take into account. Be careful in the areas sharks favor. They rarely enter shallow water close to the shore but spend much of their time waiting for prey near steep drops in the seabed or in the water between sandbanks, which sometimes lure smaller fish and marine animals into unexpectedly deep water.

Sharks have an astonishing sense of smell. They can detect the scent of blood from a long way away, so never enter shark-infested water if you have an open wound.

Shark sense

The need to stay alert when stranded in deep water and control one's behavior so as to avoid being detected by sharks has led to a proliferation of advice manuals and websites. Apparently the first was *Shark Sense*, a small pamphlet produced by the U.S. Navy and released in 1944. Distributed to all servicemen active in the Pacific area, it explained how to stay safe if marooned in tropical waters and how to fend off unwanted attention.

A night swim might seem like a fun idea, but many sharks become active prowlers in the dark. Their senses are in a heightened state of activity so that they can detect prey, whereas our main sense—vision—is almost disabled.

Save the sharks

Shark meat is sometimes considered a delicacy, but environmentalists fear that shark fishing could cause the extinction of many species.

Every year millions of sharks are killed for their fins, liver and teeth, while the rest of the animal is dumped overboard.

Studying sharks

The best place to study sharks is among them, in their natural marine habitat. Advances in diving gear and techniques, hand-held and remote camera technology, recording, tagging systems, satellite tracking, ROVs (underwater remote-operated vehicles) and other fields make studying sharks increasingly rewarding and productive.

Gradually, we can watch sharks in ever more detail and get closer to understanding what makes them tick. One of the first people to attempt serious underwater studies of sharks was the late Jacques Yves Cousteau (1910–1997). With his teams of underwater photographers, film-makers, explorers and scientists, he carried out much original research in the 1950s and 1960s. Cousteau helped to design the first scuba (self-contained underwater breathing apparatus) equipment and pioneered the use of shark cages for observation and filming.

Shark's eye view

The "crittercam" instruments are worn by wild animals for a time then retrieved. Consisting of video cameras and other information-gathering equipment, they are used on various land and ocean creatures. The "crittercam" is attached to the temporarily captured or securely held shark. When the shark is released, the camera records what it sees and where it goes. After a set time the camera strap disintegrates or unlinks, and the camera then floats to the surface, emits a radio signal and is recovered. Research around Australia, North America and South Africa is revealing the behavior of species such as great whites, tiger sharks and bull sharks.

Tagging

Shark tags vary from simple plastic clip-on versions, usually attached to a fin, to sophisticated tracking devices that emit radio signals and can be detected by boats or even satellites. Some of these radio emitters are safely "force-fed" into the shark, allowing researchers to follow it for several days, until nature takes its course and the device is expelled.

In the northwest Atlantic's Cooperative Shark Tagging Program, scientists, sports anglers and commercial fishing boats work together. They do not bring their catches back but measure the shark, fit it with a numbered tag, then let it go. If it is recaught in a different place, the distance and direction it has traveled and the amount it has grown are recorded. The tags have revealed that some sharks, such as the sandbar shark, mature very late and have few offspring. The conclusion is that when a population is fished out, it will take a long time to recover.

Tagging sharks is an excellent way to track their movements, but capturing and tagging a large and dangerous creature such as this salmon shark is an involved and difficult procedure.

Movement patterns

Gray nurse sharks have been fitted not only with number tags but also with radio-data transmitters carefully placed inside the body cavity during a brief capture. The device records information such as depth and temperature. A monitoring station on the seafloor senses the device automatically every time the tagged shark passes and downloads the data. Results show that the gray nurse shark usually swims on or near the seafloor, and is a slow swimmer, more active at night.

Diving with sharks is an alternative method of studying them. This researcher is photographing a great white shark from the relative safety of a cage.

Threats to sharks

Estimates of the numbers of sharks killed by human activity each year vary from around 50 million to more than 100 million—that's three dead sharks every second. It compares to around 8–12 human fatalities annually in the other direction.

The threats to sharks vary hugely, as they do with many wild creatures in their natural environments. A great challenge is that we can be presented with eye-catching images of logged devastated rainforests, drained cracked wetlands and oil-polluted shorelines to raise awareness and gain momentum for conservation. But because of visual limits, we cannot encapsulate the threats to the undersea habitat into such telling images.

Overfishing

A great threat to most sharks is the fishing industry and overfishing in general. Some fishing deliberately targets sharks, from hammerheads to dogfish, by various means such as curtain nets, trawls and hooked lines. The sharks are caught for their flesh, liver, oil and other products. One of the most controversial practices is finning (see panel on facing page).

Another problem is bycatch, where sharks are caught incidentally while targeting other fish. Large predatory sharks naturally congregate around schools of prey fish—and these are also being sought by fishing fleets. The vast nets indiscriminately catch them all. Trapped sharks may be released, but by then they are often fatally injured.

Today's industrialized fishing fleets are so efficient that fish stocks of dozens of species are falling around the world, and some regions are almost fished out. Sharks depend on these types of fish as their food. As the fish disappear, the sharks go hungry and are less likely to grow and breed. Also, as traditionally caught food species of fish become more scarce, commercial fishing turns increasingly to sharks.

Pollution and angling

Some sharks prefer inshore waters, often around bays and estuaries. These are the places where pollution builds up, with sewage, waste and agricultural and industrial chemicals washed into the sea from rivers or inshore effluent pipes. The chemicals enter the food chains, and as smaller fish are eaten by bigger fish these chemicals become more and more concentrated in their bodies, a process known as bioamplification. Sharks are often among the top predators of their habitat and accumulate the highest levels.

Sports angling has also been a threat to the large, desirable sharks such as makos, which put up a spectacular fight when hooked.

While sharks are sometimes eaten by predators, some, like this Greenland shark, fall victim to fleets fishing for other catches. Even if these sharks are released back into the sea, they may have been injured and die soon afterward.

Even when sharks are not caught (accidentally or deliberately), fishing still represents a threat to them, as it depletes the ocean of their primary food source—smaller fish, crabs, and similar creatures.

Finning

Shark's fin soup in an expensive delicacy in parts of east and Southeast Asia, and elsewhere, is responsible for the deaths of millions of sharks annually. Various sharks are targeted for this product, especially scalloped hammerheads. The dorsal and perhaps pectoral fins are removed, possibly while the shark is still alive, and then the shark is thrown back. Many people suggest this is not only cruel but also wasteful, since another shark must be caught to provide flesh, liver, oil and other products.

Strategies for conservation

Conservation campaigns picturing attractive and "cuddly" creatures, such as dolphins, pandas, baby seals, and even lion cubs, are designed to arouse public sympathy and support.

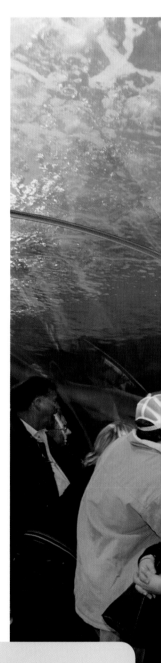

A similar campaign using the image of a fearsome shark may be less likely to succeed, but the principles are equivalent. All animals should command our respect as fellow inhabitants of our planet.

Improving the shark's image

Conservation depends heavily on education. A few species of sharks are known to attack humans, true. The same can be said of the tiger—yet there is widespread global support for tiger conservation.

Responsible education of young people at schools and colleges can obviously help, especially in nature, biology and wildlife topics. Television, books, magazines and websites can also inform about the shark's fascinating behavior and lifestyle.

Safely behind glass

Modern aquaria and sea-life centers contribute enormously to public awareness of aquatic life. Spectacular exhibits in giant tanks with walk-through tunnels allow people to stand inches away from one of the most deeply feared creatures. Most tanks feature a variety of sharks, but particularly sand tiger and sandbar sharks, which seem to take well to captivity yet look sufficiently big and frightening. Accompanying displays, commentaries and videotapes explain shark bodies and behavior.

The shark show

Shark shows truly bring education alive. At the reef, the sharks learn by simple association and habituation that the noise of the boat engine and the splash of people means food. Tourists marvel and take photographs as guards feed the sharks. Such demonstrations can certainly help to change the shark's image, but they depend on a thorough understanding of shark behavior, and there are potential problems. The general wildlife of the reef is disrupted and more sharks may be attracted to the area, which is often near a popular beach resort. It has been suggested that local sharks could even lose their own natural fear of us and come to associate humans with food.

National and international efforts

National governments, regional organizations and international authorities can be persuaded to look after the welfare of marine life and develop strategies for conservation. There is huge potential for fishing quotas and restrictions, which would not only help save sharks but also safeguard almost exhausted stocks of fished-out commercial species. However, many cultural differences remain, such as the popularity of shark's fin soup in certain regions.

Ecotourism

The ecotourism industry is worth millions. It aims to allow visitors to experience wildlife at close quarters in the most natural way possible, with minimal impact on the creatures and their habitat. Profits should be used to maintain and conserve the animals, plants and local wild areas, as well as supporting local eco-friendly employment and green initiatives. At least, this is the theory. Some "eco" tourism is little more than thinly disguised exploitation for personal gain. Many people opt to view marine life through the thick glass of an aquarium (left).

Seeing sharks first hand can inspire awe and respect in spectators. These aquarium visitors are watching gray nurse sharks and sand tiger sharks

With its strange, otherworldly features, the hammerhead shark is an impressive sight and a popular occupant of many aquariums. Viewing creatures like this can educate people as to why it is necessary to conserve our sharks.

Taking measures

There are many ways in which we can help to conserve sharks. They include supporting general wildlife organizations and also specific shark or marine life campaigns as promoted by bodies such as Shark Trust and Shark Alliance.

Overfishing is a huge worldwide problem, but governments are slow to issue quotas, especially for low-glamor species such as sharks. There remain almost no legal restrictions on catching big oceanic sharks in international waters. If restrictions do come in, then enforcement on the high seas is a perennial problem, as it is with existing fish quotas in many areas.

Some nations have introduced specific restrictions on shark fishing and catch quotas in their own territorial waters, including the United States, Australia and New Zealand. But again, progress is slow, partly because marine conservation is not at the top of many priority lists. On land, we can see when wild areas are devastated by logging or deliberate burning. But in the sea the problems seem more remote, hidden beneath the waves.

CITES

In addition to the protection of living sharks, laws can limit, license or ban trade in their fins, bodies, remains, teeth, meat and other parts and products. Such limitations are incorporated into CITES, the Convention on International Trade in Endangered Species. Most nations in the world are CITES signatories. Listing a species in CITES Appendix I means trade in these animals alive or dead, or their products, is illegal except in exceptional licensed circumstances (usually concerned with conservation). Appendix II species can be traded with permission and export permits. The only three sharks listed in CITES in 2008 were the basking and whale sharks and the great white, all in Appendix II.

Nets of death

The arguments about drift and curtain nets continue. Some conservationists want them banned altogether, but some countries rely heavily on the income generated by this kind of fishing, an industry that employs and feeds many tens of thousands of people. Redesigned, safer nets and better-enforced regulations are two positive options.

Marine parks and sanctuaries

Sharks and other sea life can benefit greatly from the establishment of marine reserves, parks and sanctuaries. These are being set up around the world, often in conjunction with eco-tourism initiatives. But protecting sharks in one area will not help if they regularly travel or migrate to another locality where they are at risk. This shows the tremendous need for more research into sharks and a better understanding of their biology, behavior and ecology.

This hammerhead shark has become entangled in a drift net and died. Conservation groups often lobby for tighter restrictions to be placed on fishing activities to prevent such tragedies.

Establishing protected areas for conservation, where fishing and water sports are prohibited, can help to maintain the shark's natural habitat. However, many sharks migrate, so conservationists need to be sure they understand a shark's migration patterns and protect each place it may visit.

Failure

In 2007 the European Union proposed the inclusion of spiny dogfish (pictured) and porbeagles under Appendix II of CITES, the agreement limiting trade in threatened species and their products. However, the proposal did not receive sufficient votes from CITES member states. Many members expressed concern over the lack of shark fishery management in European waters— while quietly remembering that the spiny dogfish is a heavily traded species that provides employment and income for some of their citizens.

THIS PLACE IS
A SOURCE OF
LIFE FOR FISHES,
CRUSTACEANS
AND CORALS.
PROTECT THEM NOW
FOR FUTURE
GENERATIONS.

Thank you!

Rare and endangered species

Sharks as a group are predators, and predators are never as abundant as their prey. Big flesh-eating sharks are top predators, and therefore naturally even rarer compared to smaller fish and other sea creatures.

Their position of apex predator, coupled with the relatively slow reproductive rate of many sharks, plus of course the immense pressures that human activity puts on the marine habitat and its wildlife, are threatening more and more shark species.

There are myriad anecdotal accounts of how various sharks have become less common in certain areas. A global view is provided by the International Union for the Conservation of Nature (IUCN) and Natural Resources. Its regularly updated "Red Lists" categorize species according to the threats they face and the severity and timescale of their plight. Categories include LC, Least Concern, through to CR, Critically Endangered, where every passing year counts.

Hunter hunted

The most famous or infamous shark, the great white, is classed by the IUCN as VU, or Vulnerable. Its list of threats include being caught for food, for materials such as teeth and fins—traded at high prices due to the species' reputation—and for sport, as a bycatch of large-scale fishing. Coupled with its slow growth and breeding rates, the great white has, in the past 50 years, gone from Hollywood villain to a species that demands active conservation measures. Other VU species include the oceanic whitetip, night shark, sand tiger or gray nurse, basking shark, longfin mako, humpback smooth-hound, tawny nurse shark and whale shark.

Species in the two more serious threat categories are summarized in the panel.

A curious case

The pondicherry shark, *Carcharhinus hemiodon*, is known from coasts around south and Southeast Asia— or it was. Growing to about 6 feet (1.8 m), its diet, behavior and ecology are little known. In fact, a capture or confirmed sighting of this shark has not occurred since the late 1970s, and its main evidence is now some 20 museum specimens. The areas where this shark lives are subject to massive fishing pressure, and there must be fears for its extinction.

Endangered and critical

Sharks in the IUCN's Endangered category, EN, include:

- *Carcharhinus borneensis* **Borneo shark**
- *Hemitriakis leucoperiptera* **Whitefin tope shark**
- *Mustelus schmitti* **Narrownose smooth-hound**
- *Sphyrna mokarran* **Great hammerhead**
- *Squatina argentina* **Argentine angel shark**
- *Squatina guggenheim* **Hidden angel shark**
- *Squatina occulta* **Smoothback angel shark**
- *Squatina punctata* **Angular angel shark**

Those in the most perilous category, Critically Endangered, CR, and in imminent danger of extinction:

- *Carcharhinus hemiodon* **Pondicerry shark** (see text)
- *Glyphis gangeticus* **Ganges shark**
- *Centrophorus harrissoni* **Dumb gulper shark** (Harrison's dogfish)
- *Isogomphodon oxyrhynchus* **Daggernose shark**
- *Mustelus fasciatus* **Striped smooth-hound**
- *Squatina aculeata* **Sawback angel shark**
- *Squatina oculata* **Monkfish or smoothback angel shark**
- *Squatina squatina* **Angel shark**

Above: The megamouth shark is very rare—in the first 30 years after it was discovered in 1976, only 39 sightings have been made. Due to its rarity, there are not enough data to tell whether its numbers are in decline, but humans may be unwittingly killing off these gentle giants.

Right: Activities such as hunting sharks for meat or goods like this jewelry are placing many sharks in danger of extinction.

Shark tourism

Despite, or perhaps because of, their dangerous reputation, many people are drawn to seeing sharks at first hand, giving rise to a new type of vacationing, called shark tourism.

There are currently two popular holiday destinations for shark tourists: South Africa, to view the great white shark, and the Bahamas, to observe reef sharks and tiger sharks first hand.

Many people simply go to these locations to view sharks from a distance—either from the shore or from a boat out at sea. Some people want to get even closer and to actually dive with the sharks in the water. The tourists wear scuba equipment and are lowered in a metal cage, and operators of the tour throw sardines, pilchards and fish heads into the water from the boat to attract sharks to the cage (a practice known as chumming), allowing the tourists to view the sharks—which may be more than 12 feet (3.6 m) in length—in the water at a range of just a few feet.

Many advocates of shark tourism believe it is a successful way of preserving sharks in the face of diminishing populations. By persuading local people to make money out of sharks without killing them, it discourages activities such as shark fishing and promotes conservation efforts to protect the sharks.

Some people, however, are fiercely opposed to shark diving, thinking it is an unnecessarily dangerous pastime. Sometimes accidents occur during shark diving itself, and the sharks get through the bars of the cage to the divers, although this kind of accident is very rare. In addition, some people think that feeding sharks to attract them to the boats is encouraging sharks to venture into waters they might otherwise avoid and reduces their fear of humans, ultimately encouraging further attacks.

The Henri Murray attack

A notorious attack that sparked the debate about shark tourism occurred in 2005, when Henri Murray, a university student in South Africa, died in a shark attack while spearfishing with his friend 200 yards (183 m) from the shore of Miller's Point in South Africa.

Spear fishers are attached to a buoy while scuba diving and use a powerful speargun to shoot passing sea creatures. When they saw the great white shark coming, the two friends shot at it with their spear guns, but it still managed to drag Murray away.

Although Murray was not participating in shark diving at the time of the incident, many people believed that it was an example of a growing number of attacks caused by the expanding shark tourism in that area, and it ignited controversy in the South African media.

Surprisingly, the number of shark tourists to arrive at Miller's Point following the attack reportedly increased—possibly because the visitors wanted to get a first-hand glimpse of the vicious killer.

Diving within the protection of a cage is a good way to get a first-hand view of sharks within their natural environment. However, sharks have been known, on occasion, to head-butt or even penetrate the viewing cages.

Shark tourism is becoming increasingly popular, but it is a double-edged sword: while it can persuade locals to make money out of sharks without killing them, there is concern that it might be provoking sharks to make increasingly frequent attacks.

Where to see sharks

PACIFIC

PACIFIC Waikiki Aquarium—Hawaii

2777 Kalakaua Avenue, Honolulu, HI 96815
Tel: +1 (808) 923-974
 Fax: +1 (808) 923-1771
http://www.waquarium.org
Shark research program (both field and
captive) with changing displays in several
galleries including South Pacific Marine
Communities, Hawaiian Marine Communities
and Diversity and Adaptations. Exhibited
species have included blacktip reef shark,
oceanic whitetip shark and sandbar shark.

NORTH AMERICA

The Aquarium of Niagara—Canada

701 Whirlpool Street, Niagara Falls, NY 14301
Tel: +1 (716) 285-3575
Toll-free: +1 800-500-4609
Fax: +1 (716) 285-8513
http://www.aquariumofniagara.org
View sharks in a coral reef exhibit also
featuring moray eels, piranha and brilliantly
colored fish.

Monterey Bay Aquarium—California

886 Cannery Row, Monterey, CA 93940
Tel: +1 (408) 648-4800
http://www.mbayaq.org
One of the world's most spectacular marine
centers; includes "visiting" accidentally caught
great whites that are then returned to the
ocean.

National Aquarium in Baltimore—Maryland

501 East Pratt Street, Baltimore,
MD 21202-3194
Tel: +1 (410) 576-3800
http://www.aqua.org
Sand tiger, lemon, sandbar and nurse sharks
encircle visitors in the giant main tank, part
of one of the world's largest and most
modern aquaria.

San Diego Shark Diving Expeditions— California

6747 Friar's Road, Suite 112, San Diego
CA 92108-1110
Tel: +1 (619) 299-8560
Toll-free: +1 888 SD SHARK
Fax: +1 (619) 299-1088

http://www.sdsharkdiving.com
Cage-diving expeditions that provide
extremely close encounters. Still and video
cameras available to hire. Also organize
specialty shark expeditions worldwide.

Underwater Adventures Aquarium— Minnesota

Mall of America, 120 East Broadway,
Bloomington, MN 55425
Tel: +1 (952) 853-0603
http://www.underwaterworld.com
A moving walkway escorts the visitor through
more than 300 feet (92 m) of crystal clear
tunnel submerged in this huge aquarium, with
sharks circling overhead.

Vancouver Aquarium Marine Science Centre—Canada

PO Box 3232, Stanley Park, Vancouver,
BC, Canada V6B 3X8
Tel: +1 (604) 659-3474
Fax: 1 (604) 659-3515
http://www.vanaqua.org
Canada's largest aquarium, dedicated to the
conservation of aquatic life through display,
interpretation, education, research and direct
action. Experienced volunteer divers can join
the staff divers in the shark exhibits.

CARIBBEAN

The Bahamas Diving Association—Florida

PO Box 21707, Fort Lauderdale, FL 33335
Tel: +1 (954) 236-9292
Toll-free: +1 800-866-DIVE
Fax: +1 (954) 236-9282
http://www.bahamasdiving.com
The Bahamas is among the shark diving
capitals of the world, and this association is a
good source of information on shark/
diver interactions taking place each month.
Caribbean reef sharks, lemon sharks, bull sharks
and hammerhead sharks can all be seen.

SOUTH AMERICA

Acqua Mundo—Guaruja

2001 Miguel Estéfno, Enseada Beach, Guarujá
- SP Brazil
Tel: +55 335-8867
http://www.aquarioguaruja.com.br
The largest aquarium in Latin America.

UNITED KINGDOM AND EUROPE

Weekend Shark Watch—Isle of Man

Tel: +44 1624-801207
Trips around the island to view basking sharks
and other notable sea life, organized by
The Basking Shark Society. Contact CCS &
Associates on the island.

National Marine Aquarium—Plymouth

Rope Walk, Coxside, Plymouth, England
PL4 0LF
Tel: +44 1752-600301
www.national-aquarium.co.uk
The UK's premier center for all things aquatic,
dedicated to raising awareness of our oceans,
the life they contain and the way we as
human beings affect them. Sharks come from
Britain, the Caribbean and Indian Ocean,
ranging from the tiny coral shark and shy
epaulette shark to the large sand tigers.

Sea Life Centres

Head Office:
Merlin Entertainments (SEA LIFE) Limited,
3 Market Close, Poole, Dorset, England BH15
1NQ
Tel: +44 01202-666900
http://www.sealifeeurope.com
Many aquaria in the various Sea Life Centres
around the UK and Europe have sharks of
various types and sizes. The displays and tours
change regularly, and there are extra Sealife
Centres in addition to those listed here.

United Kingdom—Sealife Centres and Sanctuaries

Hunstanton, Great Yarmouth, Chessington,
Brighton, Weymouth, Gweek, Birmingham,
Scarborough, and Blackpool (England), Loch
Lomond and Oban (Scotland) and Bray
(Ireland).

Belgium—Sea Life Marine Park

Koning Albert I-Laan 116 8370 Blankenberge
Tel: +32 5042-4300

Germany—Sea Life Timmendorfer Strand

Kurpromenade 5 23669 Timmendorfer Strand
Tel: +49 503-352-512

Holland—Sea Life Scheveningen
Strandweg 13 2586 JK The Hague
Tel: +31 7035-42100

Also European Sea Life Centres at
Benalmadena in Spain, Helsinki in Finland, Paris
in France and in Germany at Berlin, Dresden,
Hannover, Konigswinter, Konstanz, Munich,
Oberhausen and Speyer.

SOUTH AFRICA

Two Oceans Aquarium
PO Box 50603, Waterfront, Cape Town 8002
Tel: +27 21-418-3823
Fax: +27 21-418-3952
http://www.aquarium.co.za
Showcases life from the mighty Indian and
Atlantic oceans, including many sharks, and the
possibility for visitors to take the plunge and
see the aquarium from a fish-eye view—
guaranteed shark sightings!

White Shark Ecoventures—Cape Town
PO Box 50325 V&A Waterfront,
Cape Town 8002
Tel: +27 21-532-0470
Fax: +27 21-532-0471
http://www.white-shark-diving.com
This company offers cage diving and sighting
tours from boat decks off Gansbaai (approx.
2 hours' drive from Cape Town).

ASIA

Japan—"Kaiyukan" Aquarium Osaka
1-1-10 Kaigan-dori Minato-ku, Osaka City
552-0022
Tel: +81 66576-5500
http://www.kaiyukan.com/eng
Fifteen tanks dramatically display marine life,
with many kinds of shark, including a male
whale shark named kai-kun.

Manila Ocean Park Oceanarium—Philippines
Quirino Street, Manila, Philippines
Tel: +632 567-7777
Fax: +632 567-2309
http://www.manilaoceanpark.com
One of the world's newest aquaria and
open-water oceanaria.

Underwater World—Singapore
80 Siloso Road, Sentosa, Singapore 098969
Tel: +65 6275-0030
Fax: +65 6275-0036
http://www.underwaterworld.com.sg
A 272-foot (83 m) long travelator moves
visitors along a submerged glass-windowed
tunnel with views of coral reefs, stringrays,
moray eels, turtles, sharks and other fish.

Shanghai Ocean Aquarium—Shanghai, China
1388 Lujiazui Ring Road, Pudong New
Area, Shanghai, China 200120
Tel: +86 21-58779988
Fax: +86 21-58770088
http://www.aquarium.sh.cn
The longest underwater tunnel in the world.

AUSTRALIA

Exmouth Diving Centre—Western Australia
Payne Street, Exmouth, WA 6707
Tel: +61 8-9949-1201
Fax: +61 8-9949-1680
http://www.exmouthdiving.com.au
Guided whale shark tours (early March to
early June) for those who can swim and
snorkel. Equipment can be hired, and snorkel
lessons are also available.

Reef HQ Aquarium—Queensland
2–68 Flinders Street, Townsville, QLD 4810
Tel: +61 7-4750-0800
Fax: +61 7-4772-5281
http://www.reefhq.com.au
Alongside the coral reef exhibition area is a
separate large tank of predator exhibits.

**AQWA, The Aquarium of Western
Australia—Perth**
Hillarys Boat Harbour, 91 Southside Drive,
Hillarys, WA 6025
Tel: +61 8-9447-7500
Fax: +61 8-9447-7856
http://www.aqwa.com.au
Australia's largest aquarium and underwater
tunnel, with beautiful living coral reefs, giant
sharks, rays and turtles.

NEW ZEALAND

National Aquarium of New Zealand—Napier
Marine Parade, Napier, New Zealand

Tel: +64 6-834-1404
Fax: +64-6 833-7631
http://www.nationalaquarium.co.nz

ORGANIZATIONS

Shark Alliance
A not-for-profit coalition of nongovernmental
organizations dedicated to conserving sharks
by improving European fishing policy.

Shark Trust
UK registered marine charity dedicated to the
conservation of sharks and other marine life.
http://www.sharktrust.org

Glossary

Acoustic telemetry
The use of transmitters implanted into or tagged onto sharks to track their movement and behavior by means of the sonic pulses the transmitter emits.

Ampullae of Lorenzini
Tiny pits over a shark's snout and head that can sense electrical fields in the water.

Aorta
Main blood vessel that carries blood away from the heart.

Anal fin
Fin on the lower rear underside of body, in the midline, often near or behind the pelvic fins.

Anatomy
Structure of a living thing, including the size and shape of its internal parts or organs.

Anticoagulant
Substance that prevents blood coagulating, or thickening into a clot.

Artery
Vessel that carries blood away from the heart.

Axon
Long, micro-thin fiber of a nerve cell that carries nerve signals from one body part to another.

Barbels
Whiskers on the lower jaw of some shark species that help the fish to feel its way around the seabed.

Benthic
Base of a watery habitat, such as a stream bed, lake bed or seafloor. (Compare with pelagic.)

Bioluminescence
Production of light by living things, such as glowworms, fireflies and water-dwellers such as certain squid and fish, including some sharks.

Binomial nomenclature
The international two-part name for a species of living thing, where the first part is the genus and the second is the individual species.

Branchial
To do with gills, especially the branchial arches—the arch-shaped pieces of cartilage that form the stiff inner frameworks for the gills.

Camouflage
Disguise or concealment by blending in with the background or certain features of the surroundings to avoid detection. Both predators and prey use camouflage.

Capillary
Microscopically narrow blood vessel where substances such as oxygen and nutrients can pass through the very thin walls to the surrounding tissues.

Cardiac muscle
Specialized muscle forming the walls of the heart.

Carnivore
Animal that eats mainly other animals, usually their flesh or meat.

Cartilage
A lightweight, smooth, slightly soft and pliable but very strong material, sometimes called gristle. It makes up a shark's skeleton. In our own bodies, cartilage forms the flexible inner parts of the nose and ears.

Cartilaginous
One of three basic fish groups. Sharks, rays, skates and ratfish are cartilaginous; the other types of fish are jawless and bony.

Caudal fin
The tail—the two-lobed fin at the rear of the shark's body.

Cells
Microscopic living units that make up organisms such as plants and animals. A shark is made of hundreds of billions of cells of many kinds, such as muscle cells, nerve cells, blood cells and so on.

Cerebellum
Part of the brain that coordinates muscle movements.

Clade
The basic grouping in the method of cladistics, which includes an original common ancestor, all of its descendants and no others.

Cladistics
The hierarchical classification of species based on evolutionary ancestry.

Claspers
Two finger-shaped protrusions on the lower rear underside of a mature male shark. They were named from the mistaken belief that they clasped the female during mating. In fact, they act as guides for his sperm fluid.

Class
In the classification of living things, a group of closely related orders.

Cloaca
Body opening used for both excretion of waste materials and for the passage of sexual products such as eggs or sperm.

Collagen
Natural protein forming strong, tough fibers, found in various body parts including cartilage and skin.

Conservation
A social and scientific movement seeking to protect animal and plant species and their natural habitats from threats posed by humans.

Convergent evolution
When living things resemble each other not because they are closely related, but because they have evolved similar lifestyles.

Countershading
In animals, having a lighter color or shade on the underside compared to the upper side to counteract daylight's effect of shining more brightly on the upper side while leaving the underside in shadow. It helps with camouflage.

Denticles
Tiny, tooth-shaped scales. Dermal denticles are the sharp scales on a shark's skin. Much larger, stronger denticles form its teeth.

Dermis
Lower or inner layer of skin, below the epidermis. It contains nerve sensors, blood vessels and other living parts.

Detritivore
Living thing that feeds on detritus—dead plants and animals, carrion, rotting bits and pieces, droppings, excrement and natural "wastes."

Dominance hierarchy
System of relationships in which some animals are dominant or in charge and have first choice of food, living places, mates and other resources, while others are submissive to them—sometimes called a "pecking order."

Dorsal fin
Fin on the upper side of the body in the midline. Many sharks have more than one dorsal fin, with the largest and foremost one "cutting" the water in typical, seemingly menacing, fashion.

Ecology
Scientific study of how plants, animals and other organisms live and interact with each other, such as being predators or prey or competitors, and also how they interact with their non-living surroundings, such as rocks, air and water.

Ectotherm

Animal that gets its warmth from the surroundings or environment, as do most sharks.

Elasmobranchii

A subdivision of the cartilaginous fish, comprising sharks, skates and rays.

Elastin

Natural protein forming strong, stretchy fibers, found in various body parts including cartilage and skin.

Enamel

Extremely hard substance found in the bodies of various animals, especially forming the outer layer of teeth in numerous creatures, including sharks and mammals.

Endotherm

Animal that "burns" food in its body to generate heat and keep itself at a constant warm temperature.

Epidermis

Upper or outer layer of skin, above the dermis. It is made mainly of dead, hardened cells and acts as a protective covering.

Evolution

Change over time. In nature, living things change, or evolve, in response to changes in their environment and the living things around them—the process called evolution by natural selection.

Family

In the classification of living things, a group of closely related genera. A family name often ends with "idae."

Food chain

Series of feeding actions, when an animal eats a plant and is then eaten by another animal and so on. Food chains are usually theoretical and link to form more realistic food webs.

Food web

Set of feeding relationships forming a weblike network, showing what eats what. It usually has plants at the bottom and top predators at the summit, and it is a series of simpler food chains linked together.

Genus

In the classification of living things, a group of closely related species.

Gill

Feathery, blood-filled body part specialized to take in or absorb dissolved oxygen from water in water-dwelling (aquatic) creatures.

Gill slit

Long, narrow opening in the side of the head in sharks, where water exits after flowing into the mouth and over the gill. Most sharks have five gill slits on each side.

Gill rakers

Bony projections of the gills that help filter-feeding sharks to retain caught prey within their mouths while feeding.

Global warming

The increase in the average temperature on land and in the ocean since the mid 20th century, and its projected escalation.

Herbivore

Animal that eats mainly plants.

Heterocercal

Design of tail (caudal fin) where the two lobes are unequal in size. In sharks, the vertebral column extends into the upper lobe, which is larger. (Compare with homocercal.)

Homeothermic

"Warm-blooded"—more accurately, maintaining a constant body temperature. For example, as the surroundings cool down on a cold evening, a homeothermic animal's body temperature does not cool but stays the same. (Compare with poikilothermic.)

Home range

Area where an animal habitually roams and feeds, but which it does not actively defend against intruders.

Homocercal

Design of tail where the two lobes are equal in size. Most bony fish have a homocercal tail. Sharks have a heterocercal design.

Ichthyology

The scientific study of all 25,000 species of fish so far documented, including all kinds of shark.

Immune system

Parts of the body that work together to protect it against infection by germs, illness and disease.

Instinctive response

Type of behavior based on in-built or inherited patterns, usually as predictable reactions to specific stimuli.

Intrauterine cannibalism

A form of behavior in some carnivorous animals, whereby multiple embryos are created during intercourse, but only the one or two strongest survive until birth—the remainder are being devoured by their fellows as a source of nourishment in the womb.

ISAF

International Shark Attack File, maintained by the University of Florida—the most reputable source of information on shark attacks.

Lateral line

Row of sensors along each side of a fish's body, that detect ripples, currents and similar water movements.

Marine

Living in or associated with the water.

Migration

Long-distance journeys, usually to find more food or better living conditions. Many migrations are regular, occurring with the seasons of the year.

Myomeres

Main swimming muscles along the flanks of sharks, arranged in zigzag blocks along either side of the spinal column.

Notochord

Stiff, rodlike part that runs along the middle of the body in certain animals, such as the eel-like amphioxus. It is thought to be an early stage in the evolution of the vertebral column.

Olfactory

To do with scents and smells, or the sense of smell.

Operculum

Bony plate that covers the gills and gill openings in bony fish. Sharks lack an operculum, and so their separate gill slits are visible.

Optic

To do with eyesight or vision.

Order

In the classification of living things, a group of closely related families. An order name often ends with "iformes."

Osmoregulation

Regulating or controlling the amounts or concentrations of salts and similar chemicals in body fluids. This is especially important for aquatic living things exposed to low (in fresh-water) and high (in saltwater) concentrations of salts around them.

Oviparous

An animal that lays eggs with little or no embryonic development inside the mother. (Compare with viviparous and ovoviviparous.)

Ovoviviparous

A more primitive kind of viviparity, in which the young develop inside eggs in the mother's body, not being released until the young is about to hatch. The embryo is nourished by the egg yolk rather than the mother's body. (Compare with oviparous and viviparous.)

Paleontology

Study of fossils and other ancient clues, to explain how long-extinct animals, plants and other organisms once lived and evolved.

Parasite

Organism that obtains nourishment or shelter from another living thing, called the host, and causes harm to the host in the process.

Pectoral fins

Paired fins on the lower front sides of the body (see also pelvic fins).

Pelagic

Open water in a watery habitat, such as the open ocean, rather than the bottom or floor below. (Compare with benthic.)

Pelvic fins

Paired fins on the lower rear of the body (see also pectoral fins).

Placoid scales

Small, toothlike scales, also called dermal denticles, on a shark's skin.

Plankton

Microscopic organisms that are the food supply for most other forms of aquatic life. Plankton is not a description of a species or type of organism but of a lifestyle—drifting in pelagic or freshwater.

Phoresy

Natural "hitch-hiking" or "piggy-backing," saving energy or resources by using another organism for transport.

Physiology

Workings of a living thing, including its body chemistry and functions (see also anatomy).

Phytoplankton

Tiny plant organisms in the plankton (see plankton).

Plasma

Fluid part of blood with the cells removed, consisting of a watery solution of hundreds of body chemicals, salts, nutrients, hormones and waste.

Poikilothermic

"Cold-blooded"—more accurately, being about the same temperature as the surroundings. For example, as the surroundings warm up on a hot sunny day, a poikilothermic animal's body temperature rises by the same amount. (Compare with homeothermic.)

Predator

Hunting animal that seeks out and feeds on other animals—its prey.

Proprioception

Sense of inner position or posture, where microsensors in the muscles, joints, blood vessels and other body parts detect their positions and movements.

School

Group of sharks, or other fish or aquatic creatures moving and traveling together.

Selachian

Sharklike, or a member of the general shark group.

Selachimorph

Sharklike, or a member of the general shark group.

Skeletal muscle

Type of muscle attached to the skeleton, causing an animal's movements.

Skeleton

Strong framework of an animal, giving firmness and support. In sharks the skeleton is internal (an endoskeleton), made mainly from cartilage.

Species

Particular kind or type of living thing, and the basic unit in classification of organisms, where all members of the species look similar and can breed together to produce offspring which can also breed; members of a species cannot breed with members of another species.

Spinal column

The main supporting skeletal part along the inside of the shark's body, composed of parts called vertebrae; commonly called the "backbone," although in sharks it is cartilage, not bone.

Spiracle

Respiratory or breathing opening in various animals, found behind the eye in some sharks and also rays, where water enters to flow over the gills.

Squalene

Ingredient of the oil from a shark's liver, which has many uses in health, medicine and cosmetics. Not all of its medicinal effects are supported by modern science.

Taxonomy

Scientific study of grouping or classifying living things according to their similar features and evolutionary relationships.

Territory

Area that an animal frequents that may provide living space, food, shelter and other resources, and which it defends against intruders.

Tonic immobility

A paralyzed state, usually induced by turning the shark on its back. Scientists use this state to prevent sharks from attacking during studies. The shark can usually be woken using a chemical or electrical shark repellent.

Vein

Blood vessel or tube that carries blood toward the heart.

Ventricle

Chamber or hollow part, for example, inside a shark's brain.

Vertebra

Units that link into the chainlike vertebral or spinal column, the central supporting part of the skeleton of a vertebrate animal. In most vertebrates they are made of bone. In sharks and their kin, vertebrae are made of cartilage.

Visceral muscle

Type of muscle found in layers in internal parts such as the guts, excretory and reproductive organs and blood vessels.

Viviparous

An animal in which the embryo develops inside its mother's body. (Compare with oviparous and ovoviviparous.)

Zooplankton

Tiny animals in the plankton (see plankton).

Index